Henry Fielding

and the

Politics of Mid-Eighteenth-Century England

South Atlantic
Modern Language Association
Award Study

Henry Fielding
and the Politics
of Mid-Eighteenth-Century
England

BRIAN McCREA

The University of Georgia Press

Athens

Set in 11 on 14 point Mergenthaler Janson type
Printed in the United States of America

Library of Congress Cataloging in Publication Data

McCrea, Brian.
 Henry Fielding and the politics of mid-eighteenth-
century England.
 (South Atlantic Modern Language Association
award study)
 Bibliography.
 Includes index.
 1. Fielding, Henry, 1707–1754—Political and social
views. 2. Great Britain—Politics and government—
1727–1760. 3. Politics and literature—Great Britain.
4. Politics in literature. 5. Authors, English—18th
century—Biography. I. Title. II. Series: South
Atlantic Modern Language Association. Award Study.
PR3458.P6M3 1980   823'.5   80–14711
           ISBN 0–8203–0531–6

For Sara and Sam

"and it was still hot"

Contents

Preface

I begin by assuming that literary and political life were more closely linked in the eighteenth century than today—an assumption particularly significant for students of eighteenth-century literature, considering how basic it is to important works by contemporary scholars, most notably John Loftis, Donald J. Greene, and Bertrand A. Goldgar. Like his great literary forebears (Swift and Pope, Addison and Steele) and his most famous contemporaries (Johnson and Smollett, Richardson and Cibber), Henry Fielding would have scorned the modern notion that the man of letters should not sully his artistic integrity by participating in political rough-and-tumble. To an extent perhaps equaled only by Swift and Steele, he devoted his time and talents to political writing. My aim is to establish the social, intellectual, and political background of Fielding's political writings, and then to examine the persistent and important ways in which his political career affected his literary one. I hope to move a large body of work, upon which Fielding lavished his energies, from its present peripheral role to a more central place in studies of Fielding's life and art.

Now is a particularly opportune time for a study of this subject, because twentieth-century scholars have solved many mysteries about Fielding's biography and bibliography. Beginning with the pioneer studies of J. Paul De Castro and G. M. Godden, continuing through the investigations of Wilbur L. Cross and John Edwin Wells, and concluding in the more recent work of Rupert C. Jarvis, John B. Shipley, and the editors of the Wesleyan edition of Fielding's works, the nature and sum of Fielding's political pamphleteering and journalism have become ever clearer. We now can speak with confidence about the canon of Fielding's political writings. An assessment of those pieces in relation to Fielding's development as a writer and thinker is appropriate, indeed necessary, if our understanding of his accomplishment and genius is to continue to grow.

Because it is impossible to discuss Fielding's political career without discussing the norms and the nature of British politics during his lifetime, my first chapter will describe the political milieu in which he lived and wrote. Twentieth-century historians have disagreed about the structure of politics in mid-eighteenth-century England; I necessarily will risk taking a side in what Bertrand A. Goldgar has called "the historiographical quarrel between the Namierians and anti-Namierians."[1] I relish rather than fear this opportunity, for I believe that, in this quarrel, literary scholars may have much to teach historians. Certainly, the case of Henry Fielding shows how interest and ideology interacted in one eighteenth-century Englishman's politics. His words and actions may offer a significant and previously unnoticed particular instance against which both Namierians and anti-Namierians can test their generalizations.

With the political background (or, rather, one version of it) established, I will consider Fielding's political career in chronological order, devoting a chapter to his family background, a chapter to his years as a playwright, chapters to each of his major political journals—*The Champion*, *The True Patriot*, and *The Jacobite's Journal*—and a final chapter to his writings of 1749–54. To show how Fielding's political writings can further our understanding of his drama and prose fiction, I will direct my discussions to literary works that have been considered critically problematic, rather than to the oft-discussed masterpieces. The political writings will cast new light on several of Fielding's plays, *Jonathan Wild*, and *The Journal of a Voyage of Lisbon*. *Joseph Andrews* and *Tom Jones* will not be interpreted anew, but I will argue that they, in part, take rise from and reflect Fielding's overcoming political uncertainty. The final chapter points to problematic features of *Amelia* for which an understanding of Fielding's politics can account—features that, paradoxically, arise from his newfound political confidence.

My attempt to reconstruct the political basis of Fielding's art comes perilously close to a once-popular type of literary history that now is in disfavor. Thus my conclusion defends my approach, summarizing several truths about Fielding's life and art that it makes available to us. At a time when some literary critics construct maps of misreading, my attempt to reconstruct the ideology as well as the personal interest that shaped Fielding's political writings, and then to interpret his literary writings in light of his political ones, may seem outdated and futile. I believe that today's scholars, critics, and readers too often lose sight of their purpose, which (as I see it) is to profess not absolute truths, but an absolute commitment to seeking truth. Insofar as my method has helped me to discern several truths about Fielding, and to challenge some palpable mistakes, I stand by it.

Leaving questions of method aside, I take great pleasure in acknowledging kindnesses and help that I have received from others. An unpracticed grantsman, I have no foundations or government agencies to thank, but I honor two friends, L. H. Wilkinson and Mary Poovey, who put aside their own research to find and to copy works available only in libraries I could not visit. Alistair Duckworth, Aubrey Williams, Melvyn New, and Richard Brantley read my first draft and commented upon it in painstaking (and sometimes, for me, painful) detail. Their criticisms were as valuable as their encouragement. Of course, any first book reflects directly on a scholar's training. At the University of Virginia, I studied under men who were both learned and humane. In particular Ralph Cohen, Irvin Ehrenpreis, and Martin C. Battestin introduced me to both the rewards and the demands of study in the eighteenth century. My debt to Martin C. Battestin is special and great. He has nurtured this project from its beginnings. The only man I know who speaks with equal enthusiasm and authority about Frederick T. and "Doc" Blanchard, his rare combination of scholarly achievement and social grace is one I will always esteem.

My family has supported me financially, emotionally, and intellectually. Some scholars spice their acknowledgments with recollections of a pleasant day's work at the British Museum; I remember with similar fondness writing much of my first draft in the cool, quiet basement of my in-laws, John and Ardis Vanden Bosch. I also remember enlightening discussions of property (a word central to Fielding's politics) with my parents, Ralph and Mary Ann McCrea. Those discussions, like so many with them, helped me to ground my more esoteric research. My wife, Darla, has been an innocent victim of Fielding's politics for more years than either of us cares to remember; I love her because she will take this book, as she takes me, flaws and all. Those who have read Fielding's defense of *Amelia* will know why I dedicate this book to my children.

A Note on Texts

Until the Wesleyan edition is complete, Fielding scholars will continue to have difficulty citing reliable and editorially consistent texts. The eclectic nature of the following group is regrettable, but unavoidable.

Amelia. 2 vols. London: J. M. Dent and Sons; New York: E. P. Dutton, 1964.

The Author's Farce. Regents Restoration Drama Series, ed. Charles B. Woods. Lincoln: University of Nebraska Press, 1966.

The Champion. 2 vols. London: J. Huggonson, 1741. (See the articles by John B. Shipley and William B. Coley, cited in the bibliography, for discussion of Fielding's contributions to these volumes.)

The Complete Works of Henry Fielding. Ed. William Ernest Henley. New York: Croscup and Sterling, 1902. (Vol. 8 for *Love in Several Masques*; Vol. 10 for *The Modern Husband*; Vol. 11 for *Don Quixote in England*; Vol. 13 for the legal and social writings.)

The Covent-Garden Journal. Ed. Gerard Edward Jensen. 2 vols. New Haven: Yale University Press, 1915.

The Grub-Street Opera. Regents Restoration Drama Series, ed. Edgar V. Roberts. Lincoln: University of Nebraska Press, 1968.

The Historical Register for the Year 1736 and Eurydice Hissed.

Regents Restoration Drama Series, ed. William W. Appleton. Lincoln: University of Nebraska Press, 1967.

The Jacobite's Journal and Related Writings [*A Dialogue Between a Gentleman of London . . . And An Honest Alderman of the Country Party; A Proper Answer to a Late Scurrilous Libel*]. Wesleyan edition, ed. William B. Coley. Middletown, Conn.: Wesleyan University Press, 1975.

Jonathan Wild. Shakespeare Head edition. Oxford: Basil Blackwell, 1926.

Jonathan Wild and the Voyage to Lisbon. London: J. M. Dent and Sons; New York: E. P. Dutton, 1964. (For all references to the *Journal of a Voyage to Lisbon*).

Joseph Andrews. Wesleyan edition, ed. Martin C. Battestin. Middletown, Conn.: Wesleyan University Press, 1967.

Miscellanies, Volume I. Wesleyan edition, ed. Henry Knight Miller. Middletown, Conn.: Wesleyan University Press, 1972.

Tom Jones. Wesleyan edition, ed. Martin C. Battestin and Fredson Bowers. Middletown, Conn.: Wesleyan University Press, 1975.

The True Patriot. Ed. Miriam Austin Locke. University: University of Alabama Press, 1964. (References to *The True Patriot* will include a large roman number [to designate the issue number], a small roman number [for the page number within the issue], and a second small roman number [for the column number on the page]. A passage marked [IV, ii, i] will be found in the first column on the second page of *The True Patriot* No. 4.)

All citations of Swift's political writings are from the standard edition of the *Prose Works*, ed. Herbert Davis and Irvin Ehrenpreis (Oxford: Basil Blackwell, 1940–68); of Bolingbroke's political writings from *The Works of Lord Bolingbroke* (rpt. 1844; London: Frank Cass, 1967); of Locke's *Two Treatises of Government* from Peter Laslett's critical edition (rpt. 1963; New York: Mentor Books, 1965).

I
Ⅎⱨⅇ Political Background

Interest and Ideology
in Mid-Eighteenth-Century Politics

So young that he was still a ward in Chancery,[1] Henry
Fielding came to London in 1727 with a complicated
family background, a play that he hoped to produce, and
an uncertain future. Our knowledge of Fielding's activities during his first days in London is sketchy, but he
probably was exposed to one of the great political struggles
to occur during his lifetime. The death of King George I
on 11 June 1727, and the subsequent dissolution of Parliament, gave the electors their first chance to pass judgment
on Sir Robert Walpole since his rise to power in 1722. The
general election, held in July and August, inspired a bitterly fought campaign characterized by extensive and
vituperative pamphleteering on the part of Walpole's
friends and foes alike. In the end, the Great Man emerged
with a secure parliamentary majority, able to weather the
popular outcry against his excise proposals, to survive
foreign policy setbacks, and, most important for this
study, to dominate (himself and then through his protégé,
Henry Pelham) English politics for the next quarter-
century—the years of Henry Fielding's adult life.[2]

The flashpoint of the opposition to Walpole in 1727 was

The Craftsman, a journal dominated by the opinions and writings of Henry St. John, Viscount Bolingbroke. Bolingbroke's role in the campaign reveals much about the nature of politics in Fielding's England. Indeed, that Bolingbroke was even in England in 1727 indicates how English politicians of this era often sacrificed political principle at the altar of personal ambition. Architect of the Duke of Marlborough's downfall, friend to Swift and Pope, branded a traitor after his flight to the court of James III in 1715, Bolingbroke should have evoked only disgust and fear in good Hanoverian Whigs—particularly one like Robert Walpole, who had old scores to settle with him. Yet, in the early 1720s, Bolingbroke's campaign to return to England was accepted and occasionally promoted by his great rival. Walpole did manage "to inhibit the more generous instincts of the King"[3]—to prevent Bolingbroke's restoration to his seat in the House of Lords and, therefore, to deny the political forum he craved. But Bolingbroke's inheritance and his property, as well as his right to speak, write, and live in England, were returned to him with Walpole's public support.

The relations between Bolingbroke, Walpole, and George I will confound those who want to attribute a paramount concern for ideology to eighteenth-century British politicians. The circumstances of Bolingbroke's return provide one more bit of evidence against what has come to be known as "the Whig interpretation of history." This interpretation, popularized by nineteenth-century historians like Macaulay, Lecky, and Trevelyan,[4] simplified the study of British political development by reducing all political conflict to an ideological morality play in which forward-looking, democratic Whigs, who supported parliamentary authority and religious toleration, vanquished reactionary Tories, who worked to uphold royal supremacy and the state church. As Herbert Butterfield pointed out, the fatal flaw in the Whig interpretation was that it studied the past "with direct and perpetual reference to the present. Through this system of immediate reference to the present day, historical personages can easily and irresistibly be classed into the men who furthered progress and the men who tried to hinder it: so that a handy rule of thumb exists by which the historian can select and reject, and can make his points of emphasis." Butterfield explained clearly how such history fails to allow for differences between past and present; in its almost Manichaean concern for moral judgment, it is ultimately the enemy of "real historical understanding"— "understanding . . . not achieved by the subordination of the past to the present, but rather by our making the past our present and attempting to see life with the eyes of another century than our own."[5]

Butterfield could attack with confidence the "textbook" historians who made the Whig interpretation standard, because he wrote in the wake of Sir Lewis Namier's momentous study, *The Structure of Politics at the Accession of George III.*[6] By scrutinizing the makeup of Parliament at the death of George II and then studying borough politics during the campaign in 1761, Namier was able to prove that, by 1760, the Tory party was little more than a group of independent and powerless country gentlemen who willingly isolated themselves from the political mainstream. Namier's research showed that the political battles of 1760–61 were not between Whigs and Tories, but between groups of Whigs—men who were united in

their support of the Hanoverian succession, parliamentary independence, and the social and economic status
quo, but divided by family loyalties and personal interests. He thus shattered the beautiful but false logic with
which the Whig historians had explained the growth of
political democracy in England.

Namier's emphasis upon borough politics led him to
minimize the importance of ideology. He concluded that
widespread acceptance of the principles that triumphed in
1689, and that were reaffirmed in the Act of Succession
which made George I King of England, meant that party
distinctions were no longer important. Whig and Tory
became " 'denominations' . . . which covered enduring
types moulded by deeply ingrained differences in temper-
ament and outlook," rather than labels for "a clear party
division."[7] The disciple of Namier will see Bolingbroke's
return to England in 1725 as one more sign of ideology's
small role in his disputes with Walpole. One can hardly
praise Walpole (the defender of the Protestant succession
and the prerogatives of Parliament) and blame Bolingbroke (the promoter of Stuart hopes and the foe of democracy) when one realizes that it was George I who pushed
for Bolingbroke's return, and that Walpole resisted his
urgings at least partly because he feared Bolingbroke
would threaten his control of Parliament.

Despite its merit and influence, *The Structure of Politics at
the Accession of George III* did not answer one very important
question—a question that still bedevils historians, and
that is fundamental to any assessment of Fielding's political career. When can one say that the structure described
by Namier was in place? How early can one date the rise

of Whig hegemony and, with it, the decline of ideology as an important factor in eighteenth-century British politics? One of Namier's American disciples, Robert Walcott,[8] has claimed that the structure was in place even during the reign of Queen Anne. By tracing various family connections, he tries to prove that the great political battles of Anne's day involved shifting alliances of families (motivated largely by personal interests) and not political parties (motivated by shared ideas and principles). Walcott's work, however, does scant justice to the divisions in British society created by the War of the Spanish Succession—the divisions that politicized London social life, that spurred the famous quarrel between Jonathan Swift and Richard Steele, and that enabled Bolingbroke to forge a "Tory ideology" which briefly lifted him to power almost commensurate with his ambition.

Recent studies have tended to accuse Walcott of overstating his case and have qualified his findings,[9] but to qualify Walcott is not to answer the question that his work suggests. Historians who would not go as far as he, but who would still extend Namier's analysis to the decades immediately following the accession of George I, also confront some very basic difficulties. Those who would trace the end of Tory influence back to 1715, with the accession of George I, the failure of the Jacobite invasion, and the ignominious exile of Bolingbroke, must admit that the group Bolingbroke betrayed was long in dying. Indeed, Bolingbroke's attempts to build a strong opposition to Walpole in 1727 were thwarted largely because groups of parliamentary Tories, who could have wielded significant power, refused to cooperate with dissident, anti-

Walpole Whigs—Whigs whom they disliked and distrusted, despite Bolingbroke's urgings that past party differences be forgotten. Walpole, undoubtedly the most astute politician of his era, did not believe the Tory party had died in 1715. Throughout his long tenure, he "judiciously defused" the two great issues that had given strength and purpose to the Tory cause: he kept the land tax low, and he never countenanced attacks on the privileges of the Church of England. These policies would not have been necessary if Tory interests were no longer important or potentially powerful, and they were rewarded when Tory backbenchers supported Walpole in several crucial divisions.[10]

Similarly, those who would date the beginning of the Whig hegemony in 1725, with Walpole's consolidation of power,[11] necessarily minimize the threat that Bolingbroke posed in 1727–28 and throughout the early 1730s. As recent studies by E. P. Thompson and his followers have documented, the triumph of the moneyed urban court interests served by Walpole created both economic and social dislocation in England—a dislocation so severe that, in one instance, it threatened centuries-old customs and habits in the royal forests.[12] Lower- and middle-class resentment of these changes was strong, and Bolingbroke, who possessed an undeniable genius for speaking both to and for the declining gentry,[13] skillfully exacerbated it. The physical violence that swirled around Walpole during the excise crisis was only a small manifestation of the physical violence in England during the so-called Age of Equipoise (one of history's more elegant misnomers). Walpole stayed in power by maintaining his mastery of

Parliament (a mastery he sagely ensured by keeping Bolingbroke out of the House of Lords), as well as by bringing financial prosperity to England's ruling class. But Bolingbroke's inability to muster a strong parliamentary opposition does not mean that the political program he enunciated in *The Craftsman* generated little popular response. Even today, the conservative paradigm of a static, hierarchical, rural society attracts urbanites; in Fielding's day, benevolent patriarchal rule by the land-owning squirearchy, embodied in the government of Paradise Hall, was perhaps even more compelling. Bolingbroke's pamphlets attempted to foster this nostalgia[14] for an Elizabethan social and political structure in which every man knew not only his place, but also the rights that by custom were appropriate to it.

To see both the virtues and defects of Namier's model vis-à-vis the politics of Fielding's lifetime, we must note that the "extenders"[15] of Namier re-create the argument that Bolingbroke attempted in *The Craftsman*. Struggling to avoid the Jacobite tag and to forge a united opposition to Walpole, he asserted that universal acceptance of the Revolution Settlement and the Protestant Succession made past party differences unimportant.[16] His claim was spurious, not only because he served as the pretender's secretary of state, but also, and most important, because his vision of English society was antithetical to Walpole's. Namier's disciples and Bolingbroke to the contrary, if we clear away all the vituperation of the paper war of 1728–35, we find a conflict based on ideological differences as fundamental as those which contributed to Hamilton and Jefferson's later American version of the dispute.[17] Be-

tween 1708 and 1714, Bolingbroke rose to power by
championing a program that would end the War of the
Spanish Succession, lift the burden placed upon landowners by war taxes, abolish the national debt (and the
financial system the debt had spawned), and thus halt the
rise to political, social, and economic preeminence of the
"moneyed men." In 1727–28, and throughout the rest of
his career, Bolingbroke made the same losing case. His
central role in the political melees of the late 1720s and
early 1730s indicates that different ideologies did exist, did
come into conflict, and did force men to determine their
true loyalties and beliefs.[18]

A Whig hegemony in the Commons and Lords, if not in
the hearts and minds of the British people, existed during
Fielding's adulthood. Men who took that hegemony for
granted could be more casual about their political allegiances than could, say, Swift and Steele. But the Whig
supremacy did not mean that the Whig-Tory rubric
became meaningless or unimportant. England became
more modern, more urban during the first half of the
eighteenth century, and Englishmen, despite Walpole's
astute treatment of the gentry, did not unanimously welcome that new society. Indeed, some once-powerful landowners found the change alien to their values and interests. To opt, as Fielding did, for life in London was to
stand apart from that group and its great spokesman,
Henry St. John, Viscount Bolingbroke.

The study of Fielding's political career can suggest
answers to the questions about interest and ideology
raised by Walcott's work, but both "Namierians and anti-
Namierians" probably will find those answers unsatisfy-
ing. While Fielding was often casual in his allegiances to

the dominant Whig groups of his day, his casual attitude did not imply an absence of political ideology. When Jacobitism threatened the Whig supremacy, Fielding provided, in *The True Patriot*, an unequivocal restatement of the Whigs' shared values. And even though the Whig hegemony permitted Fielding to align himself with several groups during his career, he consistently refused to support the nostalgic politics of Bolingbroke.[19] He recognized Toryism as contrary to his political heritage and scorned claims that there were no significant differences in principle between the politicians of his day.

The complicated combinations of interest and ideology that shape Fielding's politics may exemplify the changing structure of English politics from the accession of George I to the accession of George III. In general, the change was from a politics that emphasized party ideology (the Tory versus Whig, landed versus moneyed interests conflict that dominated politics during the reign of Queen Anne) to a politics that emphasized interest (the quest for personal power by alliances of families). But this change was neither automatic nor uniform in its development. At occasional, albeit increasingly infrequent moments, issues of ideological importance confronted Englishmen. While the muting of party conflict in Parliament may have caused men like Fielding to neglect party ideology, they did not completely forget it. Fielding's own striving to reconcile interest and ideology was the most important force in his political career, and his reflections on this often perilous balance stand at the heart of his political theory.

Fielding's second cousin, Lady Mary Wortley Montagu, was probably one of the first persons he called upon when he came to London in 1727. His relationship with her raises questions about the roles of interest and ideology in his politics. With Lady Mary's help, his first play, *Love in Several Masques*, was produced at Drury Lane in February, 1728, and under her tutelage he wrote political verse.[20] Lady Mary was one of Walpole's strongest supporters, and, in Fielding's writings that she supervised, he follows her political lead. How much his early praise for Walpole reflected Fielding's own political principles and how much it reflected the pull of family ties and personal interest is difficult to say—particularly in light of his later changes in attitude toward Walpole. But if we understand the political ideology to which Fielding's youthful allegiance at least implicitly committed him, we can place this question in a context that most eighteenth-century Englishmen would have understood. For in the writings of the great Whig theoretician John Locke we can see the threads of interest and ideology from which Fielding would weave the fabric of his political career. It is no overstatement to say that Locke's work raises all the issues with which Fielding would wrestle in his own political writings.

Of course, interpretations of Locke have been many and varied, particularly in recent years. In the traditional interpretation, he stands as the great promulgator of government by contract and constitutional monarchy. But Locke has also been described as a covert Hobbesian, as a political philosopher whose concerns were actually religious, and as a thinker who was inconsistent—who could not reconcile his epistemology with his political theory.[21] Although the confusions and self-contradictions in Locke's political writings are important, at least two features remain consistent. The first is Locke's disdain for the country gentlemen who were the backbone of the Tory or Country party. Particularly in his essays on finance, Locke champions the interest of the moneyed men while mocking (and that is not too strong a word) the landowners who seek more favorable interest rates and monetary policies.[22] The second constant is Locke's reliance upon and manipulation of the word "property." Almost all commentators note that Locke uses this word in two senses: the wider includes both rights (or liberties) and financial estates, while the narrower includes only goods and lands.[23] Locke's ambiguity is convenient, perhaps calculated, because it allows him to link personal interest with more noble principles and motives. Liberties built on ambiguities, however, are not the sturdiest. Throughout the eighteenth century, men would understand Locke's theory of property in an increasingly narrow sense, until finally critics like Blake came to believe that Locke opened the way to oppression, rather than providing a basis for liberty. But the disagreements between twentieth-century interpreters provide strong evidence that the ambiguity is in Locke, and that its function, at least in part, is to avoid absolute emphasis upon self-interest—to express some optimism about man, his nature, and his capacity (however limited) for selfless behavior. Locke says that men form commonwealths to protect their property, but his shifting definitions of "property" mean that commonwealths can be protectors of individual liberties, as well as of economic and social elites. This last quality—this attempt to bridge the gap between interest and ideals—would draw Fielding to Locke.

When he acquired it we do not know, but Fielding's library included the *Two Treatises*, and he used this work to provide theoretical underpinning for his own writing.[24] Locke's political theory was congenial because it proposed that men, having established a commonwealth, could act in rational and virtuous ways; furthermore, that commonwealth was based on a voluntary contract between property holders, rather than on a divinely imposed social hierarchy. Locke's theory, with its ambiguous definition of property, countered the political absolutism proposed by Thomas Hobbes in *Leviathan* (1651) and elaborated by Robert Filmer in *Patriarcha* (1680).[25] Hobbes posited violent self-interest as dominant in all human relations and urged the necessity of an absolute sovereign to protect life. The violent effects of self-love so impressed Hobbes that he argued that the individual must be willing to place everything, except his life, at his sovereign's immediate disposal. One of the first rules of his commonwealth is that "*Propriety* [sic] *of a subject excludes not the dominion of the sovereign but only of another subject.*"[26] So long as the sovereign protects the subject's life, he can do what he wishes with the subject's "propriety."

Locke modified Hobbes and Filmer by taking a kinder view of human nature. He argued that self-interest could be enlightened instead of violent, and that men of free will could unite to create a sovereign power to protect their possessions. This sovereign, unlike Hobbes's, broke his contract with the people if he violated their property. His power over his subjects' lives was not absolute, but was bound by the conditions of the mutual agreement.

The goal of most eighteenth-century political writers was to propose alternatives to the dark, repressive Hobbesian state. But the difference between Hobbes's ideal polity and that of another writer depended on his faith in man's potential for enlightened behavior. Thus, although Tories like Swift often echoed Locke, their ideal polity reflected their doubts about man's capacity for virtue and goodness. They looked back to an Elizabethan social hierarchy where an elite class ruled with a wise, almost absolute hand, and where property ownership was static. The inflexible, unchanging quality of this system attracted a man like Swift, because his fear of violent self-love approximated (while not equaling) Hobbes's. The preeminence that the Tories proposed for the landed families reflected their kinship with the Country party of Hobbes's day. But even in this regard we must note that Swift's emphasis upon the property rights of the landed gentry echoes Locke, not Hobbes. Swift would attack the outmoded doctrines of Stuart absolutism—passive resistance and divine right. His differences with what he called the "new Whigs" (those of his day) stemmed not from his failure to accept the role that Locke assigned to property in the political process, but from his different view of what constituted property.

Writers who were more optimistic about man's potential to behave in enlightened ways could offer a more flexible model for the state. Their ideal polity became a corporation of property holders, whose concern for protection led them to disavow total self-aggrandizement. More optimistic writers could assert that any man, given possession of some type of property, was capable of enlightenment; they did not have to limit the political franchise to a small, stable, landholding elite.

Although we cannot describe the political faith that Fielding brought to London in 1727, we can say that his faith in human nature was strong and vital. This faith would manifest itself throughout his literary career, and would survive some cruel blows. To it we must turn if we are to account for Fielding's persistent refusal to be attracted by Hobbesian and Tory political theory, even as he sporadically sought the literary blessing of the Tory wits. Throughout his political writings Fielding rang changes upon the theme of property's role in enlightening self-interest and thus minimizing the need for absolutism. His political writings repeatedly combined criticism of venal, unenlightened self-love with admiration for those figures in whom he saw "Self-love and Social" joined. Like Locke, Fielding saw self-interest as a potentially legitimate and important part of the political process, not as a rude beast to be sharply disciplined.

An unseemly (for us) corollary of Fielding's emphasis upon property and interest was his inability to understand or admit the needs and rights of the poor—an inability most apparent in the social pamphlets he wrote late in his life. But this "cruel side" of Fielding will surprise us only if we ignore his debt to Locke and his distance from the optimism, universal and unqualified, that underlies democratic political theories. The "contradiction" between Fielding's repressive treatment of the poor in his social pamphlets and his espousal of the cause of freedom in his writings against Stuart absolutism is no contradiction at all. Rather, it is a sign of the consistency and narrowness of Fielding's Lockean bent—of his belief that possession of property must enlighten and domesticate self-interest before it can play a productive role in the political process. Contradiction or no, however, the important point is that Fielding's sense of the role of property in politics—his persistent focusing upon the relation between interest and principle—committed him to the Lockean school of political thought, as opposed to the Hobbesian. Whatever his motives when he wrote under the tutelage of Lady Mary, Fielding could and did provide an ideological base for his political loyalties, a base that included much more than familial or personal interests. In 1727, support for Walpole was more consistent with Fielding's subsequent political theory than was support for Bolingbroke.

Study of the political theory that shapes Fielding's writings neither explains nor vindicates his rapid changes in political allegiance during the 1730s. These changes led Fielding's contemporaries to charge him with political equivocation—a charge which recent scholarly works[27] have echoed, and with which any study of Fielding's politics must deal. This charge has both biographical and literary significance, for our recently won confidence in Fielding's integrity, and in the moral basis of his art, must suffer if we feel that his political activities were largely mercenary and venal. Namier's work is crucial in this regard, because it describes how the Whig supremacy permitted eighteenth-century politicians to be casual in their political allegiances. And Namier will provide the basis for my discussion of Fielding's changing relationship with Walpole, a relationship that particularly troubles modern students.

But first I must discuss a development that will likely confuse any contemporary student who studies the ties between Fielding and Walpole. Because it fosters a misunderstanding analogous to that which Butterfield described in *The Whig Interpretation of History*, this development may perhaps best be labeled the Tory Interpretation of Literary History. The Tory interpretation is a fairly recent development, having flourished particularly in American academic criticism since World War II. Promulgators of the Tory interpretation assume that the Scriblerians won a total victory in their war with the Dunces, and that the Scriblerian cause was just. They attribute literary greatness to Swift, Pope, and Gay, relegating Addison, Steele, and most particularly Cibber to second-rate status. Because of the prevalence of the Tory interpretation, the words "Scriblerian" and "Augustan" have become almost synonymous,[28] while the name Colley Cibber has come to stand for stupidity and folly. The Tory interpretation oversimplifies the study of eighteenth-century literature, as will be clear to anyone who recalls Leslie Stephen's description of Addison as "the typical man of taste of his time," who realizes that Cibber's *Apology*, whatever its infelicities of style, possesses sufficient rhetorical effect that it left Pope with few options for his response except ad hominem vituperation, and who remembers that probably no English playwright since Shakespeare has dominated the theatre of his age as "King Log" did.[29]

The effect of the Tory interpretation upon studies of Fielding has been particularly deleterious. Twentieth-century critics and scholars, committed to rescuing Fielding from the image created by his first biographer, Arthur Murphy, have tried to show that Fielding was like Swift and Pope—that he continued the traditions and values of the Scriblerus Club. Since contempt for Robert Walpole was part of the Scriblerian code, scholars have assumed that Fielding's anti-Walpole writings (particularly those published under the tantalizing pseudonym H. Scriblerus Secundus) reflect his true political sentiments.

To this end scholars not only have overlooked important facts—i.e., that Fielding acknowledges the literary models of Addison, Steele, and even Cibber as frequently as he does those of Swift, Pope, and Gay; that his most famous criticism of Cibber follows a criticism of Pope. What is worse, they have also tried to explain away Fielding's sporadic support for Walpole and his consistent support for Walpole's successor and protégé, Henry Pelham.

To explain away Fielding's extensive pro-Walpole, pro-Pelham commentary has not been an easy task, particularly since the serpentine machinations of those who would cast Fielding in the role of a second-generation Scriblerian have led them to ignore a basic truth. Fielding's attacks on Walpole actually were deviations from his steady loyalty to the urban and commercial way of life that flourished during the Walpole-Pelham era. This deviation occurred because of Walpole's often documented, ostentatious quest for personal gain, which made his self-interest appear unenlightened and primitive. Fielding's attacks on Walpole, however, were essentially brief interludes in his otherwise consistent support of the Whig establishment. They did not commit him to Scriblerian definitions of property; they did not remove him far enough from the Whig mainstream to make his later support of Walpole and Pelham surprising or difficult. To explain Fielding's politics in terms of his attacks on Walpole is to reverse and complicate a problem already difficult enough—the definition of the assumptions, values, and attitudes to which his Whiggism committed him. Such explanations mistakenly bestow upon a youthful flirtation the commitment and importance of a lasting adult liaison.

From 1722 until 1754, roughly the years of Fielding's adult life, Walpole and Pelham dominated English politics, except for one brief period in 1741–42. Although their methods differed in important ways, both men's power depended upon two sources. One was the confidence and support of the Commons, which for Walpole and Pelham depended first upon the confidence and support of the "Old Corps" of parliamentary Whigs. The "Old Corps" was based upon a personal loyalty to each leader, usually deriving from patronage or family ties. It was not large enough, however, to constitute a majority in the Commons, and to maintain such a majority both leaders had to curry favor among the "more or less independent members (including the completely independent section of country gentlemen)."[30] They needed effective orators to present their programs to the Commons; they were careful not to compromise or offend the principles of M.P.s who did not belong to the "Old Corps." Walpole and Pelham's second source of power was the favor of the court. Although the king could not keep a minister in power against the will of the Commons, he controlled vast amounts of patronage and could exert great influence upon elections. Ministers served at his bidding, not at the bidding of the Commons or political parties.

If we are to understand the vagaries of Fielding's political career, the most important fact of eighteenth-century political life is the makeup of the parliamentary opposition that Walpole and Pelham faced. As Namier and his followers have shown, the great parliamentary battles of the mid-eighteenth century were not between Whigs and Tories, but between groups of Whigs. Bolingbroke's ignominious exile discredited the Tories and left them without strong leadership for a decade. They became a poorly organized party of country landholders, pursuing an independent course which Samuel Johnson found attractive but which left them on the "frontier" of parliamentary power.[31]

The so-called Whigs were the ideological descendants of those who had challenged Stuart claims to absolute power. They assumed, however unconsciously, that all social institutions, including monarchies, were the "result of a voluntary contract made by men in the state of nature." But, as Locke's notions of social and political contract were adopted almost universally by the mid-eighteenth century,[32] the distinguishing trait of the Whigs became not support for the Revolution Settlement, but support for the system of finance—the new system of property—that the British had used to fund their wars against French absolutism. The well-nigh universal acceptance of the principles of 1688, coupled with the Tories' exile from power, freed the Whigs to concentrate on what Fielding would label "pollitricks" (questions of preferment, place, and personal power) instead of on politics (questions of public service and political theory). Except during those periods when the pretender posed a military threat, or when Bolingbroke posed a political one, during Walpole's years the Whigs tended to forgo theoretical discussions of property and the franchise, instead scrambling after personal gain. The weakness of the Tories and the hegemony of Locke's political theory thus caused the Whigs to split into the in group and the out, the establishment and the dissidents. The opposition to Walpole and Pelham became a combination of unreliable Tories with shifting groups of Whig factions. The Whig dissidents generally opposed particular ministerial policies and appointments; rarely could they define political ideas and ideals that separated them from the establishment.

Whig politics in the 1730s and 1740s, as practiced by both the in and the out groups, surely reflect the powerful effects of self-interest. Although the Whigs were guilty of "pollitricks," their self-interest did not conflict with the public good—at least insofar as the public good depended upon the Protestant Succession. One historian's judgment of the Whig divisions during the reign of George I is applicable to the factionalism of Fielding's day: "The first cleavage of the whig party did no permanent harm to the dynasty. On the contrary it strengthened it. Hitherto there had been only one possible opposition, composed of tories, many of them tainted by Jacobitism: now there was an alternative to the party in power as whig and as devoted to the dynasty itself as the ministers."[33]

As equally Whiggish alternatives to the ruling ministry continued into the 1730s, Henry Fielding, a man in need of patronage, not suprisingly turned to them. Fielding never barred "pollitricking" from his canon of ethical behavior, so long as the self-interest that motivated it was admitted and did not impair the public good. He perhaps most clearly expressed his view in *The Jacobite's Journal* No. 17 (26 March 1748), p. 215, when he wrote:

In a Time therefore of profound Tranquility, and when the Consequence, at the worst, can probably be no greater than the Change of a Ministry, I do not think a Writer, whose only Livelihood is his Pen, to deserve a very flagitious Character, if, when one Set of Men deny him Encouragement, he seeks it from another, at their Expence; nor will I rashly condemn such a Writer as the vilest of Men, (provided he keeps within the

Rules of Decency) if he endeavours to make the best of his own Cause, and uses a little Art in blackening his Adversary.[34]

The premise of "a Time . . . of profound Tranquility" is crucial here because it indicates the importance of an unchallenged Whig supremacy to Fielding's political thought and action. While the ins and outs battled for power within the bounds of Whig parliamentary hege-mony, changes in ministries were of little consequence. The limits within which self-interest functioned lessened its danger. Confident in the almost universal sway of Whig principles, Fielding could turn to the opposition after Walpole failed to act on his early petitions for patronage, and then, in 1741, return to Walpole's side. He could describe the switches as enlightened furtherance of his private good, which in no way betrayed his most funda-mental political principles: support for limited monarchy and new economic interests.

Fielding's awareness of a Whig consensus in Parliament enabled him to change sides without compromising his political heritage. For example, when he courted Walpole in 1729, he praised him as a "bulwark of liberty against Jacobitism and Popery."[35] The early poems praise Wal-pole because Fielding and the Great Man shared general constitutional principles. When Fielding joined the op-position, he satirized Walpole not for establishing the Hanoverian dynasty and urban interests upon a firm base, but for seeking personal gain. Fielding's last reference to Walpole as "one of the best of Men and of Ministers" (*Voyage to Lisbon*, p. 247) occurred after Walpole's death, when self-interested "pollitricking" no longer tainted his political virtues.

Since Fielding, like Locke, allowed self-interest a role in

politics, his evaluation of political figures was not inflexible. The great virtues and vices remained the same, but judgment of leaders could vary as those leaders' self-interests became more or less congruent with the public good. When Walpole besmirched his Whig principles by becoming absorbed in an all too evident self-love, he, and not his principles, became a target of Fielding's satire. When the opposition failed Fielding, not only as patrons, but by displaying a desire for personal gain as strong as Walpole's, they too fell victim. The basic situation in Fielding's political writings rarely changes, however: a place-seeker, blinded by venal ambition, time and again encounters a representative of enlightened self-interest. What does change is the figure to whom Fielding attributes the overabundance of self-interest, of "pollitricks" gone bad.

One very practical guide that Fielding used to distinguish between proper and improper "pollitricks" was the inclusiveness of a ministry. He believed the national good was served by a uniform set of political principles, yet he also realized that varying interests motivated men to work for that national good. He necessarily felt that the best ministry had a foundation broad enough to include a wide variety of interests, and thus to prevent one interest from running amok. Walpole, of course, made it his policy to exclude "from his administration those who from time to time . . . dared to challenge his power."[36] He threatened to deny the importance of the parliamentary independents to whom I have earlier referred, and to subordinate the "machine" of government to his private good. He thus became the model, in *The Champion* of 8 May 1740, for the tyrannical prime minister from whom Fielding prayed that the nation would be delivered. When Fielding saw that Walpole's major opponents, Carteret and Pulteney, were no more interested in an inclusive ministry than Walpole was, he followed his own pressing self-interest and returned to Walpole's camp. The breadth of Pelham's ministry, and more particularly its inclusion of Fielding's friends, Lyttelton, Pitt, and Dodington, met both his personal and his ideological requirements and thus earned his unqualified support.

By appreciating the importance of enlightened self-interest in Fielding's politics, we can begin to see why scholars who have tried to harmonize his discordant comments on Walpole have labored so hard and wandered so far afield. In order to cast doubt on what seems a strikingly transparent switch in Fielding's political loyalties, scholars have sometimes resorted to desperate shifts: Horace Walpole's failure to mention payments to Fielding by his father has been declared a crucial fact, and the dates given in the subtitles of Fielding's *Epistles to Walpole* have been challenged.[37] If we wish to account for the anomalies in Fielding's early political comment, we would do better to investigate the difficult balance between self-interest and principle that constituted political reality for him—to confront, rather than avoid, the financial motives that affected his relations with the Great Man. By so doing, we can perceive how the political realities of Fielding's life illustrate the realities with which the English body politic as a whole came to terms during the transition from the party conflict of the Age of Queen Anne to the one-party rule at the accession of George III. Fielding did maintain, however shakily at times, a distinction between "pollitricks" and politics. He remained true to a body of political principles that were his both by heritage and nature. He further distinguished between times of "profound Tranquility" when "pollitricks" were legitimate, and times of crisis when concern for political principle and ideology had to rise above personal interest.

A close look at his later political writings will reveal that, for Fielding, perfect reciprocity between public and private good was an absolute point on an otherwise relative scale. Most political action depends upon a balancing of these two goods, and he was not vain enough to suppose that he could stand outside the balancing process. Because self-interest usually motivates men, it necessarily for him was a part of politics, just as it was part of his changing relationship with Walpole. But this recognition of self-interest did not mean that violence and viciousness were unavoidable without tyranny. So long as self-interest was able to take a new path when a state of "profound Tranquility" no longer existed, it remained capable of being described as enlightened. And so long as self-interest remained at least potentially amenable to enlightenment, Fielding's distinctions between politics, "pollitricks," and improper "pollitricks" remained valid.

The next chapter will discuss Fielding's family background, particularly his relationship with his father, and the political heritage he derived from it. When young Harry Fielding came to London in 1727, this family background, in combination with his social position and faith in human nature, guided him toward the Whig establishment. In the years that followed, Walpole's excesses made it difficult for the budding artist to maintain consistent political loyalties. The 1720s and 1730s would not see Fielding establishing a politics of enlightened self-interest, despite his strong Whig principles. His political allegiances were casual, and his goal of success as a playwright probably foremost in his mind. However, those priorities should not blind us to the important roles of political principle and interest in his early career. Even in his plays, political conflict had a major (if latent) role. To understand that role we first must recognize the importance of his early support for Walpole—support to which his Whig family background led him. As we do this, we must remember that London was the focal point of the 1727 campaign.[38] The city to which Fielding came in 1727 was a political battleground where young and ambitious men inevitably took sides. At this crucial juncture, Fielding chose the side of Robert Walpole and the Whig establishment. In coming to London, Fielding also came to his father's side and committed himself to his father's world. This choice had political as well as personal significance. By studying the reciprocity between Fielding's loyalty to the Whig establishment and his loyalty to his father, we can learn much about his politics and the politics of mid-eighteenth-century England.

𝕱amilp 𝕭ackground

The Great War and Mid-Eighteenth-Century Memory

The year 1727 not only marked Henry Fielding's arrival in London and an important election campaign; it also marked the promotion of Edmund Fielding, the novelist's father, to the rank of brigadier general in the king's army. Besides his military background, Fielding's father also had important ties with one of England's great ruling families. His father, John Fielding, was the youngest brother of William Feilding, the 3rd Earl of Denbigh (the two branches of the family chose different spellings for their last name). Separated by birth from the earldom and its perquisites, Fielding's grandfather and father each turned to one of the standard professions open to younger sons of the nobility: the first chose a career in the church, and the second, a career in the military. The pride that Henry Fielding took in signing himself "esquire" and his descriptions of himself as a "gentleman" reflect his sense of his family's status and his aristocratic sympathies.[1]

Edmund Fielding, the younger son of a younger son, had to make his own way in the world. Opting for a military career, he could give his own son only limited and

occasional financial help. Once he separated himself from
his maternal grandmother,[2] the young poet also had to
make his own way, and thus came to London because the
city offered opportunities for rapid advancement and
financial success. Except for a few brief absences, Henry
Fielding spent his adult life in London, seeking its honors
and rewards. His ties with the aristocracy were real but
tenuous. In matters of learning and taste he might pretend
to aristocratic culture and élan, but his economic and
social positions were much closer to those of Steele and
Defoe than to those of Bolingbroke or Swift. He could not
inherit a living, and he did not try to win one by dutifully
serving an old and established institution. Instead, his
livelihood depended on mastering the ways of the city.
Though he portrayed country life as virtuous and occasionally "allworthy," he admired London's innovations
and opportunities as the small landowner (who had little to
gain from either) could not. His engrossment by the city
and its ways is expressed clearly in his *Plan of the Universal
Register Office* (1751), when he proposes to establish a kind
of eighteenth-century employment office in order to overcome the one difficulty of city life: "In large and populous
cities, and wide extended Communities, it is most probable that every human Talent is dispersed somewhere or
other among the Members; and consequently every
Person who stands in Need of that Talent, might supply
his Want if he knew where to find it; but to know this is the
Difficulty, and this Difficulty still encreases with the
Largeness of the Society."[3]

I emphasize the weakness of Fielding's ties with the
aristocracy and an instance of his positive view of London
life, because a recent study of his politics mistakenly

assumes that his family background and his classical education at Eton gave him a "solid core of aristocratic conservatism that was the anchor for his social and political beliefs."[4] This faulty hypothesis leads its originator to describe Fielding's politics as akin to the Toryism of Bolingbroke. Actually, one constant in Fielding's political writing was disdain for Bolingbroke's backward-looking model for the state. That Fielding should scorn Bolingbroke is not surprising, if we recognize that his descent—his status as the grandson of an earl's youngest brother—paid no bills for him and left him to seek success in the city. Unlike Bolingbroke, he had little to regain by a return to Elizabethan political and social norms.

We may guess at another important motive behind Fielding's contempt for Bolingbroke, if we assume that he shared with his father a fairly common conversation that begins with the question, "What did you do in the war?" If young Harry ever asked such a question, and if Edmund had any gift for narrative, then the youth probably received an exciting, unforgettable answer fully capable of shaping his lifelong political attitudes. Edmund Fielding was a gallant soldier who distinguished himself in the most extensive, expensive, and controversial war that England had yet fought: the War of the Spanish Succession. An officer under Lord George Hamilton at the Battle of Liège in 1702, and then under the famous Brigadier General Webb at Blenheim in 1704, Fielding's father served the Duke of Marlborough during his finest hour. Rewarded for his gallantry at Blenheim, he (like many in his family) made a career of the army, rising eventually to the rank of lieutenant general and commanding a regiment that took his name.[5]

The military record of Edmund Fielding might merit

only a footnote in a discussion of his son's politics were it not for the telling effects of the War of the Spanish Succession, and its forerunner, the War of the League of Augsburg, upon the politics of eighteenth-century England. As the War of the Spanish Succession wound down from the British high point at Blenheim to the less successful, more costly battles at Almanza and Malplaquet, it divided English society. It created a political controversy in which party labels took on unprecedented importance, in which Bolingbroke briefly could promulgate a Tory ideology.[6] By 1727 the war issue was passé, but the issues of urban vs. rural interests, moneyed vs. landed wealth, which the war intensified and defined, were still being debated by Bolingbroke and others. The fact that his father made his small mark in Marlborough's army perhaps led Fielding to cast a cold eye on those who brought the duke down. In *The Jacobite's Journal* No. 15 (12 March 1748), he caustically describes the jacobitical "Art of Lying and Misrepresenting," claiming, " 'Twas by such Arts as these that the brave *Marlborough* and the just *Godolphin* fell a Victim to the Intrigues of Harley and ***" (p. 190). We certainly may suspect that his treatment of Bolingbroke as an unmentionable evil was learned at his father's knee.

Because my description of the influence of the War of the Spanish Succession upon British politics will lead me away from the narrow subject of the Fielding family, I should outline the interpretation toward which I am moving. Support for the wars of King William and Marlborough inevitably required support for the Bank of England, and for the system of public credit and joint stock companies, that the British set up to finance them.[7] These financial innovations contributed to the rise of Boling-

broke's great enemy, "the moneyed men," and in some
cases hastened the political and economic decline of the
landed gentry. Thus loyalty to Marlborough and loyalty
to London's financial system were reciprocal and, most
important, were part of Fielding's political patrimony.
When he arrived in London during Bolingbroke's great
paper war against Walpole, those loyalties steered him
away from the viscount's camp, as they would throughout
the rest of his life.

The political allegiances of Fielding's ancestors and rela-
tives exemplify the division between landed and moneyed
interests, and also help us to understand why Fielding
took a certain course. The Earls of Denbigh, Fielding's
wealthy landowning uncles and cousins, were Tories.
Edmund Fielding's first cousin, Basil Feilding, 4th Earl of
Denbigh, was rewarded with a tellership of the Exchequer
during the Harley ministry (1713–15), although his Toryism was not so extreme as to include support for James II.
But Basil Feilding's brother, a second son who looked out
for himself by making a good marriage to Lady Diane
Howard, went to Parliament as a Whig and shared the
representation of Castle Rising in Norfolk with none other
than Sir Robert Walpole. Basil Feilding's son William, the
5th Earl of Denbigh, the Earl throughout Fielding's lifetime, also was a Tory and took a prominent part in the
opposition to Walpole's measures in the House of Lords.
His wife and Maria, Marquise de Villette, the second wife
of Bolingbroke, were fast friends. The Denbigh papers in
the volumes of the Historical Manuscripts Commission
include a substantial collection of letters from the Viscount and his wife to the Countess, expressing both
personal and political sympathy over a period of fifteen

years. All this as the Earl's second cousin, Henry Fielding, criticized Bolingbroke and his ideas.[8]

The larger issues reflected by the divisions within the
Fielding family appear quite clearly in Swift's writings for
the Harley ministry. Those writings show how the war
issue dominated English politics between 1710 and 1714,
giving them a rare and (in certain ways) false ideological
clarity. Swift unfailingly assumes that a state of war,
involvement in continental politics, and the maintenance
of a standing army in England and mercenaries elsewhere
increase the national debt and contribute to the growth of
joint stock companies and speculation. His repeated assertions that England's geography meant the nation to be a
maritime power and to avoid land wars (VI, pp. 22, 31–32)
mask his desire to avoid those expenses which necessitated
"that mistaken Notion of Credit, so boasted of by the
Advocates of the late [Godolphin] Ministry" (VI, p. 56).
Throughout these writings Swift heaps scorn upon those
who profit from the debt and the war, arguing that the true
sources of their wealth are increases in the tax on land
which leave "the Landed-Men half ruined" (VI, pp. 126–
27).

Swift was not alone in assuming a direct relationship
between foreign conflict, the national debt, and the new
economics. As early as 1700, during the interval between
the War of the League of Augsburg and the War of the
Spanish Succession, Congreve's Sir Wilful Witwoud—a
rude country landowner in need of refinement—plans a
trip to France, "If an how that the peace holds, whereby
that is, taxes abate" (III, iii). In 1725, Defoe, a writer much
more sympathetic to economic change and innovation
than Swift, warned

. . . the citizens and inhabitants of London . . . and builders
especially, that if peace continues, and the public affairs continue in honest and upright management, there is a time coming, at least the nation hopes for it, when the public debts being
reduced and paid off, the funds or taxes on which they are
established, may cease, and so fifty or sixty millions of the
stocks, which are now the solid bottoms of the South-Sea
Company, East-India Company, Bank, etc. will cease, and be
no more; by which the reason of this conflux of people [to
London] being removed, they will of course . . . return again to
their country seats, to avoid the expensive living at London.[9]

The Tory political program, as writers like Swift and
Bolingbroke developed it, was designed to hasten the
coming of the "time" that Defoe predicted. While they
never urged repudiation of the debt, the Tories hoped to
phase it out, eliminating along with it the economic and
political power of the moneyed men.

Perhaps Swift despised Robert Walpole partly because
the Great Man confounded the Tory formula and,
however unintentionally, showed the great gap between it
and the political, social, and economic realities of mid-
eighteenth-century England. He kept England out of war
for over twenty years, but the result was not as Defoe
prophesied or Swift hoped. Walpole's peace strengthened
the economic power of the moneyed men, made the national debt a fact of life, and witnessed the ever more rapid
growth of London. What Swift called "the pernicious
Counsels of borrowing Money upon publick Funds of
Interest" (VII, p. 69) had become standard economic policy
by 1745, when Fielding began to write *The True Patriot*, a
journal in which he directs his appeal to those whose entire
"Estate" is "in the Funds." To heighten that appeal,
Fielding on several occasions links Stuart success with

immediate and total disavowal of the national debt. Whereas Swift and Bolingbroke see the end of the debt (albeit never by repudiation) as the first step toward return to an ideal polity, Fielding sees it as part of a nightmare of social dislocation and suffering. For him the stock exchange and the national debt are as much a part of British life as the Anglican church and English common law. To rouse his audience, he will portray the young pretender as a threat to all three.

An understanding of Fielding's and Swift's different attitudes toward public finance, and a realization of how their differences are rooted in the controversy over the War of the Spanish Succession, is essential if we are to understand Fielding's politics, and to comprehend some puzzling yet ultimately very significant remarks by Swift. Donald J. Greene has emphasized that Swift, as a refugee from Jacobite violence, secretary to the Whig statesman Sir William Temple, and chaplain to the Whig Earl of Berkeley, considered himself and was considered by others to be a Whig. As further evidence against the cliché of Swift as the Tory arch-reactionary, Greene cites Swift's references to himself, in letters written after 1730, as "a good Whig" and "a zealous Whig," and Samuel Johnson's assertion that "By his political education he was associated with the Whigs, but he deserted them when they deserted their principles, yet without running into the contrary extreme." Greene uses his caveat to argue, following Namier, that eighteenth-century political labels generally resulted from "historical accident" rather than from ideological differences. He uses the example of Swift to support Walcott's claim that the terms "Whig" and "Tory" were largely meaningless.[10]

Greene's caveat mistakenly overlooks a significant qualification Swift himself makes when he describes himself as a Whig—a qualification that again points back to the wars with France and the changes they wrought in English society. In Swift's caveat (not Greene's) we can see the importance of the different notions of property that he and Fielding held; we also can discern a potentially more precise rubric for eighteenth-century political differences than Whig and Tory labels alone provide. For example, the letter of 8 January 1733 to Lady Betty Germain, in which Swift describes himself as a "zealous Whig," includes this statement: "As to myself I am of the *old Whig principles*, without the modern articles and refinements" (italics mine). Swift echoes this statement in his letter of 23 March 1734 to Francis Grant (also cited by Greene) when he writes of "septennial Parliaments [which are] directly against the *old Whig principles*, which have always been mine" (italics mine).[11] Rather than accepting Swift's claims at face value, as Greene does, we must determine the difference, in Swift's mind, between the "old Whig principles" and the modern refinements to which he refers, and must assess the meaning of that difference in terms of eighteenth-century political ideology and principle. We would do well to look again at the propaganda Swift wrote between 1710 and 1714, for in this work he assumes that Whigs will see him as a member of their opposition; then he tries to convince them that there is no substantial difference between their interests and the interests of the Harley ministry, rephrasing the issues at hand to prevent them from falling under the Whig-Tory rubric. I believe he uses the same ploy in his correspondence, and that it should not mislead us.

The title of one of Swift's major works for Oxford reveals some of the ambiguities that the war brought to his politics: *Some Reasons to Prove that no Person is obliged by his Principles as a Whig, to Oppose her Majesty or her Present Ministry*. Published in June 1712, this pamphlet takes the form of a letter to an unnamed Whig lord who has inherited "a great Patrimonial Estate." Swift opens it with a claim that Namier and his disciples echo today: "*Principles*" are not the source of the "Dispute between your Lordship and me" (VI, p. 123), because there is no real difference in principles between the two parties. Swift then stakes out his common ground with the Whigs and argues that it is broad enough to subsume all small differences:

I can truly affirm, That none of the reasonable, sober *Whigs* I have conversed with, did ever avow any Opinion concerning Religion or Government, which I was not willing to subscribe; so that, according to my Judgment, those Terms of Distinction ought to be dropped, and others introduced in their stead, to denominate Men, as they are inclined to *Peace* or *War*, to the *Last* or the *Present Ministry*. [VI, p. 123]

Swift here accepts old-fashioned Whig "opinion" concerning the virtues of the Anglican establishment and constitutional monarchy, just as, in his correspondence, he professes loyalty to the "old Whig principles" upon which the settlement of 1689 was based—a settlement Swift witnessed, unlike Pope or Fielding. But the decisive issue here is not fealty to the Revolution Settlement; rather, it is the war. Swift sees the war as the source of political division in England—a division which in all likelihood separated his politics from those of Edmund Fielding. He even goes so far as to argue that continuation of the war threatens the principles of 1689. He eagerly uses an analogy to Roman history that places the villainy of Julius Caesar (Marlborough) in sharp contrast to the virtue of Cato and Brutus (Oxford and Bolingbroke), who "joined heartily on that side which undertook to preserve the Laws and Constitution, against the Usurpations of a victorious General, whose Ambition was bent to overthrow them" (VI, p. 134).

In a pamphlet published after the fall of the Tory ministry, Swift again portrays himself serving the preservers of the Constitution. He claims that George I would do better to place his faith in the Tories, rather than in the Whigs, because the Tories "have been instructed in the Doctrines of Passive Obedience, Non-Resistance and Hereditary Right, and find them all necessary for preserving the present Establishment in Church and State, and for continuing the Succession in the House of Hannover, and must in their own Opinion renounce all those Doctrines by setting up any other Title to the Crown" (VIII, p. 92). Of course, the ironies in the last passage are labyrinthine (Swift, in most of his pamphlets, dissociates the Tories from the discredited "Doctrines of Passive Obedience, Non-Resistance, and Hereditary Right"), and generalizations about it are risky. Still, it clearly shows Swift supporting the "Establishment" founded in 1689 and the succession set up in 1701. The passage treats the old Tory slogans ironically and supports the judgment that, "Like Harley and Burke, Swift accepted the order of 1689 as finality. He worked to conserve the values of the society in which he had grown up." Swift's claims for himself as "a zealous Whig" are accurate, then, insofar as he "According to pre-1685 standards . . . would have seemed sharply anti-Tory."[12] His Whiggism appeared most clearly when, at the height of his efforts for the Oxford ministry, he affirmed the most crucial of "old Whig" principles: "That the Legislature should have the Power to change the Succession, whenever the Necessities of the Kingdom require, is so very useful towards preserving our Religion and Liberty, that I know not how to recant [of it]" (VI, pp. 92–93).

After he recites this greatest of Locke's doctrines, however, Swift immediately distances himself from the association that it would seem to imply: "The worst of this Opinion is, that at first sight it appears to be *Whiggish*; but the Distinction is thus, The *Whigs* are for changing the Succession when they think fit, though the entire Legislature do not consent; I think it ought never to be done but upon great Necessity, and with the Sanction of the whole Legislature" (VI, 93). He appropriates the first principle of the old Whigs, but then declares that it smacks of Whiggism. Through this ploy he suggests that his Whig contemporaries have lost touch with their heritage: that he, and the ministry he speaks for, are the only political force true to the principles of 1689 and 1701. Swift never tired of defending Oxford from charges that he plotted the restoration of the pretender (VIII, pp. 164–79), occasionally turning the charge against Marlborough (VIII, p. 39). But he also never fails to distance himself from the political group that worked most actively to insure the Hanoverian succession and reaped great rewards from it—the new Whigs.

Swift must qualify Locke's views on legislative control of the succession and distance himself from the new Whigs because his loyalty to "old Whig principles" is bound ineluctably with his loyalty to the social order based on landownership that he and Bolingbroke admired, and that the wars against France changed. Swift is capable of an almost egalitarian tone when he speaks of the rights of citizens. The statement that "Government without the consent of the governed is the very definition of slavery" comes from his pen, not from Thomas Paine's. But a basic assumption sets Swift's view of the rights and powers of citizens apart from the view of eighteenth-century Whigs. His "Lockean eloquence received immediately an un-Lockean qualification: since power follows property, only the consent of the substantial landowners—or a majority of them—need be counted." Swift, the "old Whig" or Tory, shares with Fielding, the "new Whig" or Whig, the premise that "power follows property." The premise that distinguishes Swift's Whiggism from Fielding's is that land is the only true property. As Swift puts it, "The possessors of the soil are the best judges of what is for the advantage of the kingdom"[13]—a statement into which Fielding would have interjected, "or of Property in the Funds."

"The modern articles and refinements" that separate Swift from the mainstream of eighteenth-century Whig politics, then, do not involve constitutional or (in cases other than that of Sir Richard Steele[14]) religious principles. The great issue that divides Swift from Marlborough, Godolphin, and the "Whigs" is the war, and more important, the economic and social changes that it brought. By thus limiting the difference between himself and the Whigs, Swift focuses attention on what he felt was the major political issue of his day—that is, the kind of economic system England was to have. He never opposes war per se, never declares that there can be no occasion when the interests of Britain might be served by fighting. Rather, he opposes the long continuance of the War of the Spanish Succession because he wants to halt the economic and social changes that twenty years of war have caused. His appeal to the Whig-lord asks that both the political principles and the social order of 1689 be preserved. But whether we concentrate on his opposition to the war or on his opposition to social change, we see Swift espousing values and views alien to those of most eighteenth-century Whigs, including Edmund Fielding.

Swift's is "a vision turned early, firmly, nobly to the past"[15]—the past in which expensive continental wars had not given rise to funds, stockjobbers, and a national debt. He can use Lockean political terminology, but he can conceive of the contract upon which government is based only as a contract between the "possessors of the soil." The reactionary tendency of his politics appears most clearly in his reversion to a theory of monarchical prerogative to justify Queen Anne's creation of twelve new peers—the action that assured approval for the Peace of Utrecht, and thus ended Marlborough's war. In this instance, Swift's "medieval" view of property brings him very close to reversing his assumptions about the need to limit royal authority. Similarly, even when Swift finds it politically expedient to collapse distinctions between his party and the Whigs, he only can extend his appeal to a Whig-lord whose "Estate" is in land. Not only do the moneyed men continue alien to his politics, but his description of this Lord, as we shall see, is also more wishful than realistic.

Despite his often misleading use of the word "Whig,"

Swift's case shows that the Whig-Tory rubric is not as meaningless as Greene and others contend. Indeed, "Whig" and "Tory" take on clear and important meanings if we use them, as Swift did, to describe fundamental differences in attitude toward economic and social changes stimulated by the War of the Spanish Succession. Swift, Bolingbroke, and the Tories look back to and idealize an economy based on the land and its products, and a mixed government based on mixed distribution of the land. The Oxford ministry worked toward that ideal by trying to end the war, to liquidate the national debt, and to check the power of stockbrokers and financiers. For the Tories, Marlborough and Godolphin became the great enemies. Swift attacks the Duke not for religious reasons, but because his successes extended the war, and because, despite his ownership of great parcels of land, he encouraged the social change that followed Britain's long military involvement on the continent. Swift retails the story that Godolphin "was originally intended for a Trade" (vii, 8),[16] for the same reason; it implies that Godolphin did not merit his position, and at the same time marks him as the type for all "upstarts."

The Whigs, in opposition to the Tories, exult in the new economic system and idolize Marlborough. They assume that commerce, rather than a traditional and largely unchanging system of landownership, is the best means of enlightening self-interest. They share Mr. Spectator's delight in the Royal Exchange, where men are "thriving in their own private Fortunes, and at the same time promoting the Publick Stock."[17] They elevate the merchant and the investor to the title of gentleman,[18] while they satirize the landed gentry, which Swift and

Bolingbroke hoped to restore to power. Fielding, who satirizes man's capacity for irrational self-love as well as the venality of Sir Robert Walpole, often sounds like a Tory. But his oft-expressed admiration for Marlborough,[19] and his unflinching appeal to men whose estates are not in land alone, clearly mark him as a Whig—as his father's son. While Swift devoted himself to fighting the changes that the war brought, Fielding was active politically after Marlborough and Walpole had ushered England, for better or worse, into the modern era.

Fielding tended to see the change as for the better. I say "tended" because his aesthetics, more than his politics, were influenced by his classical education and sense of social place. His fiction was innovative, but (witness the preface to *Joseph Andrews*) with reference to the classics. Although Fielding *is* a Whig, and his Whiggism is particularly demonstrable in his acceptance of the monied interest, his fiction does not always reflect this loyalty as, say, Samuel Richardson's does. Christopher Hill has outlined the ways in which Richardson grounds *Clarissa* in changing notions of marriage, the family, money, and their interrelationship.[20] Perhaps even more revealing, in *Sir Charles Grandison* Richardson's hero, although meant to be an exemplary aristocrat, is also (and more convincingly) an exemplary city man—an executor of wills, a framer of contracts, an arranger of marriages. While Fielding performed those very chores at his Universal Register Office, he rarely brings that world into his fiction; when he does, his tone usually darkens. In this respect his work is not as socially progressive as Richardson's. His disdain for *Pamela* and his stormy relationship with Richardson reveal his uneasiness with the changes taking place in English society and art. He is more comfortable with aristocratic, classically educated city men—the tradition of Addison and Steele—than he is with a true product of the urban bourgeoisie. But if, in his early duels with Richardson, Fielding strikes a pose of aristocratic hauteur, his later praise for *Clarissa* and efforts at rapprochement with his great rival reveal his allegiance both to a new man and to a new type of art. His admiration for the determination, intelligence, and success of upstarts like Richardson outweighed his contempt for their failings in matters of style and taste.

Of course, Swift was not politically active during Fielding's adult life, so some of my generalizations about his politics vis-à-vis Fielding's may not seem directly relevant. Swift's work is relevant, however, not only because it focuses in important ways upon the War of the Spanish Succession, but also, and most important, because it gives the first and clearest expression of Bolingbroke's Tory ideology. And Bolingbroke's role in the political melees that Fielding encountered during his early years in London was undeniably and absolutely central. Bolingbroke brings Swift's emphasis on property in land and his call for return to a prewar political and social order into the great paper war of the 1720s and 1730s. He keeps alive the issues that the war defined for Swift and himself and, in so doing, inevitably sets himself against Fielding.

In his famous *Craftsman* essays, *A Dissertation Upon Parties*, Bolingbroke echoes Swift by celebrating mixed government and tracing its origin back to an "alteration of the state of property and power" (II, p. 148) concluded during the reign of Queen Elizabeth I. As he describes this "alteration," the Tory cast of Bolingbroke's mind becomes

strikingly clear. He begins by asserting of the Norman era
that "Kings, lords, and church were in those days, and
long afterwards, the great proprietors; and by the nature
of their tenures, as well as by the bulk of their estates, they
held the commons in no small subjection, and seem to
have governed without much regard to them." Then, as a
result of a series of costly civil wars and the confiscation of
church properties, "A great part of the lands . . . were
parcelled out to those who could buy, at very cheap rates"
(II, p. 142). According to Bolingbroke, this "new foundation" of property permitted England to reach "the true
poise of a mixed government, constituted like ours on the
three simple forms [of King, Lords, and Commons]" (II, p.
148). When Bolingbroke speaks of property, he, like
Swift, refers to landed estates and their products. As he
makes the basis of mixed government a mixed (but certainly not equal) distribution of land, Bolingbroke limits
the political franchise to landowners and merchants who
trade in agricultural products and goods. On this basis he
assails the "new constitution of the revenue since the
revolution" for creating a new kind of property, and for
ruining the balance struck during Elizabeth's reign. This
"new constitution of the revenue" gives the monarch the
"means of influencing by money and governing by corruption" (II, p. 160). He labels it a threat to the British
constitution, a Dutch innovation that takes no account of
British political traditions.

Some have found that, in his history, Bolingbroke ex-
hibits perfectly what the Marxists call reification. Certainly later historians have discredited his account, and
Raymond Williams has shown that the story of a rural,
simple, virtuous England under attack by "new commer-

cialism" is a fiction, albeit an enduring one. Williams traces the story back through Massinger and More and into the classical tradition, arguing that it deluded men by obscuring the true causes of political oppression and economic exploitation.[21] Bolingbroke might rejoin that the changes during his lifetime were both real and important—that the invention of the Bank, the growth in the supply of paper money, and the proliferation of joint stock companies all give meaning and force to his redaction of the country-versus-city theme. For our purposes, however, the eternally debatable question of reification is less important than recognition of the crucial assumption Bolingbroke brings to the politics of mid-eighteenth-century England—the belief that property in land should be the basis for social and political order. If the political career he built upon this assumption reflected a reified consciousness, then Bolingbroke paid dearly for his reification. Try as he might to hide the fact, his assumption placed him in a small, shrinking minority.

The argument of *A Dissertation Upon Parties* depends upon one other assumption, shared by Whigs and Tories: that a mixed government, in which King, Lords, and Commons balance each other, best serves both public and private good. Once his audience grants Bolingbroke this premise, he proceeds to a closely reasoned argument that the new system of finance which makes its currency money, not land, threatens mixed government, and therefore is inimical to his audience's interest. Bolingbroke's claims to be nonpartisan (claims of which a Namierian might make much) should not blind us to the political ends of the *Dissertation* and the masterful rhetorical means by which Bolingbroke furthers them. He takes the old Whig arguments for limiting royal prerogative and uses them against "the new constitution of the revenue," a Whig creation. Like Swift, he appeals to the principles of 1689 as he attempts to mute political differences, but, at the same time, he makes assumptions about the nature of property that embody a Tory political view. Though twentieth-century readers may overlook his strongly partisan position, eighteenth-century readers did not.

The argument of the *Dissertation*, while rhetorically ingenious, is also limited in its appeal. Although it can appeal to landowners and merchants, the *Dissertation* inevitably dismisses bankers and stockjobbers as "upstarts." Herbert Davis's description of the audience to which Swift appeals in *The Conduct of the Allies* holds, in general, for Bolingbroke's version of the Tory argument: "It [*The Conduct of the Allies*] was particularly calculated to convince the Landed Interest that the war was being unnecessarily prolonged for the benefit of the new moneyed class."[22] Not only does the *Dissertation*, with its narrow definition of property, limit Bolingbroke's audience; it also commits him to a demonstrably false description of his society. His politics, like Swift's, matured during the years of controversial, expensive, and continuous war on the continent; and, in 1727, he proceeds on the basis of outmoded distinctions, separating the landed interest from the moneyed interest in order to argue that Britain's political survival depends on the rebirth of an independent, landed commons. As Daniel Defoe pointed out and as many subsequent commentators have affirmed, English society was not divided as Bolingbroke claimed. Landed families were heavily involved in the stock market (even Swift and Gay had money in the stocks); conversely, successful moneyed

men bought country estates with their gains.[23] Bolingbroke's arguments in favor of a landed aristocratic social
order are finely wrought, but false. That fact becomes
clear when Defoe gives as the reason for "the prodigious
conflux of the nobility and gentry from all parts of England to London": "that many thousands of families are so
deeply concerned in . . . stocks, and find it so absolutely
necessary to be at hand to take advantage of buying and
selling . . . that they find themselves obliged to live constantly here [in London] or at least most part of the year"
(p. 307). Bolingbroke and Swift's premises about property
and its role in English politics are nostalgic, rather than
realistic. The landed interest no longer existed in a pure
form and no longer dominated British life. The day belonged to London's "conflux of the nobility and gentry"
and to the moneyed men—groups with which both
Edmund and Henry Fielding had to deal.

   Fielding's decision to come to London involved not only
a choice between the country and the city but also one
between his father's family and his mother's. For the first
twenty years of his life, Fielding's relations with his father
were uncertain. After the unexpected death of Henry's
mother, Sarah Gould Fielding, in 1718, his father married
"a widow described . . . as an Italian and a Roman
Catholic, who had kept an eating house in London." The
marriage stirred hostility between Edmund Fielding and
his in-laws, finally leading Henry's maternal grandmother
to sue his father for custody of her daughter's children and
their small estate. During the long years of litigation over
his custody, young Henry apparently sided with his
grandmother, even, according to one story, fleeing to her
side when his father threatened to prevent him from visit-

ing her.[24] The beginning of his reconciliation to his father, in 1727, was fraught with great portent for him. On one hand, Fielding's physical separation from his grandmother, from the Gould family, with its wealth and standing in British legal circles, may signal his declaration of independence. Certainly, once he arrived in London, Fielding long deferred the legal career for which the Goulds had destined him. The reconciliation with his father also meant that Fielding left behind the Gould estate at East Stour. As he pursued literary and then legal success in the city, Fielding would look back to his rural upbringing with great fondness. But, after he cast his lot with his father, a happy rural seat was never again to be possible for him. Recognizing his father, Fielding accepted a financially uncertain patrimony. If the recently promoted brigadier general could afford to send his son to Leyden, Henry soon learned how unreliable soldier's wages were. After his sudden return from his studies abroad, he had to make his own way.[25]

The most crucial aspect of Fielding's reconciliation with his father, however, is the social attitude it reflected. Edmund Fielding returned to England from Blenheim, rewarded for his gallantry and success, and won Sarah Gould, a woman who was above him. The long legal battle for guardianship of their children was only one sign of what seems to have been the Goulds' consistent dislike of their son-in-law. Successful, landowning, and titled, they did not take to a man whose only fortune was his valor, one who lacked an estate, despite his illustrious ancestry. Fielding's grandmother won the custody battle, but apparently she did not win young Henry's heart and mind.

His choice, of course, was neither absolute nor final. Fielding's father married four times and completely squandered his son's patrimony. Later in his life Fielding would once more rely on the Goulds, particularly his uncle Davidge and his cousin Henry, and with their help would practice law. But in 1727 Fielding finds in his father (whom he once, supposedly, fled) a patron. Perhaps the clearest sign of Fielding's sympathy for his father's plight as a half-pay officer is the long list of deserving but unjustly treated military men characterized in his work: in *The Modern Husband*, Captains Merit and Bravemore; in *Joseph Andrews*, the father of the young woman Wilson ruins (III, iii, pp. 206–7), Paul in the story of Leonard and Paul, (IV, x, p. 315), and Gaffar Andrews; in *Tom Jones*, the virtuous lieutenant who would not prostitute his wife for promotion (VII, xii, pp. 370–71), and the father of Mrs. Miller (XIV, v, p. 757); and, most important, Captain Booth in *Amelia*.

Thus while we cannot say why or for how long Fielding was reconciled to his father, we can and must observe the political significance of this step. Loyalty to Marlborough was part of Fielding's partrimony, probably the part that most powerfully set him apart from the Scriblerians, whose literary work he admired. And loyalty to Marlborough implied loyalty to the City that his wars had shaped—to the Exchange, the Bank, the Debt, and the Funds. Swift, Bolingbroke, and Defoe all understood how the war had changed English life. Bolingbroke and Swift, finding the change for the worse, designed a political program to fight it. Men like Edmund Fielding profited from the change and assumed it was for the better. As a twenty-year-old would-be playwright, Fielding may not have thought about or understood the political significance of a war long past. But he liked his father, admired Marlborough, and was excited by and committed to city life. If we understand the political attitudes latent in his youthful likes and dislikes, we can understand why, upon his arrival in London, he took up the cause of Robert Walpole and wrote panegyrics on George II.[26]

Fielding's political patrimony guided him away from Bolingbroke and toward the Whig establishment. Confronted with Walpole's abuses of power, his political loyalties would change. In his plays he often imitated the Scriblerians. But even as he pursued theatrical success, Fielding remained his father's son, making assumptions about property and politics that separated him from the Tory wits and linked him with Steele, Addison, and Cibber, the leading lights of the Whig literary establishment. To account for Fielding's plays, to understand fully their shifting poses and tones, we must recognize the political pressures and the principles that helped to shape them.

III

Fielding's "Undistinguished Career as a Dramatist"

Literary and Political Uncertainty

Although he could not know it at the time, by coming to London Fielding was taking the first step in his career as a playwright—a career he would pursue, with few interruptions, for the next ten years. Fielding's plays are of uneven quality, but Charles B. Woods has summarized succinctly and accurately the general response to them. After noting the anomalous opinion of George Bernard Shaw, he writes: "The plays of Henry Fielding have rarely received high praise, despite the fact that some of them were extremely popular on the eighteenth-century stage. Nearly everyone who has commented on them during the last two centuries has felt obliged to concern himself with a question that may be put in this way: why should a writer of Fielding's abilities have had such an undistinguished career as a dramatist?"[1] Woods describes Fielding as "an experimental dramatist" who wrote at a time when audiences encouraged and rewarded innovation. He implies that Fielding's banishment from the stage by the Licensing Act prevented him from discovering a dramatic mode in which his abilities could better serve him.

My explanation for Fielding's "undistinguished career as a dramatist" differs in emphasis, but not in direction, from Woods's. Fielding was "an experimental dramatist," but I will try to show that he experimented primarily because he was a young and uncertain writer, not because a great wave of theatrical change engulfed him. At the heart of his literary uncertainty was a political uncertainty —an inability to choose between two different political groups and two different conceptions of the nature of man. As Fielding's political views changed, so did the plays he wrote, as well as the companies that performed them. His impressive abilities were wasted as he shifted mercurially between opposing political and literary camps.

Students of Fielding's theatrical career immediately face a revealing problem. Inexpensive, well-edited paperback editions of his farces and satires are available; however, pending the publication of the Wesleyan edition of Fielding's plays, his conventional five-act dramas are available only in the much maligned and outdated Henley edition. Similarly, students will find several helpful essays on the techniques and themes of Fielding's dramatic satires, but no equally insightful and extensive critiques of conventional efforts like *Love in Several Masques* or *The Modern Husband*.[2] Only a few of Fielding's plays still are read and discussed, partly for qualitative reasons (the satires are funny, fast paced, and serve as both political and literary documents) and partly because of the assumptions that most scholars today bring to eighteenth-century literature (critics reared on the Tory interpretation find Fielding's imitations of Gay much more relevant than his imitations of Cibber). Most recent studies of Fielding's plays, however learned, have been fundamentally incomplete. They have discussed only two short periods in his theatrical career—the years 1730-31 and 1736-37— and have failed to elaborate the significance of 1727–29 and 1732–35, years Fielding spent pursuing success at Drury Lane.[3] They have not explained how Fielding's years in the theatre add up to a career, and have failed to answer the question set by Woods.

This chapter will assess how Fielding's conventional Drury Lane comedies and his more famous farces are parts of a dramatic whole. It will trace Fielding's changes in playhouses, models, and patrons, noting the shifts in political allegiance they reveal. It will then suggest how this political uncertainty affected *all* of Fielding's plays, and how it contributed to their one basic similarity: clumsy, unsuccessful use of double plots. By elaborating the political reasons for Fielding's failure as a dramatist, this chapter will point once more to the important relationship between literature and politics in eighteenth-century England, and it will assess for the first time the significance of Fielding's years at Drury Lane.

Love in Several Masques, the play Fielding brought to London in 1727, was produced at Drury Lane on 16 February 1728. In the preface to its 1728 edition, Fielding reminds his reader that it appeared during the runs of two great popular successes, Gay's *Beggar's Opera* and Cibber's *Provoked Husband*, asserting that its failure to go beyond three performances is not a fair sign of its quality. His apologia is revealing because he professes admiration for both of the plays against which he was competing, thus pointing not only to the transitional nature of his career as a playwright, but also to his fundamental political uncertainty. The dramatic modes and politics of Gay, a charter member of the Scriblerus Club, and Cibber, the butt of the Scriblerians, were largely antithetical. A young playwright who admired both writers obviously had contradictory impulses and ambitions, and obviously would have trouble pleasing a town that expected a distinction between Scriblerian satire and Drury Lane comedy.[4] Contemporaries complained that his exemplary comedies drew too dark, too satirical a picture of the society against which the exemplary figure defined his virtue. Many of Fielding's early farces lost satiric momentum as they paused to develop sentimental situations and characters.[5] In both types of plays, Fielding repeatedly tried to combine satire and sentiment in a double plot, reflecting the bifurcation of his artistic vision in the 1730s.

Fielding's admiration for Gay as well as for Cibber points to more than conflicting ambitions; it also reveals a decline in the importance of party labels (at least the party labels of Anne's reign) in the theatre of his day. Drury Lane remained the theatre of the Whig establishment, and Fielding had to take his sharp anti-Walpole satires elsewhere. His movements to and from Drury Lane thus reveal shifting literary and political values, but the identification of Drury Lane with support for Walpole and of the Little Theatre in the Haymarket with the opposition can be misleading. During the years of Whig hegemony under Walpole, dramatists, like politicians, were able to concentrate upon questions of interest, rather than questions of ideology. Many of Fielding's contemporaries wrote both for Drury Lane and for the Haymarket, theatrical companies eagerly borrowed each other's successes, and plays by Colley Cibber were produced at all theatres, not just at Drury Lane. The theatrical wars did flare occasionally, but popularity and success were the goals of dramatists and producers—goals that young Fielding shared. While his shifts between Drury Lane and the Haymarket were not atypical, their frequency does set him apart from his contemporaries (most of whom lacked Fielding's gifts and his opportunities) and reveal his literary and, ultimately, political uncertainty.

The theatrical careers of two of Fielding's now-forgotten contemporaries shed light upon his. Henry Carey is now remembered, if at all, as the author of *Chronohotonthologos*, a farce introduced at the Haymarket in February 1734, but performed by the Drury Lane company of actors, who, under the leadership of Theophilus Cibber, were rebelling against the Drury Lane management. Throughout the early 1730s Carey wrote for and had benefit nights at Drury Lane. His *The Contrivances; or, more Ways than One* was a popular Drury Lane afterpiece (and was also performed at Goodman's Fields and Lincoln's Inn Fields). In December 1732, Drury Lane produced Carey's afterpiece *Betty; or, The Country Bumpkins* barely a month after the opera *Treminta*, for which he wrote the libretto, was on the boards at Lincoln's Inn Fields. In July 1735 Carey produced another afterpiece, *The Honest Yorkshireman*, at the Haymarket. He took it there (according to the preface to its 1736 edition) only after the Drury Lane managers held a copy of it for nine months, promising to perform it but then returning it at the end of their season. Carey's experience with *The Honest Yorkshireman* closely parallels Fielding's with *Don Quixote in England*. This, coupled with his and the entire Drury

Lane company's shift between theatres in 1734, lends credence to the view that Fielding's shifts were fairly typical.

An even more obscure contemporary of Fielding's was Charles Coffee, whose *Phebe; or, The Beggar's Wedding* was one of the most popular afterpieces of the early 1730s. Written for and first produced at Drury Lane, it was performed on all the major London stages, including the Haymarket. On 27 April 1730, while Drury Lane was performing *Phebe*, Coffee introduced "a new farcical ballad opera," *The Female Parson; or, Beau in the Suds* at the Haymarket. Three days later the Haymarket company performed both *Phebe* and *The Female Parson* for Coffee's benefit night. In August 1731, Coffee returned to Drury Lane with the hugely successful afterpiece, *The Devel to Pay; or, The Wives Metamorphos'd*. This work, taken from a Goodman's Fields afterpiece, also would eventually be produced by all the London theatres. In January 1733 Drury Lane produced Coffee's *The Boarding School; or, The Sham Captain* with little success. Coffee, then, not only moved between theatres, but also created entertainments so successful that they were universally produced. It was not at all uncommon for two theatres to offer *The Devil to Pay* on the same night. [6]

The quest after popular success not only led to universal production of efforts by minor figures like Carey and Coffee; it also meant that the classics were shared by London theatres, regardless of political considerations. Nicholas Rowe's *Tamerlane*, which "depicted the Whig ideal of a constitutional monarch . . . and was not performed at all from 1710–1714," [7] was performed regularly on November 4 and 5 at all the London theatres, including, in 1733, the Little Theatre in the Haymarket. All the theatres offered periodic performances of *Cato*, of *Venice Preserved*, and of Shakespeare's history plays. However much Pope may have tried to link his misrule of the theatre with Walpole's misrule of England, Cibber exerted almost universal sway. His masque, *Damon and Phillida*, was one of the most popular afterpieces of the era. *The Provok'd Husband* also was performed by all major companies. (Anyone eager to politicize the theatre of Fielding's era should note the 18 December 1733 production of this play at the Haymarket theatre, for the benefit of John Dennis, with a new prologue by Alexander Pope!) So were plays such as *Love Makes a Man*, *The Comical Rivals*, and *The Double Gallant*. Cibber's preeminence was such that the Haymarket company ceded its stage to him and his son Theophilus during their conflict with the Drury Lane patentees in 1734. Likewise, popular works of Fielding's, including *The Mock Doctor*, *The Miser*, *The Virgin Unmask'd*, and *The Intriguing Chambermaid*, were part of Drury Lane programs even while he was managing the Haymarket Theatre and satirizing the Cibbers. After passage of the Licensing Act, they remained in the Drury Lane repertoire.

Clearly, bold statements about Fielding's moves to the Haymarket revealing literary and political heterodoxy and his returns to Drury Lane revealing orthodoxy are not completely accurate. The state of the theatre was not the same as it had been during 1710-14, when Addison carefully chose his prologue and epilogue for *Cato* in order to win both Whigs and Tories, when Richard Steele's pamphleteering temporarily cost him his state offices, and when productions of *Tamerlane* ceased. Nor was it as

political as it had been in 1720-21, when two Whig factions warred for control of Drury Lane, and when Steele's
loyalty to Walpole was tested and then rewarded.[8] Whig
hegemony meant that, at least until 1736-37, the London
stage was not divided between Whig and Tory camps.
Writers were more or less free to find an audience where
they could, although certain material cound not be produced at Drury Lane. Fielding's *Welsh Opera* never would
have sullied Cibber's stage, and *Pasquin* and *The Historical
Register*, despite their popularity, were not picked up by
other companies.[9]

Fielding was a much more successful playwright than
Coffee or Carey; in terms of performances, he was second
only to Cibber among the authors of his era. His shifts in
playhouses thus created controversy. When he alluded to
political motives for those shifts, he knew a large audience
stood ready to grasp his implications. In addition, Fielding
was, at times, ready to push his satire so far that it made
political comment and risked political retribution. When
the Prince and Princess of Wales attended a performance
of *The Historical Register* and *Eurydice Hissed* on 18 May
1737, the plays became both political and literary events,
with the Earl of Egmont particularly noting the parts of
this "satire on Sir Robert Walpole" that the Prince applauded most heartily.[10] Whatever ambivalence we may
note in Fielding's politics during 1736-37, *Pasquin*, *The
Historical Register*, and *Eurydice Hissed* clearly served the
cause of the opposition. Their sharp political bite separated them from the less controversial fare at London's
other theatres and attracted record crowds.

With a balanced sense of the politics of drama in mid-
eighteenth-century England, we can go on to assess the

meaning of Fielding's changes in playhouses, patrons, and literary models, and can interpret anew his plays. If our Namierian realization that party labels declined in importance in the 1730s will check our tendency to force political significance upon Fielding's changes,[11] so our analysis of the peculiar shape of Fielding's theatrical career will check our tendency to dismiss political considerations.

The production history of Fielding's plays suggests that his theatrical and political loyalties were, indeed, bound. Fielding's writing for the royal patentees at Drury Lane generally avoided explicit political comment, while his writing for the Haymarket company derived much of its power and appeal from thinly veiled allusions. Most of his Drury Lane plays were five-act comedies in the tradition of Sir Richard Steele and Colley Cibber; representing the trials of an exemplary individual or couple, these works inculcated moral precepts. The Haymarket plays generally were three-act farces in the tradition of the Scriblerus Club, satirizing human weakness and representing a scene of corruption and folly to which figures of exemplary virtue were alien.[12]

As he changed theatres and dramatic modes, Fielding also changed patrons. The first chapter sketched some of the political implications of Fielding's relationship with his first patron, Lady Mary Wortley Montagu. Loyal to her Whig heritage,[13] Lady Mary strongly supported Walpole and his ministry, and (as Isobel M. Grundy has shown) encouraged her young cousin to attack Pope and praise Walpole. In the two poetic fragments written under Lady Mary's supervision, Fielding's combination of praise for her "political idol" and disdain for her "literary enemy" underlines how closely literary and political activity were connected for him.[14] Lady Mary helped Fielding place *Love in Several Masques* at Drury Lane; he dedicated the play to her and prefaced it by admitting his lack of experience and thanking Cibber and Wilkes for "their civil and kind behaviour previous to its representation" (VIII, preface, 9). Lady Mary's patronage apparently was not strong enough to make Cibber and Wilkes accept Fielding's second play, *The Temple Beau*. Consequently, he produced that five-act comedy at Goodman's Fields and then, under the pseudonym H. Scriblerus Secundus, began to write farces for the Haymarket company. With one exception, he signed the *nom de plume* to all his Haymarket plays of 1730–31 and abandoned it when he returned to Drury Lane in 1732.

Although Pope did not confer his public blessing upon the plays of H. Scriblerus Secundus, the Haymarket farces were so popular that Fielding could do without a patron. When he returned to Drury Lane with *The Modern Husband*, however, he appealed for Walpole's patronage in terms similar to those he had used three years earlier in the fragments written under Lady Mary's supervision. When production delays at Drury Lane in 1733 led Fielding back to the Haymarket with the political satire *Don Quixote in England*, he signaled the revival of his heterodoxy by dedicating the play to Chesterfield, who had recently joined the opposition. A tentative and unsuccessful return to Drury Lane in 1735 produced a dedication of *The Universal Gallant* to the 3rd Duke of Marlborough, the politically ineffective grandson of the great Whig hero.

Fielding's rapid shifts in patrons, playhouses, and modes have a baldness and simplicity that do not express fairly the literary and political uncertainty of the individual plays. Even when he rejoined Drury Lane and dedicated his first mature comedy to Walpole, Fielding could not avoid Scriblerian satire and farce. Even at his most farcical and satiric, he never lost faith in the potential of men to behave in exemplary ways.

An artificial and complicated situation that Fielding sets up in *Love in Several Masques* defines a literary and political uncertainty that will manifest itself throughout his theatrical career. After almost marrying Mr. Wisemore, Lady Matchless comes to London to avoid him and to punish fools, fops, and fortune-hunters. Wisemore, whose only fault is a tendency to describe at length his own virtues, comes to town to win Matchless. In Act IV, Scene ii, the disguised Lady Matchless meets him in the park and, pretending to be a woman of great wealth, offers fame and fortune to him in return for his favors. Their subsequent dialogue summarizes Fielding's uncertainty about the nature of man, a doubt that affected all of his subsequent plays. Wisemore claims: "Grandeur is to me nauseous as a gilded pill; and fortune, as it never can raise my esteem for the possessor, can never raise my love. My heart is no place of mercenary entertainment, nor owns more than one mistress" (VIII: IV, ii, 64). Matchless says in an aside, "Generous, worthy man!" but turns to Wisemore with the words, "Romantic Nonsense." She offers more resistance to his exemplary virtue: "Then know, thou romantic hero, that right is a sort of knight-errant, whom we have long since laughed out of the world. Merit is demerit, constancy dulness, and love an out-of-fashion Saxon word" (VIII: IV, ii, 65).

Matchless's double response to Wisemore encapsulates

the conflicting pressures that will shape Fielding's stage-craft. Just as Matchless cannot decide whether Wisemore merits praise or scorn, so Fielding can neither accept nor reject the dramatic convention of the exemplary figure. The literary outgrowth of this indecision manifests itself quite clearly in *Love in Several Masques*, for, once Matchless temporarily rejects Wisemore's worthy behavior, social satire replaces the earlier emphasis upon his virtues. Three town fops who covet the fortune of Matchless move to center stage, and the focus of dramatic attention turns to their schemes to win her. Exemplary comedy returns only after Wisemore, through disguise and cunning, wins Matchless and dismisses his rivals from the stage. Indeed, Wisemore creates such a powerful "prevalent example" that, in the play's last scene, two other virtuous couples come to understandings and agree to marry. The conclusion of *Love in Several Masques* makes an "example" of Wisemore's rude nobility, but only after the town norms of deceit and disguise taint it. Because Fielding believes in the "good sense and good nature" (VIII: IV, ix, 73) of Wisemore and Matchless, he writes a comedy, after using the three fops in order to flirt with satire. His faith in virtue, however, was neither strong nor constant during his years as a playwright. When that faith weakens, satire, farce, and political heterodoxy follow. The cynicism of Matchless's second response becomes the norm by which Fielding judges characters and events; figures of exemplary virtue disappear, instead of the town fops.

The speed and extent of Fielding's changes in attitude become apparent when we turn to his third play, *The Author's Farce* (1731). In this popular success the exemplary figure, Witmore, is the friend of a hack writer named

Harry Luckless. Like his antecedent and namesake, Wisemore, Witmore utters virtuous sentiments, criticizes debased modern customs, and practices active charity, assisting the debt-ridden Luckless when he can. Luckless submits to the town's ways and writes a puppet show portraying the Court of the Goddess of Nonsense, seemingly winning both theatrical and political success. During its performance Luckless learns that he is actually King Harry the First of Bantam. As King Harry leaves for his native land, with an entourage that reads like the cast of *The Dunciad*, Witmore disappears. Sir Farcical Comic (Colley Cibber), Mrs. Novel (Eliza Haywood), Don Tragedio (Louis Theobald), Marplay and Sparkish (Cibber and Wilkes) all are promised places in Bantam; Witmore goes unrewarded and unmentioned, his sober virtue apparently foreign to the kingdom of pure farce.

The fate of Harry Luckless provides a comical but important indication of Fielding's conflicting literary impulses. Witmore's presence amidst the concluding farcical scenes would strike a discordant note, so Fielding, at the expense of probability, eliminates him, just as he disposed of the three fops in *Love in Several Masques*. To foster the absurdity and satire of the conclusion of *The Author's Farce*, he must suppress one element in the play's double plot. Similarly, the didacticism that pervades the final scenes of *Love in Several Masques*, leading to a curtain song "not without a moral," can flourish only after he abruptly ends the satiric plot. These disappearing acts are arbitrary and unsatisfactory solutions to the problems created by Fielding's mixture of exemplary and satiric plots; they reveal an artist who cannot manage his material. Of course, even in Fielding's day the debate over double plots already had become moot. I wish not to revive it, but merely to indicate how Fielding's double plots point to an uncertainty that persisted regardless of his literary mode.

A writer of well-established loyalties, Steele at his best could use a double plot and still maintain a unified, consistent effect. In *The Conscious Lovers* the courtship of the servants, Tom and Phillis, provides a subplot for the main action, the courtship of Bevil, Jr., and Indiana. Steele does not dwell upon Tom's escapades, but when he does portray them, he avoids diverting or fragmenting the response of his audience. In accord with Addison's dictum that the "Under-Plot . . . bear such a Relation to the principal Design, as to contribute towards the Completion of it, and be concluded by the same Catastrophe,"[15] Steele uses Tom to clarify the virtues of Bevil, Jr., focusing on the coxcomb's failures to help explain the hero's successes. Because Fielding's "Under-Plots" resulted from his own internal divisions, he never could imitate the technique effectively used in *The Conscious Lovers*.

Fielding's awkward use of an "Under-Plot" is perhaps clearest in *The Modern Husband*, the five-act comedy with which he returned to Drury Lane in 1732 and which he dedicated to Walpole. The exemplary figure in this play is Mrs. Bellamant, a woman who scorns the diversions of the town and is faithful to her husband. To intensify the effect of her virtue, she necessarily must be tested; Lord Richly, an eighteenth-century version of the Restoration rake, who uses money and political influence in an attempt to seduce her, thus becomes a potentially useful character. But once Richly and his cohorts, the Moderns, appear, Fielding concentrates on their knavish schemes, rather than on Mrs. Bellamant's virtues. Because of his Scriblerian urge to attack the venality of the new, "moneyed" men (Richly has made his fortune manipulating South Sea stock), his "Under-Plot" overshadows his major plot. The play, which shifts abruptly between scenes of virtuous and of debased behavior, fails to develop unity of purpose and effect. The portrayal of "modern" vices does not define or elaborate Mrs. Bellamant's virtues, so she comes to us *sui generis*, a shining miracle set apart from the life around her.

Typical of the disjointedness of *The Modern Husband* is an early scene (x: i, viii, 20–21) in which Captain Merit and Captain Bravemore prepare to ask for Richly's patronage. The two captains discuss the corruption of a town that permits merit and bravery to go begging. The scene develops an effective satiric point, but Fielding, after creating interest in the soldiers, never returns them to the stage. Like the fops and Witmore, they vanish. As the plot divides into two unrelated actions, Fielding's attempt to curry political favor fails. Richly is a product of the new economic order that flourished during Walpole's long tenure, and Fielding's contempt for Richly is one thing we can be sure of in this otherwise confused effort. Effusive dedications to the contrary, Fielding's satiric "Under-Plot," his harsh description of a great man's levee, showed that he was not ready for political orthodoxy.

But if orthodoxy was difficult for Fielding, political heterdoxy offered no escape from his dilemma. In 1734 he left Drury Lane and brought *Don Quixote in England* to the Haymarket theatre. Most scholars describe this play as a sharp satire of corrupt campaign practices—practices opposition propagandists continually attributed to Walpole and the Pelhams. Its dedication to Chesterfield, and the description of the earl as "one who hath so gloriously distinguished himself in the cause of liberty, to which the corruption I have here endeavoured to expose may one day be a very fatal enemy" (XI: dedication, 7), imply that political comment will be the main business of the play. Contrary to Fielding's claims, however, political satire extends through only five scenes. The rest of the play describes the trials of an exemplary couple, Fairlove and Dorothea, who must overcome the prejudices of their parents and financial obstacles in order to marry.

We can appreciate how the exemplary and satiric plots pull against each other if we observe how Fielding splits the hero's character. In the political satire, Quixote is his naive and innocent self. His simple virtue enables him to serve as a satiric foil for the greedy voters, who urge him to run for Parliament in order to force a currently unopposed candidate to bribe them. Quixote's innocence exposes the venality of citizens, who feel that "if we had but an election once a year, a man might make shift to pick up a livelihood" (XI: III, iv, 53).[16] In the exemplary plot, however, Quixote is a wise and pragmatic figure, warning Sir Thomas Loveland, Dorothea's father, to balance financial and romantic considerations in choosing a husband for his daughter. Quixote's advice brings about the marriage of the exemplary couple. Thus, as Fielding moves away from his opening commitment to Scriblerian satire, he creates two Quixotes: a Don who is simple, idealistic, and mistakes inns for castles; and a surprisingly practical Don, who countenances (without submitting to) financial considerations and appeals to common sense.

Don Quixote in England, taken as a whole, reflects its

hero's double personality. It includes Fielding's most famous air, "The Roast Beef of England." First written for the farcical *Grub-street Opera*, it expresses the Scriblerian theme of burgeoning corruption in English society and politics. But the play also portrays, in Sir Thomas Loveland, a decent and perceptive member of the political establishment.

Between *Don Quixote in England* and *Pasquin*, Fielding produced only one play, an unsuccessful Drury Lane comedy entitled *The Universal Gallant*; so it appears that his literary and political uncertainty persisted until he composed his final dramatic satires. As early as his first effort for Drury Lane, Fielding could not decide whether to satirize or admire rustic old English virtues. Correspondingly, he could not fix his attitude toward the "moneyed" men. Richly is a villain, but the attack on him involves no elevation of rural swains. And Wisemore, the self-proclaimed rustic, gains a "matchless" wife by learning the city's ways. Thus the plays themselves manifest Fielding's ambivalence toward Walpole and the society he dominated.

The conflict between Scriblerus Secundus and "Steele Secundus" also left Fielding open to criticism by his contemporaries. That criticism can help us to understand the background of literary and political transition against which Fielding pursued success as a playwright. A history of Fielding's "press" hardly is possible here, but *The Grub-street Journal*'s attacks on him provide important insights into the difficulties he faced as he changed theatres.

When Fielding returned to Drury Lane in 1732 with *The Modern Husband*, after his great success at the Haymarket with *The Author's Farce* and *Tom Thumb*, he proclaimed not only his return to seeking patronage from Robert Walpole, but also his return to entertaining by "rules" and "reason." He described his successful farces as the "unshaped monsters of a wanton brain" (x: prologue, 9) and claimed that he was leaving them behind him. The return to Drury Lane, then, not only involved a recantation of Fielding's earlier literary satire (Cibber and Cibber, Jr., both of whom Fielding had attacked in *The Author's Farce*, had major roles in *The Modern Husband*), but also involved the retraction of his recent attack on Walpole in *The Welsh Opera*.[17] Fielding, who had scored his successes as a farce-writer by mimicking the Scriblerians, suddenly became a target for *The Grub-street Journal*, a publication which expressed opposition views in politics and literature and with which Alexander Pope had ties.[18]

Ronald K. Paulson and Thomas Lockwood have summarized the literary and political motives behind the *Journal*'s sudden antipathy for Fielding. It concentrated attention on Fielding only after he returned to Drury Lane in 1731–32, "associating himself with Colley Cibber (a subject of the *Journal*'s attacks since he became laureate) and with a patent theatre that would not attack the ministry."[19] But the *Journal*'s reasons for attacking Fielding were more complex than Paulson and Lockwood allow. It never charged Fielding with choosing the wrong side, never attacked him on the basis of a party label. Instead, it assailed his Drury Lane comedies for not conforming to the norms which his own claims for them implied. Fielding's exemplary comedy, according to the *Journal*, did not measure up to the standards of Drury Lane—the standards of Steele and, most significantly, Cibber. In their more systematic and lengthy criticisms of Fielding, the

Journal's writers set upon him not because he was, "Like any ambitious young playwright . . . first drawn to Drury Lane."[20]

The letter signed by Dramaticus in *The Grub-street Journal* No. 117 (30 March 1732) gives a lengthy critique of *The Modern Husband* that avoids ad hominem vituperation and raises theoretical questions about decorum and probability. Dramaticus introduces his standards for comedy early in the letter: "Our best Comedies are those that mix the serious and merry together: of this kind are *The Careless Husband*, *The Conscious Lovers*, *The Journey to London* etc. The decency of polite life is preserved in these pieces; and the whole interspersed with characters that enliven the scene, and feast the mind with an agreeable mixture of light and solid meats."[21] Dramaticus then censures Fielding's as a pale and ineffective imitation of the comedies of Steele and Cibber. "As to Emilia and Gaywit [the young exemplary couple in *The Modern Husband*], they are but faint sketches after Lady Grace and Mr. Manly in *The Journey to London*; as Mr. and Mrs. Bellamant [Fielding's older exemplary couple], are of Lord and Lady Easy in *The Careless Husband*" (p. 35). We may be surprised to find a *Grub-street Journal* writer setting up Colley Cibber as one standard of comedic excellence, but the motive behind this praise reveals itself when we observe the criticisms of Fielding to which it leads. Dramaticus's comments on Steele and Cibber actually damn by faint praise, for he defines their comedy as inimical to serious comment upon social vices. He claims that, while Steele and Cibber always "preserve" the "decency of polite life," Fielding does not. He attacks Fielding for "lowness" and thus refuses to countenance the combination of Drury Lane sentiment and Scriblerian satire that Fielding attempts.

The logic of Dramaticus's praise for Cibber is apparent in his remarks on Fielding's Lord Richly and Mr. and Mrs. Modern—the embodiments of all that is wrong with contemporary society. He writes: "I know not why he has made Lord Richly a great man, unless it be for the sake of describing a levee; nor why this great man should be the greatest rogue that ever lived: I don't conceive but that the Play had gone on full as well without it. The making of a great man absolutely and totally bad, both in the public and private station, in his morals and behaviour, is so poor, so scandalous, *so mean a piece of satire*, that . . . all good and wise men will despise the odious picture" (p. 35, italics mine). He continues, "As to the *Modern Husband* and his Lady, they are such wretches that they are *as much below Comedy*, as they are our pity" (p. 36, italics mine). The complaint that "the play had gone on just as well" without these characters is actually a complaint that Fielding made his play of disparate elements. While the satiric purpose behind Fielding's portrayal of Richly is obvious even today, Dramaticus's convenient obtuseness enables him to attack the comedy of Steele, Cibber, and the newcomer Fielding. If we follow his premises to their logical conclusion, Dramaticus is arguing that relevant, effective satire is foreign to, or "below," Drury Lane comedy. Scriblerian satire and Drury Lane sentiment are, he assumes, irreconcilable. The young playwright can write like Steele and Cibber (and focus upon Mrs. Bellamant), or he can write like Scriblerus Secundus (and savage "modern" corruptions). He cannot, Dramaticus warns, work both sides of London's literary streets. Dramaticus's rhetoric was a complicated variation of the praise-by-blame ploy, for the *Journal* could hardly attack Fielding for satirizing modern vices about which it also complained.

Yet it had to protest his making Drury Lane theatre, the bastion of social conventionality and Whig supremacy, the platform for his satire.

Fielding's uncertainty appears in an attempt of his to answer Dramaticus. The play at issue in this case was *The Old Debauchees*, a truly second-rate effort in which two exemplary figures, Young Laroon and Beatrice, finally overcome the wiles of a corrupt, lascivious priest. Dramaticus returned to keynote the *Journal*'s campaign, leveling the standard charges of lewdness and lowness against the play and its afterpiece, *The Covent Garden Tragedy*. He again tried to take from Fielding the rights and prerogatives of a satirist, in the issue of 13 July 1732 attacking the anti-clerical rantings of one character in *The Old Debauchees* while also setting up two maxims that any satirist would immediately reject: "You may imagine perhaps, Mr. Bavius, that much the greatest part of this fine language being spoken by *Old* Laroon, a vicious Character, and only of the Popish Clergy, it can have but very little efficacy in exposing ours. But there are two maxims which you are to take as a key to the whole: That whatever scandalous thing is said of a Priest, you are to regard only what is spoken, and not the person who speaks it; and that *Priests of all religions are the same*" (p. 54). By the logic of this argument, not only would Swift be liable to charges of blasphemy, but the rhetorical strategy of Dramaticus and of the *Journal* itself, which employed praise by blame,[22] would also lose its effect. We might anticipate that Fielding's defense would emphasize the satirist's need to manipulate a variety of voices and poses, to have his characters express views that he does not accept. But in *The Daily Post* of 31 July 1732, rather than rejecting the premises of Dramaticus, Fielding turns to the example of Steele. He does not defend his plays as satires; instead, he argues that scenes from low life are not inimical to comedy. He builds his defense around a reference to Steele's essay in *The Spectator* No. 266 (4 January 1712): "Sure the Scene of a Bawdy-house may be shewn on a Stage without shocking the most modest Woman; such I have seen sit out that Scene in the *Humorous Lieutenant*, which is quoted and recommended by one of the finest writers of the Last Age" (p. 62). This appeal to the authority of Steele and "the Ladies"[23] in effect wins the argument for Dramaticus by indicating that Fielding accepts his premise—his description of Drury Lane drama as limited to polite comedy, in which characters encounter menacing but not distressingly evil social vices. Once Fielding accepts this stereotype for the Drury Lane stage, he places himself in the impossible position of trying to prove that the dark social comment of plays like *The Modern Husband* or *The Old Debauchees* is neither very powerful nor very dark. He commits himself to stifling one impulse behind his drama—the Scriblerian desire to lash the town into virtue. Fielding's position for debate becomes hopeless because, like it or not, his portrayal of Lord Richly and his equation of marriage with prostitution in the epilogue to *The Old Debauchees* question values held by his audience. As Dramaticus was clever enough to observe, Fielding could fit his comedy to Drury Lane standards only by denying a part of it.

Fielding shared a view of the London stage similar to that of Dramaticus. The preface to *The Modern Husband* implies, and his later defense of *The Old Debauchees* clearly shows, that when Fielding moved to Drury Lane, he saw that the change inevitably commited him to a different type of drama. Like Dramaticus, he felt that this drama arose from a faith in humanity's potential for virtuous, exemplary behavior that was antithetical to "low" satire. For Fielding, as for Dramaticus, the return to Drury Lane meant that Steele and Cibber, not the Scriblerians, should be the models for his art. For Fielding, as for Dramaticus, return to that playhouse meant return to support for the Whig hegemony, as Sir Robert Walpole embodied it. Yet Fielding's inability to stifle his Scriblerian impulse—indicated in *The Modern Husband* by his concentration on the vices of Richly and the Moderns—shows that the established literary and political categories were inadequate guides in his search for a literary mode and political position. In his duel with Dramaticus, Fielding appears as a transitional figure trapped by outmoded classifications and assumptions. In the 1740s he would escape by creating his own critical and political vocabulary, but in the 1730s he was too uncertain to abandon outdated dichotomies.

In his two major dramatic satires of 1736–37 and their afterpieces, Fielding seems to emerge from his uncertainty and to speak with a strong, unequivocal voice. In *Pasquin* he returns to the figure of the Court of the Goddess of Nonsense, but he uses it to attack standard Scriblerian targets like Cibber and Theobald. He sets up an analogy between stage and state and, like Pope, uses signs of corruption in the drama to satirize corruption in the state.[24] In these late plays Fielding abandons the double plot and provides a series of related farces, all of which contribute to an attack on the status quo. In *Pasquin*, for example, the romance between Colonel Promise and Miss Mayoress, which in past Fielding efforts might have developed into a sentimental "Under-Plot," enhances the political satire. In *The Historical Register* Fielding makes nary a gesture toward exemplary comedy; he observes venality and bad taste to be so universal that he portrays them in four different situations without changing his basic direction. In the final years of his theatrical career, then, Fielding appears to avoid the missteps of his youth and to place himself firmly in the Scriblerian camp. A sign of this new rootedness is that he no longer shifts between farce and comedy but creates a new mode, "Dramatic Satire" (*Pasquin*, p. 1).

There are, however, signs that the Scriblerians did not welcome Fielding to their camp. For example, *The Grub-street Journal* No. 239 (15 April 1736) included a "sharply worded note that Pope had not, as rumour had it, been present at a performance of *Pasquin*." Not content to deny Pope's presence, the *Journal* added an extra fillip: "We think it very probable that a person of his uncommon sense and wit will not have any curiosity to see it acted at all."[25] To understand the motives behind this attack, we must turn to Fielding's portrayal of the opposition in his final dramatic satires, for there we again see a political uncertainty akin to that which earlier led him to resolve dramatic situations by means of disappearing acts.

An early dialogue in *Pasquin* helps us to understand Pope's disdain for the play. An alderman and the mayor discuss the parliamentary candidacies of Sir Harry Fox-Chace and Squire Tankard. The alderman supports Sir Harry and the Squire because their "Estates in our own Neighborhood render 'em not liable to be bribed." The mayor controverts the alderman's arguments; Trapwit, the play's author, justifies the alderman's speech by claim-

ing, "you must have one Fool in a Play" (I, 6). When Sir
Harry and the Squire appear, Fielding shows them to be
rude and bibulous men who are as ready to offer bribes as
the Court party candidates. Thus the landowning country
gentleman whom the Scriblerians wished to return to
political preeminence becomes the subject of sharp satire.
Writers like Bolingbroke, Swift, and Pope, who dedicated
their political program to destroying the power of the new
moneyed "upstarts," could have applauded Fielding's portrayal of the Court candidates, Lord Place and Colonel
Promise, for these characters typify the very Walpolian
abuses that the Scriblerians repeatedly attacked. But his
treatment of Fox-Chace and Tankard, the landed men,
removes Fielding from Bolingbroke's opposition "circle."
More openly satiric versions of Sir Roger de Coverley, Sir
Harry and the Squire only extend the standard Whig
satire on members of the Country party and adumbrate
the character of Squire Western, another Tory from
whose latent Jacobitism and bellicose rusticity Fielding
will distance himself satirically.

Fielding attacked Walpole and the Court influence in
Pasquin without closing ranks with the Tories. A similar
political ambivalence surfaces in *The Historical Register for
the Year 1736.* After lashing the political and literary failings of Walpole's England, Fielding again shows the men
of the opposition to be as mean spirited and greedy as
Walpole. The only significant difference between the
"Patriots" and the harlequin Quidam is that Quidam
(Walpole)[26] is cleverer. I do not mean to suggest here that
Fielding's final dramatic satires were so evenhanded as to
be innocuous, or that Walpole was mistaken if he did,
indeed, push through the Licensing Act in response to

Fielding's plays.[27] Walpole was much more recognizable than his covey of rivals, and much more likely to be associated with the conditions Fielding described. Fielding's satires, no matter how unflattering to the opposition, still served its purposes, and, with opposition support, became great popular successes.

Yet Fielding's portrayal of the opposition in his dramatic satires surely reflects a continuing political uncertainty. In these plays he is very much a man in search of a party and a cause. He assails both the moneyed men, who were the heart of the Whig hegemony, and the landed men, who were the center of Tory hopes. By implication, he calls for a new opposition untainted by nostalgic Tory dreams as well as by Walpolian venality; however, he finds no realization of this ideal anywhere on the contemporary political scene. The literary counterpart of this political uncertainty appears when we note that Fielding's experiments in the mode of "Dramatic Satire" allowed him to avoid a double plot, but only at the cost of completely fragmenting his action, rather than unifying it. The final satires are loosely connected series of vignettes, signifying neither a successful transition to a new literary mode nor a successful transition to a new political allegiance.

In their divided satire the late plays reflect an ambivalence similar to that manifested in the disjointed double plots of the early plays. Given the persistent uncertainty evident in the late plays, the course of Fielding's political career—opposition writer, disenchanted opposition writer, Walpole supporter—becomes, at least in hindsight, inevitable. Total disillusionment and bald political satire could not resolve the duality that first appeared in

Lady Matchless's response to Wisemore. Thus *Pasquin* and *The Historical Register* were not final resting points for Fielding, but were instead new indicators of a still changing position. The latter play was first performed with Lillo's bourgeois tragedy, *Fatal Curiosity*—a juxtaposition which may indicate that Fielding had not resolved the satire-sentiment split so much as he had isolated extreme examples of each type. He could combine the models of Scriblerus Secundus and "Steele Secundus" in the programs at the Haymarket, not in the plays he wrote for that theatre. In perhaps the best summary of his political and literary uncertainty in 1736–37, Fielding himself wrote in the prologue to *Pasquin*:

> So does our Author, rumaging his Brain
> By various Methods try to entertain;
> Brings a strange Groupe of Characters before you,
> And shews you here at once both *Whig* and *Tory*;
> Or *Court* and *Country* Party you may call 'em:
> But without Fear and Favour he will maul 'em.
>   [Prologue, 5]

To "maul" both Whigs and Tories was not to create a political identity. The divided satire of the final plays shows that, as late as 1737, Fielding's political values and allegiances remained confused. That confusion led him to experiment with dramatic modes and to produce strange amalgams of traditionally disparate characters and plots. As Fielding shifted his political allegiances, the types of plays that he wrote changed radically, as did the companies that performed them and the audiences that viewed them.[28] Always "rumaging his Brain," always experimenting, Fielding wasted his impressive literary gifts as he moved mercurially between dramatic modes. But even though the plays are an undistinguished group, we must not overlook the important role of the 1727–37 decade in Fielding's literary career. The skillful integration of satire and sentiment achieved in *Tom Jones* became possible only after many unsuccessful practice runs. By acknowledging and understanding the political sources for the clumsy, experimental quality of Fielding's plays, we can better appreciate his accomplishment in *Tom Jones*, and better understand why he almost simultaneously attained political certainty and literary mastery. What was at stake for Fielding during the 1730s was the conception of human nature that he would bring to his art. On the eve of the Licensing Act, he continued to fluctuate between Scriblerian pessimism and Addisonian benevolism, still uncertain whether he belonged with the Tories or with the Whigs. Only after years of political and personal turmoil would he attain the balanced, mature wisdom that enabled him to overcome his political and literary doubts.

I V

ᚷhe ᚷUncertain ᚷOpposition

The Champion *and* Jonathan Wild

Many writers have assumed that the Stage Licensing Act of 1737 was designed to silence Fielding,[1] and that his submission to it reflected his recognition that to fight Walpole and the state would be futile. But today we can question whether the Act really was the last blow in a long battle between Fielding and Walpole. Does this account do justice to Fielding's circumstances in 1737? The Act left all manner of options open to him; if he had wished to become the darling of the opposition, he could have published a banned play[2] and perhaps repeated Gay's success with *Polly*. Or, since his dramatic satires had not committed him to the opposition, he might have returned again to Drury Lane. Plays like *The Mock Doctor*, *The Miser*, and *The Lottery* remained part of the Drury Lane repertoire after the Licensing Act, and their continued success indicates that Fielding could have returned to the stage then (as he eventually did)[3]—at least with the right kind of play. But instead he chose to accept the closing of the Haymarket Theatre. On 1 November 1737 he entered the Middle Temple to pursue his deferred legal career, and for two years his pen was silent. He did not return to literary and political prominence until he began work on *The Champion* in November 1739.

Fielding's silence will disappoint those who want to view stage licensing as an act of political tyranny, rather than as the culmination of a long movement toward reform of the London stage, and who would like to cast him as the heroic opponent of Walpole's villainy. But such Manichaean theories overlook the complex intermingling of interest and ideology in the politics of mid-eighteenth-century England, as well as Fielding's fundamental and persistent loyalty to the Whig establishment. We must recognize the likelihood that his "vanishing act" probably involved his own financial interest. While this recognition may cost us the pleasing portrait of a heroic, democratic Fielding, it helps us to discern the ways in which he embodied and reacted to the political realities of his day.

In *The Champion* No. 13 (13 December 1739) Fielding recounts a dream vision of Helicon. While a "little Man" (obviously Alexander Pope) embraces the Muses, an interloper (obviously Colley Cibber) tries to invade their territory. He begins to climb the hill, but tumbles down crying, "A Cup of Sack is a better thing stap me Vitals" (I, 87). A Great Man and his company then arrive on the scene, and, after the former squeezes the hands of (bribes) the sentries, the party begins a rapid ascent. At this point the Muses "applied to the little Gentleman to defend them; but he, to the great Surprize of every Body, crept under one of their Petticoats"(I, 92). As the Muses turn to others for help, the narrator awakens "in the Inner-Temple" (I, 93) after receiving from the Great Man a "Squeeze by the Hand, that . . . put an End to my Dream" (I, 92).

Leaving aside for the moment Fielding's apparent comment on Pope, we may feel that this vision offers an allegorical rendering of the less savory aspects of Fielding's relationship with Walpole.[4] Certainly the dream's biographical implications are tantalizing. Fielding seemingly admits to beginning his legal studies after receiving a payment from Walpole, and thus perhaps explains his acquiescence in the Licensing Act. The recent discovery of an issue of *The Champion* (4 October 1740) in which Fielding admits to taking money from Walpole "to stop the Publication of a Book [probably *Jonathan Wild*], which I had written against his Practice"[5] makes the idea of money passing between them less startling. Indeed, the "squeeze" referred to in the dream may have been only one of several payments.

Much of the problem with Fielding's acceptance of money from Walpole is ours, not his. Raised on the Tory interpretation of literature, we tend to regard Walpole as unspeakable, a venal man with whom no self-respecting poet would deal. This is to overlook, of course, Walpole's gift of £200 to Pope for work on his translation of the *Odyssey*, as well as some strong hints that the two men struck more than one bargain.[6] Although Walpole's record as a literary patron was undistinguished, the great literary figures of his day, Scriblerian and otherwise, had to deal with him—sometimes to their regret, but hardly to their disgrace. The Tory interpretation is particularly misleading in Fielding's case because it has led scholars to narrow his theatrical career to his scenes of anti-Walpole satire. Thus, when suddenly Fielding is revealed taking money from Walpole to suppress a book, or to acquiesce in the Licensing Act, he is liable to criticism not only for lining up on the wrong side but also for vacillating. Yet in the previous chapter we saw that Fielding never set himself unequivocally against Walpole. Furthermore, Bertrand A. Goldgar's research[7] has shown that Fielding's contemporaries did not make the political applications so popular with modern scholars. Patronage by Walpole was natural, given Fielding's family background and youthful political loyalties. Only the misguided preconceptions of modern scholars turn his relations with the Great Man into a crucial test of his political and moral character; the charge of tergiversation becomes plausible only if commentators persist in distorting plays like *Pasquin* and *Don Quixote in England*, turning them into tracts and overlooking their rich political uncertainty.

My goal here is not to defend Fielding more than two centuries after the fact, but to define the source for some important modern misconceptions about his enduring literary works. The Tory interpretation has given rise to all sorts of misdirected controversies about Fielding's political virtue, distorting our vision not only of his life, but also of his art. The previous chapter attempted to reduce that distortion by refocusing attention on parts of Fielding's theatrical career dismissed by the Tory interpretation, and by describing the relation between Fielding's political indecision and his experimental, misshapen dramatic efforts. This chapter will describe how political uncertainty influenced *Jonathan Wild*, another work that has too often been categorized as entirely anti-Walpole. Evidence from *The Champion* indicates that Fielding's uncertainty continued into the 1740s, even after he joined the opposition. Recognition of this persistent uncertainty, which his recitation of standard opposition slanders against Walpole masked, rather than resolved, should help us understand Fielding's return to Walpole's failing cause

late in 1741. That return, announced by the publication of
The Opposition: A Vision (December 1741), has sparked
controversy among Fielding scholars because it implies
that Fielding's pen could be bought. By studying Fielding's politics in *The Champion* we can accomplish two goals.
First, we can establish a context for *The Opposition: A Vision*
which will defuse much of the controversy[8] that has centered on it. Second, we can define a political source for the
unique character of *Jonathan Wild*.

 The Opposition becomes a problematic work only if we
assume that Fielding's role in *The Champion* was that of a
dedicated opposition propagandist. Although most Fielding scholars share this assumption, it may not be valid. In
The Champion Fielding did not necessarily direct a forceful,
anti-ministerial campaign; rather, he permitted his co-ad-
jutator, James Ralph, to set the political tone. The Advertisement to the 1741 reprint of *The Champion* outlines
Fielding's role in the journal. In it Ralph declares, "Several
Persons having been concern'd in writing the Champion,
and it not being reasonable that any one should be
answerable for the Rest, it has been thought proper to
signify to the Reader, that all the Papers distinguish'd by a
C. or an L. are the work of one Hand; those marked thus
** or sign'd Lilbourne, of another, to whose Account,
likewise, except a few Paragraphs, the *Index of the Times* is
to be plac'd" (I, x). Research by John Edwin Wells showed
that the pieces initialed C. and L. are Fielding's, as
scholars had long supposed.[9] A classical motto prefaces all
the essays thus signed, and in many Fielding elaborates
wittily or learnedly upon the motto, avoiding specific or
forceful political comment. Even in those essays where
Fielding comes to a political point, he rarely fails to pause

and explain the relevance of his classical epigram. Ralph, on the contrary, does not allow displays of learning to divert him from his political task. In general his essays lack mottoes, or use English mottoes whose relevance to his subject requires little explanation.[10]

The Advertisement provides another important bit of information. Almost without exception, we are told, the "Index of the Times" is the product of Ralph's hand.[11] If we locate the most ringing and vitriolic denunciations of Walpole, we discover most of them in the Index. The rebuke to Walpole's *Gazetteer* in the Index to *The Champion* of 1 December 1739 presents Ralph in a moderate but nonetheless bitter vein: "Whereas the Author of the Gazetteer of Yesterday, has had the Modesty to charge *Novelty* and *Innovation* on the important Affair, at present in Agitation, with respect to the *Place-Bill*; this is to inform him, that in the Reign of Charles II no less than *Two Parliaments*, both Whiggish (who had see the fatal Effects of a *Court-Influence* by the Means of *Pensioners* and *Place-men*) had the very same Expedient in Debate . . ." (I, 55). Ralph becomes more typically daring in his vituperation when he deals with the great opposition *bête noire*, the standing army. In the Index to the issue of 18 December 1739, he comments: "We hear from *Scotland*, that certain Soldiers, who were in pursuit of a Deserter, took it into their Heads to seize a loaded Cart, under the Pretense that it contained prohibited Goods, and a Skirmish following between them and the Peasants in the Neighborhood, one of the last was shot dead on the Spot.—*The blessed Effect of a Standing Army*" (I, 116). Instances in which Ralph rails against the army, royal excursions to Hanover, and Walpole's use of places and pensions are numerous.[12] The

Index includes the most specific and unequivocal political
writing in *The Champion*, and it is not Fielding's work.

A pattern of organization characterizes most issues of
The Champion: an allusive, learned, and often nonpolitical
essay by Fielding precedes a section of direct, often bellicose, political comment by Ralph. In his first five leaders
Fielding avoids political issues; instead, he introduces the
Vinegar family,[13] discourses upon the custom of "Hereditary Honour," wonders how talent can be misapplied,
analyzes why virtuous people must maintain a virtuous
appearance, and offers a redaction of Pope's *Essay on Criticism*. Given the dearth of political comment in these opening essays, Fielding's discussion of the misapplication of
talent in the issue of 20 November 1739 may reflect his
own doubts about the endeavor to which he has committed himself. Certainly support for such a hypothesis
grows if we note that Ralph immediately picks up the issue
and seemingly tries to buck up his partner. In the 29
November 1739 issue he argues "that a Man may have
very great Talents, Wit, Learning, Memory, and Elocu-
tion, and yet apply them so awkwardly, that they may
prove detrimental to himself, and offensive to those who
keep him Company" (I, 43). Ralph implies that, in a time
of political crisis, literary gifts that serve no political purpose are wasted. In the issue of 4 December 1739 Fielding
appears to acquiesce in Ralph's view. He prints, and
promises to be guided by, a plea from his bookseller to
"infuse Gall in your Ink, and, instead of Morality, Wit,
and Humour, deal forth private Slander and Abuse" (I,
58).[14] The ironic dismissal of "Morality, Wit, and Humour" indicates how tentatively Fielding responded to
Ralph's urgings.

Fielding's success in dealing out vituperation varied throughout the remaining issues of *The Champion*. In that of 6 December 1739, which follows the letter from the bookseller, he successfully turns a general discussion of the role of fortune in men's lives into a sharp comment upon Walpole's rise to power. But he contributes to the issue of 11 December 1739 an essay upon human nature that is a miniature of his "Essay on the Knowledge of the Characters of Men" and defies any but the broadest of political applications. The essay that heads the 13 December 1739 issue includes a letter in praise of *The Champion* for "not being totally devoted to Politics" (1, 87).

Probably the most revealing single instance of the two writers' persistent differences in attitude and tone comes in the issue of 10 January 1739/40. The issue opens with a letter that bears Fielding's mark and criticizes Vinegar for taking on an "Office too great for any one Man to execute" (1, 174). Fielding then proceeds to develop an analogy between Vinegar and Walpole. He makes an effective satiric point by using the word "Office" in a general sense and concludes by observing, "How ridiculous must it seem then, to see a Fellow of low Capacity, and a mean Behaviour, investing himself with this Office, placing his Family over all the Professions, and shaking a Club at the whole Nation" (1, 175). Ralph, however, not content with this transparent satire, adds a brief note in which Vinegar claims, "tho' the Darts in this Letter, are feather'd with my Name, they are levell'd at a much *larger* Mark" (1, 178). Ralph's metaphor aptly describes his relationship with his co-worker: he repeatedly gives political point to Fielding's allegories and allusions. When he is not pressing Fielding to apply his talents more relevantly, he is busy establishing a background that makes Fielding's essays more politically volatile.

To emphasize Ralph's role in *The Champion* is not to deny that Fielding remained capable of alluding to and addressing political issues. His appeal to the voters of London in the issue of 18 December 1739 offers straightforward and strident political comment, and his derivation for the word "trunk" in the issue of 31 May 1740 slanders Walpole with great verve. But these instances are in the minority. From the uncertain opening of *The Champion* until the conclusion of his active participation in it, Fielding's attitude toward the journal's politics remained quite consistent: "Lastly, as to Politics, our Readers are to regard them as their Physic, not their Food; and they may be assured Dr. Lilbourne [Ralph] will dose them as often as it is requisite" (II, 331–32).

If we recognize that the Index is the political cutting edge of *The Champion* and that Fielding's leaders tend to be witty, classical, and learned, rather than dogmatic, contemporary, and opinionated, we can see that he moved into the opposition camp hesitantly and indirectly. He generally resisted Ralph's urgings that he apply his talents more "effectively," and while he inevitably associated himself with the Index's calls for Walpole's ouster, he did not sign them. Indeed, if we speculate that Ralph published the key to *The Champion* at Fielding's request, we can appreciate how eager Fielding was, in 1741, to dissociate his position from Ralph's, and how clear a distinction between them existed in his own mind.[15] Without engaging in speculation, however, we can say that during his tenure with *The Champion* political views tended to be of secondary interest to Fielding. They did not add up to a firm party position that he could compromise or trim.

Fielding's political uncertainty appears in at least three self-contradictions that run throughout his articles. The first, and most pervasive, involves his conflicting descriptions of the "times": if the reader of *The Champion* wonders whether the period described is the "best of times" or the "worst of times," his confusion merely reflects Fielding's. The second indication of Fielding's uncertainty is visible in the wide range of political and literary models offered by Hercules Vinegar, his family, and his correspondents. Scholars have noted the brilliant satires on Cibber in *The Champion*, but they have failed to emphasize that Fielding comments on Pope almost as much, and that his comments often are sharply critical of the "small Man." Similarly, the journal includes criticisms of Bolingbroke, as well as the more famous attacks on Walpole. The third and most fundamental self-contradiction in *The Champion* appears when Fielding combines blame for Walpole with praise for the merchants and citymen who consolidated their political and economic power during Walpole's long tenure. By 1739-40 Walpole's pacifist foreign policy had cost him support among the merchant classes; this change made it easier for Fielding to attack the Great Man, yet to avoid aligning himself with the Tories. Still, Fielding's complaints about the luxury of the times do not lead him to systematic or extended criticism of the new economic system. Living in an era in which the political labels of Anne's day were losing importance, Fielding writes for the opposition; however, unlike Swift and Bolingbroke, he appeals to, instead of dismissing, London's moneyed men and merchants.

The signs of political uncertainty in *The Champion* also

indicate that Fielding had not resolved the philosophical problem he set himself as early as *Love in Several Masques*. He still could not accept either Hobbesian or benevolist doctrine about the nature of man and society. His self-conflict is particularly apparent in his comments upon the times. In No. 41 (16 February 1739/40) Vinegar discourses on charity, with words that should give pause to those who describe *The Champion* as ever on the attack: "I have the pleasure to observe that the most amiable Characteristic of the present Age is Charity" (1, 275). He goes on to give his opinions about the most deserving objects of this virtue. In No. 33 (21 February 1739/40), Fielding, albeit in an essay that proposes a hospital for fools, refers to the building of hospitals as a praiseworthy example of the age's "Species of Charity" (1, 292). Of course, Fielding also will repeat the old Tory complaints, referring to "this luxurious Age" and describing it as a time "when a prodigious Debt, a useless Army, an immense Fleet, and dreadful Taxes to support them, when a dilatory War, formidable Enemies, and suspicious Allies, hover over us" (1, 268). Nevertheless, recognition of some instance of charity or "publick Spirit" usually rescues him from complete pessimism.

This is not to minimize the importance of Fielding's descriptions of the times as morally, politically, and artistically decadent. *The Champion* is full of such descriptions, and one could argue that they become longer and darker as the journal progresses.[16] The point is that such descriptions are, for Fielding, a deviation from his normally more optimistic and temperate attitude toward man and society. Railing against the times, Fielding developed a Scriblerian tone. His problem in the journal was to reconcile his divergent perspectives on man and society and to develop a tone consistent with his belief that, "though I am unwilling to look on human Nature as a mere Sink of Iniquity, I am far from insinuating that it is a State of Perfection" (1, 80).

If Fielding's comments on the times often are self-contradictory, his references to political and literary figures are even more confusing. As we saw in the previous chapter, during Fielding's life taking a side in the great literary conflicts of the day still had political consequences. Support for Cibber and Drury Lane's version of literary orthodoxy implied support for Walpole; support for Pope in his battle against the Dunces usually meant joining the opposition. At first glance, Fielding's attacks on Cibber in *The Champion* and his praise for Pope as one "whose Works will be coeval with the Language in which they are writ" (1, 34) seem to jibe nicely with the traditional description of *The Champion* as an opposition journal; Fielding's literary loyalties appear to be properly congruent with his political ones. But we have already noted one less than laudatory description of Pope (the "little Man" who fails the Muses in the dream vision of Helicon), and a closer look at Fielding's comments on Pope and Cibber reveals an uncertainty that parallels his political doubts.

For example, in *The Champion* No. 80 (17 May 1740), the lead essay describes the "Proceedings of the Court of Censorial Enquiry." Colonel Apology, obviously a pseudonym for Colley Cibber, is brought to trial for an "Assault" on the English language. Apology's defense skillfully "bites" Cibber, for he claims, "It is impossible I should have any Enmity to the *English* Language, with

which I am so little acquainted" (II, 227). Fielding, however, qualifies his attack on Cibber—a qualification overlooked by scholars who have been raised on the Tory
interpretation. The Court acquits the Laureate after
Vinegar observes that several parts of his *Apology* are
"excellent" (II, 227), and that the book as a whole is "entertaining." Of course, Fielding's suspension of his attack on
Cibber hardly proves political or literary doubt, but
another case in Vinegar's court lends support to the thesis
of uncertainty.

The first case in the "Court of Censorial Enquiry"
involves an A. P. Esq., who is brought to trial for neglecting his satiric "Talents." Fielding clearly refers to Pope,
and the charges are as serious as those he will level against
Cibber. Vinegar puts the case in properly complicated
legal syntax: "the said A. P. the said good Talents and
Design neglecting and no Ways regarding, but having too
much Fear before his Eyes, one *Forage*, alias *Brass*, alias *his
Honour* . . . all Sorts of Roguery to commit and perpetrate
did allow and suffer . . . and by these Means he the said
A. P. did encourage, aid, abet, and receive the said Brass,
etc" (II, 223). Extenuating circumstances arise in this case,
which, as in Cibber's, lead to an acquittal. But the stigma
of cowardice remains as firmly attached to Pope as the
stigma of ignorance does to Cibber. The juxtaposition of
the two trials, then, shows Fielding standing apart from
the assumptions and labels that had governed political and
literary life in previous generations. Taken together, his
portraits of Pope in *The Champion* Nos. 13 and 80 distance
him from the greatest Tory wit, even as he is satirizing
Cibber and Walpole. At two other points in the journal,
Ralph, with his flair for reducing an issue to direct, per-

sonal confrontation, baldly attacks the philosophy of *An Essay on Man*, scornfully describing "the *Ubiquitarian Creed*, which consists of but one Article, *viz.* that *Whatever is, is right*, and which he [the Ubiquitarian] deems as infallible as that of Rome" (I, 103; II, 313). The criticism of Bolingbroke implicit in an attack on the doctrine of *An Essay on Man* gains political point when one Index equates Walpole's moral turpitude with Bolingbroke's.[17]

As Fielding's criticism of Cibber and Pope left him in a literary noman's land, so his attacks on Bolingbroke as well as Walpole left him in a political one. Ultimately, the model for his "new" political position would be the Whiggism of Addison and Steele—a Whiggism that lauded economic innovations opposed by Tories like Swift, Bolingbroke, and Pope. Thus, while Vinegar always qualifies his praise of Pope or his attacks on Cibber, he is unstinting in his praise for his two great predecessors in the genre of the periodical essay (I, 154, 175). But because he is uncertain of his loyalties and trapped by outmoded dichotomies, Fielding spends more time in *The Champion* working out his attitudes toward Cibber and Pope than he does emulating Addison and Steele.[18]

Fielding's occasional praise for Addison and Steele points to the third sign of his political uncertainty in *The Champion*. In their works, London merchants like Sir Andrew Freeport and Mr. Sealand attained social and literary legitimacy.[19] The Scriblerians (Bolingbroke and Swift in particular) opposed this change in the "cit's" status and felt that economic and political power should rest with landed country gentlemen. Fielding's sympathies with the citymen are apparent, particularly when we note his admiration for the exemplary comedy, pioneered by Steele and Cibber, which capped the London merchant's rise to literary respectability. He took care to separate his criticisms of Cibber's *Apology* from his favorable opinion of the early plays, even going so far as to suggest, in *The Champion* No. 75 (6 May 1740), that "some future Theobald" might suspect *The Careless Husband* and *Love's Last Shift* were not by the same hand that wrote the *Apology*. This admiration for bourgeois drama is paralleled in *The Champion*'s repeated appeals to the merchant class. In the first issue Fielding refers to *The Conscious Lovers* and then claims, "I have often wondered how such Words as *Upstart, First of his Family*, etc. crept into a Nation, whose Strength and Support is Trade, and whose personal Wealth (excepting a very few immense Fortunes) is almost entirely in the Hands of a Set of sturdy Scrubs, whose chief Honour is to be descended from Adam and Eve" (1, 9). "Upstart" was a word the Scriblerians, especially Swift, favored, and Fielding's criticism of its use provides one measure of his distance from them.

The Champion No. 15 (18 December 1739) includes the essay that best summarizes Fielding's departure from the political labels of the prior generation, combining a strong criticism of Walpole with an appeal to the citizens of London that describes them as the head and heart of the British political system. The essay is distinctive because it gives to wealthy citymen political virtues that, it claims, their poor country cousins cannot share. It supposes that the wealth of Londoners makes them less liable to bribery and corruption—an integrity the Tories reserved for landowners. All of these themes appear in a passage that, despite its length, merits quotation in full.

Corruption, which hath for many Years been creeping upon us, and working its way imperceptibly under Ground, will if it once finds an Entrance into your [London's] gate, rush downwards like a Torrent, and overwhelm the Nation; for who can stem it, if the Citizens of London yeild to its force? Or where shall it meet with a Dam, if your Walls are none? Can we suppose that those who are able to bribe the richest City in the Universe, will not be capable of succeeding in a beggarly Borough? Or can we expect that a poor County Shop-keeper . . . shall have Virtue enough to refuse what is even necessary to his Livelihood, whilst the opulent Tradesman or Merchant of *London*, avaritiously or perhaps wantonly gives up his Conscience, his Country, nay his own real Interest to hire. [I, 107]

The Scriblerians assumed the system that fostered the growth of London was inseparable from political and moral corruption. For them "Paper Credit" was the "last and best Supply/ That lends Corruption lighter Wings to Fly" (*Epistle to Bathhurst*, ll. 69–70). In *The Champion* Fielding committed himself to a journal that lined up with Bolingbroke on almost every political issue of the day. He associated himself with Ralph's outspoken support for the Place Bill, sniping at the standing army and criticizing royal visits to Hanover. He echoed Swift's complaints about the national debt. But Fielding did not attack the social, economic, and political changes the debt fostered. To complain about the debt and at the same time to praise the beneficiaries of the economic system built on it was to accept changes the Tories found unacceptable. To blast Walpole and at the same time to avoid protesting the changes that took place during his ministry was to prepare the way for a return to his camp.

Unlike Scriblerian pamphlets and journals, *The Champion* does not argue that the system requires radical economic, social, and political change. Rather, Fielding aims to assure his readers (most particularly Londoners) that the system is basically good, and that one man is subverting it. Fielding refers to Walpole, and to the office of prime minister, as a *fortuitous* addition to British politics. Fielding only repeats an opposition commonplace when he defines a prime minister as "A Magistrate who, though not consistent with our Constitution, nor countenanc'd by our Laws, hath often found means to insinuate himself into the political Machine" (II, 188). But his descriptions of Walpole as a man whose rise was owing to "fortunate Accidents" (II, 318),[20] rather than to economic and social changes, mean that his attacks on Walpole skirt the conservative ideology basic to Scriblerian attacks. Fielding chooses to portray the Great Man as a foreign harlequin, thus avoiding the issues of class distinction and agrarian versus commercial interests raised by Swift and Bolingbroke.

Fielding used several rhetorical ploys to separate Walpole from the urban Whigs. One involved the use of a foreign label or analogue for the office of prime minister. This motif begins in No. 46 (28 February 1739/40), when Vinegar urges a correspondent who proposes to lecture on "the Art of Prime Ministry" (I, 315) "to travel abroad with his Nostrums; for I apprehend that they will meet with little Encouragement here, where we neither have or can have a Prime Minister" (I, 319). Fielding and Ralph make the same point by comparing Walpole to tyrannical first ministers separated from their readers by time, such as Wolsey (II, 90) and Cromwell (I, 66–67), or by nationality, such as Richelieu (II, 321). Fielding used an analogy to the Turkish "first minister," the "Vizier,"[21] to further distance Walpole from British political traditions. Ralph picked up the analogy and also used it to link Walpole's

power and position to a foreign culture (II, 91; II, 135).
Walpole, with his Turkish, French, or anachronistically
English absolutism, thus becomes an anomaly in an other-
wise sound society.

   Fielding's frequent comparisons of Walpole to the Harlequin, John Rich, have a similar effect. For Fielding, the
great virtue of this analogy is that Rich's theatrical success
depended upon illusion and disguise. By constantly
equating Walpole with Rich, Fielding could imply that
the citizens of Britain had been gulled rather than cor-
rupted—that, if they were undeceived, they could make
the political system function properly. Thus in No. 76 (1
May 1740) Fielding describes the British government as a
self-contained system in which "the several Officers and
Magistrates, from the King to the Constable [are] but the
several Wheels of State, in a subordinate Manner, making
up one grand Machine, like a Piece of Clock-work in right
Order, [that] moves steadily and regularly by fixed and
certain Laws" (II, 187). Fielding first illustrates Walpole's
relation to this machine in terms of Archimedes' hypothesis about being able to move the globe if he could only find
a place to stand. In terms of the lever analogy, Walpole's
power becomes a foreign "Body, which hath no function
assigned to it" (II, 188) but which "intervenes" in the
machine's operation and causes "Confusion and Disorder." Fielding then summarizes Walpole's "mechanical"
accomplishment by comparing him to "the Master of a
Raree-Shew [Rich] who sets Kings on their Heads, makes
the *Czar of Muscovy*, the *King of France*, and all other great
Personages dance at his Command in whatever Manner he
pleases" (II, 188). Here again Fielding portrays Walpole as
an interloper, not as a creature produced by the machine

itself. Complaints about the luxury of the times notwith-
standing, Fielding makes Walpole the agent of "Confusion
and Disorder," the gremlin who disrupts an otherwise
smooth-running machine.

Swift and Bolingbroke believed that, to restore the
political principles of 1689, economic and social reform
were necessary. Power had to be returned to the landowning country gentleman if change was to be lasting,
because Walpole (Harlequin) was simply an avatar of his
audience's own venality. Fielding, however, sees Walpole's power in very different terms. In No. 74 (3 May
1740) he forecasts the end of Harlequin's reign in the
theatre, with obvious glances at Walpole's fall from political power. The "dexterous Harlequin" wins the applause
of "the viler Riff-Raff" (II, 177), but his reign suddenly
ends in the midst of it:

> . . . the silent Pit is sullen and indignant at the Farce; nor in the
> Box . . . breaks forth a whispering Applause. Mark thou the
> End, a Set of solemn Figures enter on the Stage, the Power of
> Harlequin is at an End, aloft they lift the impious long success-
> ful Sorcerer and thrust him down the Throat of a tremendous
> Dragon . . .—Rejoice, then, O wicked Man, in thy Tricks, and
> let thy Heart cheer thee in the Success of thy Tricks, but know
> that for all these Tricks, we shall bring thee to Judgement. [II,
> 177]

The vituperation of this passage is Scriblerian, particularly the bitter and resounding repetition of "Tricks." But
this should not cause us to overlook that regular dramatic
actors, with the silent support of London's upper classes,
bring Harlequin down. The analogy to Harlequin once
again permits Fielding to attack Walpole without attacking the urban bourgeoisie.

The rhetoric of *The Champion*, then, reflects Fielding's attempt to find a political position between the circles of Bolingbroke and Walpole. Troubled by the place-seeking, electoral fraud, and manipulation of Parliament that characterized Walpole's rule, Fielding sided with Caleb D'Anvers in calling for an end to specific abuses: witness the support in *The Champion* for the Place Bill and triennial Parliaments, and the attacks on the excessive national debt and burdensome standing army. But his praise for the merchants and theatregoers of London indicates (and his rhetorical strategy affirms) that Fielding did not share the Scriblerians' anachronistic ideal for society and politics. In *The Champion* Fielding was far closer to the Whiggism of Addison, Steele, and (eventually) Henry Pelham than to the Toryism of Bolingbroke, with its emphasis upon property in land. Freed from the spectre of Walpole's unseemly abuses of power, Fielding would return to support Whig hegemony. He and the shrinking Tory opposition had little in common besides a target.

The signs of persistent political uncertainty in *The Champion* become particularly important when we ponder *Jonathan Wild*, the work of Fielding's that is most difficult to categorize. Nearly seventy years ago John Edwin Wells guessed that Fielding moved from working on *The Champion* to writing *Jonathan Wild*. Wells pointed out that "most of the chief matter of *Jonathan Wild* is forshadowed in Fielding's signed papers [in *The Champion*]," discussed specific instances of verbal and thematic echoes in the two works, and argued that "Fielding wrote in his paper of June 12 [1740] a farewell; that thereafter he appears to have ceased to contribute regularly to the *Champion*; and that the actual writing of *Jonathan Wild* was logically his next step." We now have very strong evidence that Fielding wrote *Jonathan Wild* before 4 October 1740,[22] and thus Wells's guess seems even more likely, particularly since *Jonathan Wild* shares structural incongruities with Fielding's plays—incongruities in part attributable to the political uncertainty that Fielding, in *The Champion*, still had not worked out.

In the previous chapter, we saw how Fielding's attempt to join satiric and sentimental plots in his plays reflected his fundamental literary and political uncertainty. At the time of *The Champion*, Fielding, for all his vigorous vituperation, still had conflicting political impulses. *Jonathan Wild*, which is, as J. H. Plumb has observed, "one of the odder great books in English fiction,"[23] is the literary counterpart of its author's political oddity. Like the plays, the book brings together two plots that are not easily joined. One traces the rise and fall of the thieftaker Wild, and, in so doing, satirizes eighteenth-century manners. The extent to which Fielding imitates the Scriblerians when he focuses on Wild is seen best in Book II, chapter iv. Entitled "Of Hats," it imitates *A Tale of a Tub* and the *Variorum Dunciad* in its penchant for falsely learned comment, and emulates Parts I and II of *Gulliver's Travels* in its satire of political parties through the literalization of a clothing metaphor. The other plot, as in Fielding's plays, recounts the trials of an exemplary couple. Significantly enough, the exemplary figure, Thomas Heartfree, is not a country swain who brings rural virtues to a decadent city; instead he is a London merchant, a jeweller whose "character . . . is probably based on that of George Lillo,"[24] the bourgeois dramatist whom Fielding had patronized at the Haymarket Theatre and eulogized in *The Champion* (I,

113). Just as Fielding adapts Scriblerian techniques in his satiric plot, so in this plot he adapts the techniques of sentimental, exemplary comedy.[25]

Fielding's uncertainty in *Jonathan Wild* appears in features other than his shifting between plots and techniques. Satire and sentiment in *Jonathan Wild* are rarely pure. Wild's failures in crime and in love give his character a comic impotence that prevents him from becoming the personification of evil.[26] Mrs. Heartfree's recounting of her voluptuous adventures detracts from the sobriety and the effect of the exemplary plot. The most specific sign of Fielding's political uncertainty is that Wild, early in the book, acts out the sins of Robert Walpole, but, once in prison, acts out the sins of the opposition. He challenges the governor of the prisoners for purely personal motives and disappoints the debtors to whom he promised reform.

Fielding's description of Wild and Heartfree as "characters of a stamp entirely different" (p. 54) points to the dual nature of *Jonathan Wild*. The absolute distinction between the two sets of characters helps Fielding to draw a "contrast between greatness and goodness,"[27] and thus to point a moral about the former's dangers and the latter's virtues. But to draw such a stark contrast Fielding must sacrifice unity of purpose and effect. In a book designed to "inculcate" the moral that villainy cannot long succeed, the most singular and memorable figure remains the villain. The attractiveness of Wild's energy, coupled with the fecklessness of Heartfree's pure virtue, shows that Fielding sees neither pure villainy nor pure good nature as likely or desirable—although, of course, virtue is preferable. Fielding's ideal for character, as he announced it in the preface to his *Miscellanies*, integrates greatness and goodness and thus reaches the "*true Sublime* in Human Nature" (1, 12), No such ideal character appears in *Jonathan Wild*. In the prose fiction satire, as in the plays, Fielding only can counterpoint goodness and greatness; he cannot join them.

The absolute distinction between goodness and greatness in *Jonathan Wild* has an effect similar to that of *The Champion*'s rhetoric. Wild, like Walpole, is venal and base, but he understands how things work. He is "the master of the [puppet] show (the great Man) who dances and moves everything" (p. 148). Wild abuses his power and misleads the London Merchant, in whom Fielding reposes all virtues except greatness of mind. Heartfree's bewitchment by Wild protects him from complicity in Wild's crimes; his obtuseness is like the obtuseness Fielding attributed to Londoners in *The Champion*. It is convenient in that it allows Fielding to portray Wild's vices without admitting how dependent they are on luxury, which itself is essential to Heartfree's trade as a jeweler. Fielding, who by heritage and interest is loyal to commercial values, protects and praises Heartfree, the representative of those values, by portraying him as the victim of trickery, rather than of his own effort to make a profit.

Despite Walpole's excesses, Fielding remained a Whig in the tradition of Steele, a supporter of the mercantile and commercial interests that came to dominate English life during the eighteenth century. Walpole's abuses, however, tainted the tradition and made it difficult to locate and support. Fielding's first uncertain step in resurrecting it was false but necessary: the London merchant had to be portrayed as manipulated by a man who did not share his values and virtues. In reality, the case was quite different.

Heartfree welcomed Wild to his home because they had gone to school together, and he joined him in a scheme to make a large profit in diamonds. Walpole was not a foreigner, but the scion of an old Norfolk family, and his trickery consisted merely of a fine understanding of the ins and outs of changing British politics. Written with the same need to isolate Walpole-Wild that shaped the rhetoric of *The Champion*, *Jonathan Wild* emerged an odd but fascinating work. Much of its oddity derives from Fielding's decision to make gullibility and passivity his hero's greatest virtues—a decision with political as well as literary motives.

Against the background of Fielding's uncertain politics in *The Champion* and *Jonathan Wild*, we can better define the significance of perhaps his most controversial political piece, *The Opposition: A Vision*. In this, two mules named Ralph and Vinegar are abused by venal travelers and rescued by a "large man." Fielding "seems to say that his days of starving in a false cause are over; Walpole's generosity has set him free and fed him."[28] While we now have clear evidence that Fielding was not above taking Walpole's money, we can learn much from the motivation of those scholars who argued against the obvious message of *The Opposition*. Wilbur Cross, always anxious to cast Fielding in the best possible light, dismissed it as "a good natured rebuke of the leaders of his party."[29] William B. Coley, after culling Horace Walpole's correspondence and notebooks for references to payments of Fielding and finding none, declared that the pamphlet does reveal political disillusionment, but not an unscrupulous switch to Walpole's side.[30] However, anyone who attempts to purify *The Opposition*, or any aspect of Fielding's political career, must not overlook one important fact: besides admitting to payments from Walpole, Fielding declared on several occasions that obstinate adherence to party should not always outweigh a writer's financial interest. His most frequently quoted defense of the writer's right to change sides comes in *The Jacobite's Journal* No. 17.[31] Similarly, in *The Champion* No. 26 (12 January 1739/40), he argues that the word "Turn-coat" has been abused, asserting that it originally referred to "certain prudent Persons" who could understand "the true Merits of a Cause" because they had been "on both Sides of it" (1, 180). He goes on: "Any ill Usage from his Party, any Refusal of what he [the writer] thinks himself entitled to, no doubt justify . . . Exchange" (1, 181).

Of course, Fielding's claims for his right to change sides would be mere self-vindication if his behavior violated the standards of his day. But we should not be confused about the question we face, and bring irrelevant assumptions to it—particularly the assumptions of the Tory interpretation. It is precisely because Fielding's behavior violates standards set by the Tory interpretation that scholars like Cross and Coley have felt compelled to misread *The Opposition*. Yet, now that we know Fielding accepted money from Walpole, we can dispense with the impossible task of making him a good Tory and focus instead on the true issue. In light of the norms of his day, were Fielding's shifts in political allegiance venal and base? Namier's work is crucial in this regard, for it sets a background against which we can study Fielding's actions without engaging in damnation or deification. Insofar as the structure of politics described by Namier was in place during Fielding's day, Fielding could change sides without compromising his principles. In other words, however much Fielding,

like the Scriblerians, attacked Walpole's crude political
dealings, he never was driven by Walpole's excesses to
reject his Whig heritage. When the Whig opposition mis-
treated him, he could (and did) return to Walpole's camp
with all good grace. He suspended work on *Jonathan Wild*,
stopped making even occasional contributions to *The
Champion*, and garnered subscriptions to his *Miscellanies*
from Walpole and Walpole's allies.[32]

Fielding's most important change in *The Opposition* is not
in his political allegiance; rather, it is in his destruction of
the convenient but false image of Walpole as the bewitcher
of a callow British electorate. In *The Opposition*, Walpole is
neither a deceptive Harlequin nor a foreign intruder, but a
typical Norfolk man. As Fielding began to draw a truer
picture of the Great Man, so he began to move toward a
more mature support for the Whig hegemony that Walpole nurtured. In the early 1740s, to return to Walpole's
camp was to return to what would become the Pelham
camp. Fielding would support the Pelham ministry for the
last ten years of his life precisely because it saved Britain's
political, religious, and social institutions when Prince
Charles Edward threatened them.

Fielding's reconciliation with Walpole, his dispensing
with the Walpole-as-Harlequin, Walpole-as-Vizier fic-
tions, was his first step toward political certainty and
stability. His growing certainty would contribute to his
first successful literary experiment, *Joseph Andrews*. However, it would not be fully realized until the climactic
event of Fielding's political life caused him to redefine his
political heritage and his political values. Fielding's response to the Jacobite rebellion would complete the
change that *The Opposition: A Vision* began.

V

ℭrue ℙatriotism
and ℙolitical ℭertainty

With the publication of *The Opposition: A Vision* Fielding
returned to the Whig establishment, escaping the equivocal position to which his attacks upon Walpole had led
him. By returning to his earliest, most natural political
allegiance, he began to resolve the uncertainty manifest in
his plays and in *The Champion*. The progress of his change
from 1742 to 1745 is difficult to trace exactly, for in those
years Fielding's principal concerns were literary, familial,
and legal, and he offered little in the way of political
comment. In 1742 and 1743 he devoted considerable time
to preparing and publishing the first three editions of
Joseph Andrews, as well as to the publication of his *Miscellanies* and the production of his *Miss Lucy in Town* and *The
Wedding Day* at Drury Lane. During this time his family
was struck by illness and death; he lost his elder daughter
in March 1742, and his beloved wife, Charlotte, after a
long illness in November 1744. In addition to his family
problems, financial difficulties demanded his immediate
attention. And, in the midst of these activities, he was still
attempting to establish a legal reputation, riding the
western circuit and seeking briefs. After Walpole's fall in

February 1742, it is little wonder that Fielding turned from the confused political situation and tried to set his own house in order. Not until 1744 would he muster the time or interest for even ephemeral political comment.[1]

But we can gain some insight into Fielding's changing politics during this period (as well as their literary importance) by noting several important features of *Joseph Andrews*. Published barely three weeks after Walpole resigned the Treasury, it is Fielding's first successful literary experiment—a work that anticipates his supreme accomplishment in *Tom Jones* and possesses great virtues of its own. Here, for the first time, Fielding successfully combined satire and sentiment and conveyed to his reader the sense of knowing good nature that dominates the prefatory chapters in *Tom Jones*. The reasons why Fielding suddenly found his voice, suddenly achieved literary mastery, may never be completely clear to us; they probably were not completely clear to him. Perhaps his difficulties in 1741–42 tempered his wit with a more serious view of life, and thus enriched it. Perhaps, spurred by Richardson, he finally discovered a medium more suited to his literary gifts. But we should also remember that Fielding's misshapen plays and his odd masterpiece, *Jonathan Wild*, reflected his political uncertainty. Unable to settle upon a political allegiance, he could not resolve an important philosophical question (Was man by nature an exemplary or a weak being?) and an important literary question (Would he write farces and ballad operas, or would he write sentimental comedies?). In *Joseph Andrews*, as Fielding gave clear signs of his return to the Whig establishment, so he also began to use his literary gifts more purposefully. Martin C. Battestin has shown how Fielding's revisions of *Joseph Andrews*—revisions that turned a rough, crudely structured first edition into a finished masterpiece —paralleled and spoke to his disenchantment with the opposition.[2] Battestin clearly indicates that Fielding's changes accomplished two ends for him, smoothing transitions in his narrative, and defining more clearly his suspicions of the men who had replaced Walpole. These revisions thus point once more to the close tie between Fielding's political and literary careers.

Of course, *Joseph Andrews* is not as fine or as finished a work as *Tom Jones*. Its infelicities are revealing, however, because they harken back to problems in Fielding's earlier work. The famous and oft-discussed digressions, for example, differ greatly in their aptness. Wilson's account of his life provides a synechdoche for the action and the major themes of the book,[3] but the stories of Leonora and of Leonard and Paul are not as well integrated. Besides the major digressions, *Joseph Andrews* includes numerous minor ones that allow Fielding to scour satiric butts but do not further his action. The dialogue between two young gentlemen about coaches, dogs, and shooting (I, xvi, p. 74), the debate between two men over the character of a magistrate who decided a case between them (II, iii, pp. 98–100), and the discussion between the poet and the player concerning the state of the theatre (III, x, pp. 259–64) offer Fielding satiric opportunities, but the characters disappear immediately thereafter. These pauses, and the less successful major digressions, are analogous to the scene between Captain Merit and Captain Bravemore in *The Modern Husband*. They reveal a Scriblerian desire to lash vice—a desire that Fielding is mastering and shaping, but that he still does not totally control.

Fielding's uncertainty *is* lessening, however, as is clear in his combination of satire and sentiment. In its treatment of Colley Cibber and Lord Hervey, *Joseph Andrews* looks back to the techniques and themes of Scriblerian satire; in its portrayal of Adams and Fanny and Joseph, particularly in their frequent moments of emotional rapture, the novel recalls exemplary sentimental comedy. But for the first time in his career Fielding merges those two traditions, principally by using two techniques. The first is his offering of multiple definitions for key moral terms—in this case, "charity" and "chastity"—thereby mediating cynical and idealistic uses of the words.[4] Mrs. Tow-wouse, Parson Trulliber, Peter Pounce, and Adams (among others) define charity; from their definitions emerges a Fielding-esque sense of the word, at once noble and knowing, philosophical and practical. Second, he adopts a pose of narrative omniscience and then uses his access to the minds of the characters in order to offer rich, complicated descriptions of their motives—descriptions that again link practical (sometimes base) motives with noble ones. Witness the ongoing *psychomachia* of Lady Booby, the conflict in her between lust and honor, between passion and her concern for reputation.

The political counterpart of Fielding's growing literary certainty appears not only in the specific political allusions outlined by Battestin, but also in Fielding's treatment of social rank and class. He appears to have fixed his attitude toward the landed country gentleman, attacking unworthy members of the class, but protecting the Booby family and asserting his "adequate Regard" for the race (III, ii, pp. 191–92). Still a city man, he cannot sing the praises of this group, but the unrestrained contempt for

them apparent in his plays now has bounds. This reconciliation is part of his larger affirmation of the social order.
Characters in *Joseph Andrews*, be they masters or servants,
cannot identify themselves without reference to their
betters and lessers. It is true that, throughout the novel,
characters and events seem to challenge class distinctions.
But although Joseph is more virtuous and manly than any
nobleman we meet, and although his physical charms
inspire the same response in a great lady and in her servant, this egalitarian thrust is blunted once he discovers
his true identity and his rightful place: Fielding leaves the
theme of social climbing to Richardson and satirizes
Pamela as an unworthy candidate for such elevation.

Despite instances in which Fielding's satiric impulse
breaks free, *Joseph Andrews* never challenges the social
order ruled by Boobies. Adams will rebuke his betters in
church, but not outside it, and is famous for his sermons
on submission. He will be misled and deceived by self-
interested politicians, but he will not question the system.
Although his exemplary virtue is a standing rebuke to
those less worthy, it ultimately is not the center of the
story, any more than are Fielding's satiric portrayals of
venality and hypocrisy.

Joseph's growth from Adams's pupil to his guide is at
the heart of the book.[5] His growth parallels that of Fielding the artist. Joseph combines knowledge of the world
—the perception of man's vanity and depravity that underlies Scriblerian satire—with exemplary virtue and
benevolent sentiments. He has listened to Alexander Pope
and has lived in the City, emerging the wiser from both
experiences. Joseph's character, the hybrid Fielding was
incapable of nurturing in *Jonathan Wild*, is the first impor-

tant product of Fielding's liberation from the conflicting loyalties to which his political uncertainty exposed him. While the balance struck in *Joseph Andrews* is not as complete or as elaborately wrought as that in *Tom Jones*, it clearly is of the same kind—an integration of satire and sentiment of which Fielding's earlier work is largely devoid.

Emerging from his family tragedies and literary triumphs, Fielding encountered a political situation in 1744–45 that involved a conflict between Whig factions. George II, who personally favored the counsels of Carteret, now Earl of Granville, could find little support in the Commons for his favorite. He had been forced to award Henry Pelham the Treasury. But George, particularly in his foreign policy, still followed Granville's advice, and so long as Granville remained the royal favorite, the government was hamstrung by personality conflicts and an uncertain chain of command.[6] Throughout these years Fielding, following the lead he had taken in *The Opposition*, supported the Whig establishment, leadership of which had passed to Henry Pelham in 1742. This loyalty explains his otherwise puzzling pamphlet, *An Attempt Towards A Natural History of the Hanover Rat* (1744). In it he leveled some harsh charges against the royal family, attacking in particular their use of English funds to fight their own battles on the continent. Since he would, within a year, be writing panegyrics upon George II and his family, this pamphlet may seem another sign of political indecision. But, as Gerard Jensen pointed out,[7] it served the interests of Pelham and the Whig Old Corps in their battle against Carteret's influence. It was one of many warnings that George II should begin to put English interests first, mend his fences with the Commons, and

give up Carteret's grand schemes for triumph on the continent—warnings that Prince Charles Edward would soon
vindicate, however unintentionally.

Even after the Stuart threat faded, George II remained
reluctant to recognize and reward Pelham's virtues. Not
until February 1746, when the Pelhamites resigned their
posts and Granville and his ally, William Pulteney (now
Earl of Bath), were unable to form a ministry, did George
finally accept Pelham as his minister.[8] This action reconciled Fielding to the Hanoverians; it stimulated his hyper-
bolic praise for George and his family in the final issues of
The True Patriot and helped him to develop an allegiance to
the House of Brunswick that would not vary during the
rest of his life.[9] On a larger scale, the Jacobite threat, in
conjunction with the political crisis of the "48 hour ministry," forced English politicians, including George II,[10]
out of the politics of self-interest into which they had
lapsed. These two events created a political climate in
which men redefined their loyalties and values, in which
ideology once again became important. While Fielding's
changes in sides during the 1730s and early 1740s lend
credence to the view that political labels were losing importance, his response to the rebellion provides crucial
evidence that the structure of politics which existed upon
George III's accession was not completely in place earlier.
For, as Fielding defended the Protestant Succession and
the Pelham ministry, he did not invent his case. Rather, he
turned to traditional Whig spokesmen like Addison, and
traditional Whig theoreticians like Locke.[11]

Fittingly enough, on 19 August 1745, when Charles
Stuart proclaimed the restoration of the Stuart dynasty in
a brief ceremony at Glenfinnan, Scotland, the King of

England was enjoying one of his frequent vacations in Hanover. While Bonnie Prince Charlie gathered an army, George II rejected the Pelham ministry's pleas that he return to England (and bring with him some of the British troops fighting on the Continent), preferring instead the counsel of Granville, who minimized the rebel threat. The surprising early successes of Charles Stuart's ragtag army resulted from good luck and from widespread apathy among the English people—apathy the Hanoverians had helped to create. As one historian has noted, "the frequent visits of George I and II to the electorate, often highly inconvenient for the easy and rapid conduct of business, and their evident predilection for their Hanover interests and subjects were extremely unpopular" in England.[12] A growing anti-Hanoverianism in the country, apparent in Fielding's own *Hanover Rat* pamphlet, was the key to the rebels' success, especially since they received much less French and Spanish help than they had expected. The English had rejected Stuart absolutism and Roman Catholicism in 1688, but almost sixty years later, with an unattractive foreign family on the throne, Englishmen easily could lose sight of those earlier issues. Many stood ready to accept, if not actively to work for, the return of a House whose ability to alienate them probably exceeded even that of the House of Brunswick. When Prince Charles marched into England, then, his success depended upon the Britons' failure to see him as a threat to their political customs and values. The young Stuart could not hope to conquer; he only could hope that a nation tired of costly foreign wars and Hanoverian neglect would turn to him.

We cannot determine Henry Fielding's whereabouts in

the summer of 1745 as precisely as we can those of George
II and Charles Edward. Rupert C. Jarvis has discredited
the old story that Fielding, shocked by the loss of his wife,
was rescued from silence and melancholia by his response
to the rebellion. He proves that Fielding wrote an ironic
pamphlet on the occasion of Walpole's death and argues
that he was "hacking for Cooper, his old publisher, during
the very period which has hitherto been universally accepted as his period of silence." But even though the
rebellion may not have restored Fielding to himself, it
clearly gave him great motivation to write. In October he
quickly produced three anti-Jacobite pamphlets, and by
early November he was at work on *The True Patriot*.[13]
Fielding's strong response to the rebels' early successes
shows how his political uncertainty vanished as they
forced him to reassert the old Whig principles. The '45
became the definitive event in his political life, mainly
because the rebels' greatest weapon was not force of arms
but force of apathy. As they moved closer to London, they
created a situation in which political ideas once again
became important—in which pro-ministry writers like
Fielding found their task to be the definition of the Whig
principles and values that Britons shared. *The True Patriot*
attempted to teach all Britons, including George II, that
those principles and their true interests were inseparable.
In reacquainting his audience with a political ideology it
almost had forgotten, Fielding rediscovered his own political heritage and left behind the equivocations of his days
as "the Champion." Whatever its other consequences, the
'45 ended Fielding's days as a political gadfly. It had a role
in his political life analogous to its role in *Tom Jones*,
providing the great backdrop against which Henry Fielding came of political age.

I speak of *The True Patriot* and *Tom Jones* in the same breath because Martin C. Battestin has recently contested the standard "history" of the novel, which hypothesizes that Fielding did not start work on it until his political duties eased in mid-1746. Battestin has argued convincingly that Fielding started *Tom Jones* in the early months of 1745.[14] If we accept Battestin's account, there follow two important conclusions for the student of Fielding's politics. First, Fielding's sense of the threat posed by the Jacobites was so strong that he put aside his masterpiece to accept once more the difficult tasks and uncertain rewards of political journalism. Second, Fielding wrote *The True Patriot* when his literary talents were mature. Born of this convergence of serious intent and literary mastery, *The True Patriot* expresses Fielding's most deeply held political beliefs with the wit and skill that will ultimately characterize *Tom Jones*. It includes, particularly during the period when Fielding gave it his full attention,[15] much of his finest political writing, and justifies Arthur Murphy's claim that it "displayed a solid knowledge of the British laws and government, together with occasional sallies of humour, which would have made no inconsiderable figure in the political compositions of an Addison or a Swift."[16]

Murphy's last comparison is, in terms of political ideology and party, oxymoronic, though it effectively suggests the nature of Fielding's accomplishment. In *The True Patriot* he finally reconciled two dissimilar eighteenth-century views of politics and of man's political nature. In writing the journal he not only worked out his own political doubts and discovered values and allegiances that he could support with certainty; he also defined a centrist political theory that wove together the two great divergent threads in the political thought of his era.

The format of *The True Patriot* reveals the disparate
political attitudes that Fielding integrated. The basic
format, as Miriam Austin Locke has observed, is conventional: "Each number consists of four pages of three
columns each—a format which had become traditional for
publications of this sort during the middle decades of the
century."[17] An opening essay, usually designed to stir
patriotic feeling, is followed by sections of foreign and
domestic news which justify the journal's subtitle, "The
History of Our Own Times." The last page records
births, deaths, and marriages, and also contains advertisements. But in two instances Fielding departs from the
standard form of earlier political journals. The first is the
"Apocrypha" section, which runs through the first eighteen numbers. A new version of Vinegar's "Court of
Censorial Enquiry," this section gives Fielding a forum for
attacking the faulty information and bad writing that he
finds in rival journals. More important, his calm scrutiny
of reports and rumors and his sardonic comments on
solecisms reflect a calm and urbane attitude that he was
trying to encourage. The second departure from standard
form is small but significant: in twenty-two of thirty-two
numbers (Nos. 1, 11–27, 29–32), Fielding includes a section of stock quotations; in twenty-one (Nos., 12–32) he
records bankruptcy pleas. With one exception,[18] the stock
quotations follow the bankruptcy pleas and form a "financial section" that precedes the advertisements.

The last variation is important because it shows Fielding acknowledging the national debt and the stock exchange—the favorite targets of Swift and Bolingbroke—as
parts of British life. Joining stock quotations with bankruptcy proceedings may be consciously ironic, and may

indicate that his acceptance of the new economic order is less than wholehearted, just as the financial speculations of Bolingbroke, Swift, Pope, and Gay may indicate that their attacks on the new order include show as well as substance. In any case, the inclusion of a "financial section" in the journal, and the persistent pleas in early issues for insuring government funds and public credit,[19] sharply separate Fielding's politics from those of Bolingbroke and his circle. While Fielding's concern for correctness and style in the "Apocrypha" section surely indicates his respect for traditional, humanistic standards and values, his recognition of the new economic order in his "financial section" indicates that he felt obliged to pursue his ideal of culture in circumstances different from those which Bolingbroke approved. Isaac Kramnick has argued that "Bolingbroke lived in an age when the old order, though challenged, still seemed appropriate and possible."[20] Fielding wrote *The True Patriot* after the moneyed men had consolidated their hold on power. Pursuing a politics of enlightened self-interest, he defined the role of property in politics against a changed socio-economic background.

The transitional nature of Fielding's politics in *The True Patriot* is apparent not only in the format of the journal, but also in the disparate political models at which he glances. He opens the journal with "a few Hints *who* I am" (I, i, iii) and starts by claiming, "First, then, It is very probable I am Lord B---ke. This I collect from my Stile in Writing and Knowledge in Politics." In the second issue, when he introduces a letter from an "Old Gentlewoman" who asserts that "the Bank, South-sea, and East-India Stock, is the strongest Box they [her fellow widows] can put Money into" (II, ii, i), Fielding refers to Addison's

papers on British women in *The Freeholder*. In neither case
does he explicitly state that he takes Bolingbroke or Addison as a political model; both allusions are whimsical and
amusing, rather than serious. But the combination of
divergent political views that Fielding achieves (however
ironically) in these allusions, hints at his goal in *The True
Patriot*. He will try to emulate Bolingbroke's "Stile in
Writing," his aristocratic urbanity and taste, in an England that accepted the economic system Addison admired
and Bolingbroke (at least in his writings) attacked. The
two men are alluded to, rather than taken as models,
because they stand for opposing extremes that Fielding
must integrate, rather than for adequate political philoso-
phies. The early references to them, coupled with the
journal's formal innovations, show that the rhetoric of *The
True Patriot*, and its definitions for political terms, will be
shaped by tensions similar to those which dominated
Fielding's years in the theatre. The young Fielding could
not reconcile the twin roles of Scriblerus Secundus (apparent in his attacks on Walpole and the moneyed men)
and sentimental dramatist at Drury Lane (apparent in his
grateful praise for Cibber and Walpole). In 1745, an older
and wiser Fielding developed a definition of true patriotism which balanced his previously antithetical political
impulses and allowed him to be consistent in his political
loyalties for the rest of his life.

The rhetoric of *The True Patriot* tries to link the reader's
self-interest with the preservation of the Hanoverian
dynasty and the Pelham ministry. The attempt to convince the reader that his good corresponds with the good
of the party supported by an author is as old as political
journalism and appears in a wide range of eighteenth-

century political writings. Swift, for one, claimed to appeal "to all others indifferently, whether *Whig* or *Tory*, whose private Interest is best answered by the Welfare of their Country" (VI, p. 45). Bolingbroke used a similar strategy when, in his *Dissertation Upon Parties*, he defined a "faction" as those individuals who band together to pursue "an interest distinct from the interest of the whole" (II, p. 26); he did so again in *The Idea of a Patriot King*, when he attacked his age as one in which "so many betray the cause of liberty, and act not only without regard, but in direct opposition, to the most important interests of their country" (II, p. 388). Addison briefly illustrated the Whig version of the strategy when he claimed that the design of *The Freeholder* was "to reconcile Men to their own Happiness by removing those wrong Notions and Prejudices which hinder them from seeing the Advantage of themselves and their Posterity in the present Establishment."[21] Fielding merely added to the tradition when he made "happiness" the topic of essays in the sixth and seventeenth numbers of *The True Patriot*, "proving" that for the majority of Englishmen happiness and the Hanoverian succession were one and the same.

Although Whig and Tory writers of the Augustan period appeal to self-interest, this appeal is far more difficult for conservative writers like Swift and Bolingbroke than it is for Addison, who is more optimistic about human nature and man's capacity for rational, virtuous behavior. The effect of Addison's optimism is most apparent in *The Freeholder* No. 5 (6 January 1715/16), when he reasons: "As Self-love is an Instinct planted in us for the Good and Safety of each particular Person, the Love of our Country is impress'd on our Minds for the Happiness and Preservation of the Community. This Instinct is so remarkable, that we find Examples of it in those who are born in the most uncomfortable Climates, or the worst of Governments" (p. 23). Because he assumes "this Love of our Country is natural to every Man" (p. 24), he also assumes that it "ought to cast the Balance" (p. 29) as Englishmen decide between the pretender and George I. He asserts that a dynasty whose religious and political principles are foreign to English norms obviously cannot be "conducive to the Welfare" (p. 29) of the community, and he claims that certainly the bloodshed and suffering of civil war would be equally inimical to the public good. Having made these points, Addison believes no further argument is necessary or possible. He concludes his essay by dismissing self-interest, instead of appealing to it.

Jesus Christ is one of the several biblical models used by Addison to illustrate this "Love of Country." Addison devotes the heart of his essay to recalling specific instances in which Christ "declared his Superior Good-will to his own Nation" (p. 27). The effortless, unstrained quality of his arguments in No. 5, and in the *The Freeholder* as a whole, depends upon his belief that, in respect to "Love of Country," the majority of Englishmen are like Christ. This liberal estimation of human nature's capacity for selfless behavior influences the rhetoric of the entire journal.

Bolingbroke and Swift did not share Addison's faith in man's innate "Love of Country." In their view, all human behavior is motivated by a self-love that must be strenuously curbed and directed. Bolingbroke typifies this attitude as he repeatedly portrays himself standing against a trend toward "partiality" and "faction . . . that . . . is the immediate effect of self-love, the strongest spring in the human, nay, in the whole animal system" (II, p. 148). Swift's attacks on Marlborough depend on his proving that "the true Spring or Motive" of the Duke's policy "was the aggrandizing [of] a particular family" (VI, p. 41), and his famous advice to Thomas Sheridan perhaps best summarizes the great gap between the Tory and the Addisonian views of man: "You should think and deal with every Man as a Villain, without calling him so, or flying from him, or valuing him the less. This is an old true Lesson."[22] Although Bolingbroke and Pope quarreled with Swift's bald refusal to expect selfless behavior from men, it shapes the rhetoric of the Tories. Because of their intense awareness of those qualities that make man a fallen rather than a Christ-like creature, they cannot dismiss self-love. Instead, they must appeal to it and join it to a specific concept of the national good.

Addison, with his high estimation of man's potential for "Love of Country," can define the national good very broadly. He is content to observe the incongruity between James III's Roman Catholicism and arbitrary political principles on the one hand, and English norms on the other. He leaves it to his readers to make inferences about those consequences—economic, social, and political— which will affect them most specifically if the Stuarts return to the throne. Even in *The Freeholder* No. 16 (13 February 1716), when he considers the suspension of the habeas corpus act—an issue with considerable impact upon the daily lives of Englishmen—he builds his argument upon an appeal to historical precedent,[23] and thus distances the issue from knotty questions of personal interest. Swift and Bolingbroke do not hesitate to use analogy, but they use it to define an ideal polity—a polity whose model is Elizabethan economic and political life. Given their belief that self-love is the "spring" which moves men, they feel they must prove to the reader that his "private Interest" will be furthered by the reestablishment of the social and economic hierarchy they admire. Consequently, in their political writings the rhetoric depends more on syllogism than on analogy, and they cannot define the national good as vaguely as Addison does. They consistently relate the "private Interest" of their audience, which becomes a minor premise, to a major premise in which they define the true public welfare. The Tories' definition of their ideal polity as an aristocratic social, economic, and political order based upon property in land is crucial: it at once limits and structures their argument. They can appeal very strongly and clearly to people with very specific interests, but they cannot address an increasingly large and influential group of moneyed men.

These differences in rhetoric provide a helpful guide to the counterforces that shape the rhetoric of *The True Patriot*. After his earlier disappointments, Fielding was too sensitive to the foibles and flaws of human nature to believe that he could appeal successfully to "Love of Country." Like Swift and Bolingbroke, he appealed to the self-love of his reader and attempted to gain his point by linking self-love with social good. His appeal necessarily was limited by this strategy, because there were interests that his major premise about the national good did not include. The need to distinguish Fielding's political writing from that of Bolingbroke and his circle, however, becomes obvious when we see that he legitimized new economic interests—which the Tories consistently spurned. Bolingbroke and Swift's simplistic distinctions between "Usurers and Stockjobbers" and the "Landed Interest"[24] reflected their inability to accept the fundamental economic, social, and political realities of their day. Addison joined his emphasis on man's capacity for benevolent, selfless behavior with a keen appreciation of economic realities which Swift and Bolingbroke found hard to accept. By coupling the Tory emphasis on self-interest with Whig economics, Fielding integrates, as was his wont,[25] two types of realism. In doing so, he makes a political transition of which Bolingbroke was incapable and which he, as a young man, struggled so fitfully to attain. He turns to the old Tory rhetoric without joining the Tory cause, and he revivifies the Whig tradition first espoused in *The Freeholder* without committing himself to Addison's liberal estimation of man's capacity for altruism and beneficence.

The rhetoric of *The True Patriot* illustrates the persistence with which Fielding tries to integrate Whig and Tory evaluations of man's political nature. One of his most revealing devices is the series of definitions he offers for the word "patriot"—definitions that generally prove inadequate, and that the reader must combine and balance in order to establish a model for "the true Patriot." Early in the journal Fielding sets the problem: "this word *Patriot* hath of late Years been very scandalously abused by some Persons . . . Ambition, Avarice, Revenge, Envy, Malice, every bad Passion in the Mind of Man, have cloaked themselves under this amiable Character, and have misrepresented Persons and Things in unjust Colours to the Public" (II, i, i). The situation here parallels that in the great comic novels, where Fielding sets himself the task of separating sham from reality.[26] In the novels, as he works to unmask hypocrisy and deceit (the naked fact of Square's carnality), so here he will reveal the "bad Passion" of political operators. To discriminate the "true" meanings of words like "charity" and "prudence" in the novels, Fielding sets up collages of "scandalously abused" versions of them. The debased conceptions of Mrs. Tow-wouse ("Common Charity a f--t"), Parson Trulliber, and Peter Pounce clarify the nature of Adams's "true" charity. And we learn about "true" prudence by learning what it is not from Blifil, Lady Bellaston, and Jones himself. As the reader of the novels must discriminate carefully between versions of moral terms, so the reader of *The True Patriot* must not assume that Fielding endorses the versions of patriotism expressed by his speakers.

The need for caution is clear once we perceive how radically definitions for patriotism vary among Fielding's mouthpieces. In No. 9 an Italian opera singer writes "de Patriat, dat is to say, van Parson who take Part vor de Mony" (ix, i, i), while in No. 25 another correspondent, Philander, takes precisely the opposite tack: "He only is the *true Patriot*, who always does what is in his Power for his Country's Service, without any selfish Views, or regard to private Interest" (xxv, i, ii). In other issues Oliver Oldcoat asserts that a patriot "*is one who opposes the ministry*" (xxix, i, iii), and Stephen Grubb reduces patriotism, as he does religion, liberty, and love, to a matter of pounds and shillings (xi, i, i-iii). Miriam Austin Locke prefaces her edition of *The True Patriot* with Philander's words, in tandem with a quotation taken from No. 2: "For what less is meant by Patriotism, than the Love of one's Country carried into Action" (ii, i, i).

The admirable faith in "Love of Country" expressed in the last definition does tempt one to view it as Fielding's definitive comment on patriotism. But to accept as final this definition, or Philander's, is to oversimplify Fielding's position and overlook the rich blend of variations on patriotism that he is creating. Philander's namesake, as he appears in No. 21, is a romantic and an idealist, but he also is an adulterer. And Fielding turns to the Addisonian version of patriotism in No. 2 only to counter the most debased modern versions of the word. Although the idealistic definitions of patriotism are not qualified as systematically or as strongly as the cynical definitions (Oliver Oldcoat clearly is a fool, and the opera singer is obviously a knave), Fielding's persistent appeal to his reader's self-interest shows the irrelevance of absolute idealism to political situations. If Philander were even close to the truth, Fielding would not need to exert so much effort appealing to the Stephen Grubbs of the world and talking about security of property.

To identify Fielding with Philander makes him sound too much like Addison and mistakenly minimizes the importance of his appeals to the reader's self-love. Such an identification also overlooks another definition very different from Philander's. In No. 3 the editor, speaking in his own voice, relates a nightmare vision of the results of a Jacobite victory. As he apologizes for the personal bent of his narrative, he offers an important variation upon Philander's definition: "It is natural, on all occasions, to have some little Attention to our private Welfare, nor do I ever honour the Patriot the less (I am sure I confide in him much the more) whose own Good is involved in that of the Public. I am not, therefore, ashamed to give the Public the following Dream or Vision, tho' my own little Affairs, and the private Consequences, which the Success of this Rebellion would produce to myself, form the principal Object", (III, i, i). This version of patriotism, not Philander's, is the keystone around which Fielding arches debased or misguided versions of the word. Philander's definition is admirable but impractical; the opera singer's definition is perhaps pragmatic, but its total disavowal of principle clears the way for a Hobbesian political world. The narrator stands between them.

Most important about this treatment of the word "patriot" is that it reveals Fielding using techniques he had used with success in *Joseph Andrews* and would perfect in *Tom Jones*. In the comic novels, the intrusions of the narrator establish a norm by which readers can judge different versions of much-abused words; likewise, here the editor intrudes in his journal and establishes a standard for patriotism by which readers can judge other speakers. In the novels Fielding enriches the meaning of crucial moral terms by accumulating different versions of them, whereas here he enriches the meaning of "patriotism" by putting the word in so many different speakers' mouths. Underlying this practice and perfection of technique is a balanced, mature assessment of human nature—a confidence that, while man's motives are diverse (sometimes venal, sometimes noble, sometimes deserving satire, sometimes praiseworthy), self-interest is not the sole guide for human behavior. Fielding's greatest political work prepares the way for his greatest work of art, for it resolves not only his political but also his philosophical and literary uncertainties. The relationship between Fielding's politics and his art, relatively harmful in his plays and in *Jonathan Wild*, here appears in a brighter light. In both cases, however, the relationship is close, even crucial. Only its effect changes.

The editor's version of true patriotism manifests Fielding's refusal to accept in toto the definitions of either Addison or Swift. The editor sees a role in politics for "Attention to our private Welfare," but, unlike the opera singer and Stephen Grubb, he uses the word "little" to describe it. He is not "ashamed" to reveal how a Jacobite victory may affect his private interest, but he also claims a more general significance for his story: "For, I believe . . . there are few of my Readers who will not find themselves interested in some Parts of it" (III, i, i). He describes himself as more sure of a patriot whose personal interest is readily apparent, and thus prepares us for what might otherwise seem his startling acceptance of "the Saying of a great Man, *That no one served the Public for Nothing*" (XVII, i, i).[27] But by defining the true patriot as an individual "whose own Good is involved in that of the Public," the editor avoids an absolute emphasis on self-interest. The great question that remains for him, however, is just how potentially multifarious private interests coalesce under one public good. The Tories could "involve" private and public good only in the case of those landowners and merchants whose fortunes depended on the products of a landed, rural society. Addison and the benevolists did not struggle to define a means for such involvement, because they had faith in man's Christlike, innate "Love of Country." Fielding, a transitional figure, recognizes the importance of self-interest but involves it with social good in less reactionary ways than Swift and Bolingbroke.

As Fielding tries to revive the Whig supremacy—to make the majority of Englishmen see that their interests and those of the rebels are antithetical—the axis along which he repeatedly joins self-interest with the preservation of the political status quo is security of property. In taking this line, he returns to the heart of Locke's political theory, with its assumption that "The great and *chief end* . . . of Mens uniting into Commonwealths, and putting themselves under Government, *is the Preservation of Property*" (p. 395). Fielding's interest in property is practical as well as theoretical, for, insofar as he is able to prove that Charles Edward threatens the property of Englishmen, he, like Swift, can appeal to their self-love and direct it to the political system established in 1689. The great threat that the Stuarts present to the political status quo, as well as to property, rests in their potentially arbitrary use of the absolute power that Fielding claims they bring with them. According to Locke, freedom is the individual's "*Liberty* to dispose and order, as he lists, his Person, Actions, Possessions, and his whole Property, within the Allowance of those Laws under which he is; and therein not be subject to the arbitrary Will of another, but freely follow his own" (p. 348). The source of freedom, then, is an effective body of "*stated Rules* of Right and Property" (p. 405) which no one, the sovereign included, can breach. If the citizen is to be truly free and safe, Locke adds, "whatever Form the Common-wealth is under, the Ruling Power ought to be governed by *declared and received Laws*, and not by extemporary Dictates and undetermined Resolutions" (p. 405). By Fielding's day, the Tories accepted these Lockean principles. Indeed, as we shall see, even Bonnie Prince Charlie publicly announced his repudiation of the principles of political absolutism favored by his forebears.

In *The True Patriot* No. 3, the editor clearly looks back to Locke when he replies to the Jacobites who are persecuting him, "*That the Life of no Man was worth preserving longer that it was defended by the known Laws of his Country*; and that if the King's arbitrary Pleasure was to be that Law, I was indifferent what he determined concerning myself" (III, i, i). Fielding's linking of the Stuarts with "arbitrary" absolute power is crucial. He cannot let them escape this charge, because from the arbitrary exercise of absolute power follow all the evils he foresees in his nightmare—the disavowal of the national debt and ruin of the funds subsequent to it, the usurpation of the traditional English judicial system by foreigners. The desire for absolute power that Fielding traces throughout the Stuart heritage, and the threat that the potentially arbitrary use of that power poses to the "stated Rules of Property," make the Pretender's cause equally dangerous to public and private interest. Thus, when the rebel chief wrote an address to the people of England in which he denied the charge of absolutism, Fielding immediately fired back, "I am very sorry to see you . . . disclaiming all Pretensions to absolute Power. Those who know anything of your Father, and of your own Behaviour in *Scotland*, will . . . give little Credit to this Declaration" (III, ii, i). In No. 4 Fielding explicitly states that the purpose of the editor's nightmare was "to give a lively Picture of the utter Misery and Desolation it would introduce, and the Insecurity of our Estates, Properties, Lives and Families under the Government of an absolute Popish Prince, (for absolute he would plainly be)" (IV, i, i). He strengthens the tie that binds Charles Stuart to "the absolute Power which he infallibly brings with him" (IV, i, ii) and reemphasizes how such power is contrary to the interests of property owners.

Fielding assigns himself a more difficult task in No. 4, one which points to both his similarities and his differences with Swift, when he attempts to develop a reciprocity between the interests of the unpropertied and the interests of the Pelham ministry and the royal family. Like Swift, Fielding finally cannot conceive of the political function of self-interest outside the context of a property settlement. His limited ability to appeal to self-interest becomes quite apparent when he writes, "I am however aware, that there yet remains a Party to be spoken to, who are not strictly concerned in Interest in any of the preceding Lights; I mean those Gentlemen who have no Property, nor any Regard either for the Religion or Liberty of their Country" (IV, i, i). The conclusion of the sentence typifies his treatment of the unpropertied in the rest of the essay: they are, in effect, denied a serious political role. He lashes them with Swiftian irony and innuendo, speaking of their "principal Trade" as "the honest Method of selling ourselves, which hath flourished so notably for a long time among us" (IV, i, ii).

Fielding's satire in the fourth issue begs the conclusion that the poor must be excluded from the political process. *The True Patriot*, like several of Swift's pamphlets, has as its goal the end of divisions among good Whigs. Fielding's quest for the inclusiveness, like Swift's, is limited by his emphasis upon the role of property in politics. Unlike Swift's, however, Fielding's greatest political journal defines "property" very broadly—as anything more than a forty-shilling-a-year freehold. While he cannot make a serious appeal to the poor, Fielding can side with "every good and worthy Protestant in this Nation, who is attached to his Religion and Liberties, or who hath any Estate or Property, either in Church-lands or *in the Funds*, (which includes almost every Man who hath either Estate or Property in the Kingdom)" (IV, i, i, italics mine). The parenthetical expression reveals Fielding's deviation from Swift's model. Swift, with his backward-looking political ideal, never could appeal to the "Monied-Interest." Rather than answer Sir Richard Steele, the type of the new Whig, Swift responds to Steele's arguments with ad hominem vituperation and bitter innuendo, only deigning to deal seriously with landowning Whig lords.[28] Addison, on the other hand, entitles his great political journal *The Free-holder* and makes the forty-shilling property owner the center of the political system. When he opens the journal by claiming, "A Free-holder may be either a Voter, or Knight of the Shire; a Wit, or a Fox-hunter; a Scholar, or a Soldier; an Alderman, or a Courtier; a Patriot, a Stock-jobber" (pp. 2–3), he enfranchises groups that Swift would have excluded from power.

In *The True Patriot*, Fielding's definition of property aligns him with Addison, but his appeal to the propertied follows the pattern of Swift and Bolingbroke. His syllogism has a broader major premise than that of the Tories, as he accepts economic changes that Addison and Steele celebrated and that Swift and Bolingbroke scorned. Although he shares with Swift some fundamental Lockean principles, different assumptions about the nature of property make Fielding's politics very different from the Dean's. Fielding is a Whig, given his notion of property. Swift is, all Namierian caveats to the contrary, a Tory.

Although one writer has castigated it for its inaccuracies and histrionics, we must return to the editor's nightmare in No. 3 to illustrate more specifically Fielding's appeal to men of property, and his definition of what constitutes property. On one level the nightmare appeals to the crudest sorts of self-interest: the editor portrays the Jacobites as ravishers of wives and daughters and beaters of children, a picture at odds with historical truth.[29] Once this visceral appeal is made, however, the narrative addresses itself to the reader's legal, economic, and religious interests. The editor cites English common law in his defense against charges of treason, only to learn from a judge who speaks "in broken English" that the new king has arbitrarily suspended the law. Sent to prison, he meets an old friend who has been reduced to theft to feed his family. The friend explains his fall very simply: "you must know, *my whole Estate was in the Funds*, by the wiping out of which I was at once reduced to the Condition in which you now see me. I rose in the Morning with £40000 . . . at Noon I found a Royal Decree had reduced me to downright Beggary . . . My Wife is dead of a broken Heart, and my poor Girls have neither Cloaths to cover them nor Meat to feed them" (III, i, iii, italics mine). A succession of Roman Catholic priests then descend upon the narrator and threaten him with even more severe punishment if he does not convert. The message of the vision, of course, was abundantly clear to any Briton who valued his legal rights, his religion, and his property.

The revealing feature of this nightmare is that it ties Fielding to a specific political outlook only in its description of the friend's "Estate." Swift and Addison, writers of very different political allegiances, both claimed to defend the Anglican establishment and eagerly portrayed their opponents as threatening it. They also defended the established legal system and code.[30] Thus the described abuses of the Church and the common law had standard, almost universal political appeal. Fielding displays his allegiance to those who emerged victorious in 1715 only when he places the "whole Estate" of the editor's acquaintance in the "Funds." When Bolingbroke uses "Estate," he refers to the land holdings of the nobility and gentry (II, pp. 142, 148). He understands changes in political power in terms of changes in landownership, and he classifies men like the one Fielding describes sympathetically as threats to the proper distribution of property—the distribution that emerged during the Elizabethan era. Swift also attacked this type of man for profiting from the huge national debt and the war, both of which, he claimed, led to taxes that left "the Landed-Men half ruined." (VI, pp. 126–27). The son of a military man who had no land, Fielding was not sympathetic to the views of Bolingbroke and Swift. His portrayal of the ruined "Monied-Man" sets him apart from them and reveals his basic Whiggism.

Once Fielding controls self-interest by directing it to an enlightened quest after security of property and life, he is able to align that interest with the basic assumption of the Whig hegemony—the Lockean call for government by "*stated Rules* of Right and Property," instead of by royal fiat. He constructs a syllogism in which private interest is subordinated to a Whig supremacy that protects traditional religious and legal liberties, as well as new economic interests. If his reader does not question his major premise —his description of what a government should do—then political parties and private interest groups become unnecessary; the syllogism makes "Self-love and Social" the same. Only because he assumes that his audience accepts his premise can the editor, echoing Swift, make proud claims for his impartiality. He asserts that the author of *The True Patriot* "hath not sought the Protection of any Party, by adhering to the Principles of any, farther than is consistent with the true Interest of his Country, which no Party, it will be found, hath effectually consulted at all Times. Indeed this absurd and irrational Distinction of Parties hath principally contributed to poison our Constitution . . ." (xiv, i, iii). While this passage might seem to clinch any argument a Namierian might choose to make, we should note that Fielding's brave talk was possible only given one widely accepted definition for the "true Interest" of the nation. Syllogisms by themselves do not compel assent, nor do they end political conflict. Swift wrought his rhetoric more finely and asserted his freedom from party ties more vehemently than Fielding did, but his premise that the national good would be best served by enfranchising only the landed men was irrelevant, even antithetical, to the interests of most Englishmen with property and power. Addison's appeals to a vague love of country inevitably were more attractive to London's moneyed men than were Swift's carefully crafted appeals to interests they did not share. Like Swift, Fielding, despite his claims to speak impartially to all men, addressed a group that was limited by his assumptions about property and its role in politics.

When Fielding, following Locke, assumes that the best way to involve self-love with social is through a political system that takes security of property and person as its goal, he commits himself to at least one view that many moderns will find disappointing. Because those who have the most property obviously have the greatest interest in maintaining the system under which they prosper, Fielding concludes that the wealthiest men will tend to make the best public servants. Although this conclusion is particularly central to *The Jacobite's Journal*, several passages in *The True Patriot* anticipate its later importance. In No. 17 Fielding points out that "some Situations, some Degrees of Poverty and Distress . . . might require divine rather than human Prudence, to adhere with Integrity to the Good of the Public" (XVII, i, iii). But a rich man must be a fool not to perceive that his own and his "Family's Ruin are necessarily involved in the Ruin of his Country" (XVII, i, ii). Without Addison's faith in innate love of country, Fielding sees the poor only as threats to the careful intertwining of "Self-love and Social" that is at the root of good politics. He must exclude them from a political role because the possible sacrifice of national interest to private good would be all too tempting for them. Because Fielding believes the wealth of propertied men shields them from this temptation, he praises Pelham's ministry for including "Men of distinguished Property and Probity, who have a large stake in their Country's Welfare" (XXXI, iii, i).

While Fielding's appeal to the interest of property owners is systematic and persistent, it is not absolute. In two numbers he re-creates his (at that time) most famous fictional character, Parson Abraham Adams, and has him comment upon the rebels' success. Adams attributes it to the "just Judgement of God against an offending People" (VII. i, i) and calls the citizens of England to moral regeneration. Instead of appealing to material or financial interests, Adams appeals to spiritual ones, replacing concern for property with concern for the soul and attacking the "self-interested Motives" of most Englishmen. He is appalled by the response of "a very great and generous Friend of mine," who says of his contribution to a national defense fund, "It was rather Sense than Goodness, to sacrifice a small Part [of his wealth] for the Security of the Whole" (vii, ii, i). Fielding will not contradict Adams's Addisonian appeal to the selfless Christian instincts of the British people, nor his call for them to live less luxuriously. But Fielding's main appeal necessarily is to those who "know the World better" (xiii, i, i) than Adams, and the tone of the journal as a whole remains practical rather than idealistic. Adams's benevolism, like Philander's, provides only one of many possible versions of patriotism.

A change in the relation between Adams and his creator appears quite clearly when we note that in *Joseph Andrews* Adams never reaches London. His virtue remains pure, unqualified by his brief exposure to the values of a world different from the rural community of faith he has created. But in *The True Patriot* Adams refers to a winter passed in London, and his attacks on the city and its customs set up an explicit conflict which the comic novel only implied. As a political journalist, Fielding must appeal to those Londoners whose values are foreign to Adams; he tries to elicit from the "very great" the response that Adams finds unworthy. The peripheral position of Adams in the journal, and his disillusionment with a world he previously had known only by report, reveal a distance between him and his creator. Despite his own full awareness of the city's ills,[31] Fielding is a Londoner. When he speaks in his own voice, he sets a standard for patriotism very different from that of Adams. In *Tom Jones* the literary counterpart for this distance is that Fielding makes his hero grow (unlike Adams, but like Joseph Andrews). Before he

achieves Sophia, Jones must add concern for his interest
and reputation—prudence—to his benevolence.

The perspective that Adams brings to *The True Patriot*,
while it is not one that Fielding adopts, does serve an
important purpose. It balances the emphasis upon self-
interest and property and prevents the journal from becoming completely mercenary in its appeal. The importance of Adams, as well as of the spectrum of definitions
for patriotism that the journal offers, becomes apparent
when we encounter Stephen Grubb, the correspondent in
No. 11. Grubb believes that "every Man, Woman, and
Thing . . . have their Price" (xi, i, i); he calculates the
value of love and faith on a balance sheet, and refers with
surprise to Adams's earlier questioning of the supreme
"truth" that *"there is no real Value in any Thing but Money"*
(xi, i, i). Even the debased "Prudence" of which Grubb
boasts (xi, i, i) leads him to suppose that men will support
the ministry once they "seriously consider the Preservation . . . of their Property; and advance their Money in its
Defence" (xi, i, iii). But this prudence, circumscribed by
absolute self-interest, is canny, rather than truly enlightened; its analogue in *Tom Jones* is the mean-spirited cunning of Blifil.[32] Grubb is too selfish to "involve" his private
good in the public good, and Fielding leads the reader to
reject his views. He shows Grubb to be at once heartless
and foolish, completely lacking Adams's beneficence and
idealism.

Stephen Grubb's prudence makes him a "Patriat" by
the misguided standards of the Italian singer, but he fails
to meet the standard for patriotism offered by the editor in
a later number: "what is . . . Patriotism better than true
Wisdom, and by what Action can we deserve the Appella-

tion of *wise*, so justly as by using our utmost Endeavours to preserve our Properties, our Liberties, and our Religion?" (xvii, i, i). The frequently repeated phrase that points to Grubb's failings is "our Properties, our Liberties, and our Religion." "Properties" invariably heads the list, a position which reflects Fielding's awareness that self-interest motivates men. To stop at "Properties," however, and not add religious and national ideals to pure materialism, is to advance only slightly beyond Hobbes's state of nature. Grubb's greedy concern that the government protect his property provides only a minimal base for a social contract; it depends more on avarice than on reason. Grubb's version of prudence is a deviation from the "true Wisdom" that Fielding admires—a deviation as serious as that of people who fail to see the threat the rebels pose to their properties and lives.

Fielding's triad of "our Properties, our Liberties, and our Religion" shows that Adams's benevolent idealism, while not a norm in the journal, is not alien to its values and goals. Unenlightened self-interest, in the person of Grubb, is as far from Fielding's position as is the simple benevolence of Adams. That the ministry serves both pragmatic and idealistic interests only strengthens Fielding's arguments for it. The triad also manifests once again Fielding's grounding in the tradition of Locke. For, while Fielding narrows Locke's use of "Property" (the word here refers only to estates in money and land), by linking "our Properties, our Liberties, and our Religion," he resets the Lockean problem of at once recognizing self-interest but limiting its influence. Locke used verbal ambiguity to deal with this problem; Fielding takes the riskier course of promoting a ministry which both mercenary and altruistic parties can support. It was riskier because the Pelhamites, however virtuous, remained mere men. When they lapsed, or died, Fielding would have to confront again the problem of self-interest and its role in politics.

Despite the two important interludes with Abraham Adams, the strategy of *The True Patriot* remains an attempt to link syllogistically private and public good.[33] Once Fielding "proves" that the emphasis on property rights and civil liberties of the Whig settlement provides the best means for linking "Self-love and Social" and gives his new, expanded definition of property, he can support that settlement without demur. The editor repeats the commonplace, popular since 1689, that Englishmen live "under the *best* Constitution, if *well* administer'd, that has been made known to the World" (xviii, iii, ii). Because the House of Brunswick embodies the principles of 1689 and 1701, standing against the threat of Stuart absolutism to both property and person, it receives fulsome praise in the closing issues of the journal. Pelham's ministry, by its early recognition of the danger facing the nation and its "broad-bottomed" re-creation of the Whig hegemony, proved itself the proper administrator for the "best Constitution." Fielding thus parallels his praise for the royal family with praise for the ministry. In the last issue to which he gave his full attention, he defines "New Patriotism" (xviii, iii, ii) simply and precisely as support for the Pelham ministry. Locating great virtues in the ministry, Fielding can claim that it has given people "a knowledge of our true Interests" (xviii, ii, i), and that it has made distinctions between true and false patriotism (so difficult at the start of the journal) easy.

To see the watershed that the rebellion and *The True*

Patriot constitute for Fielding's politics and his art, we can profit from a brief look at his *Miscellanies*, his last major published work prior to the '45. The first volume provides something like a compendium of the political confusion and uncertainty we have seen in Fielding's other writings. In several of the essays and poems, particularly "Liberty," "Of Good Nature," and "An Essay on Conversation," Fielding sounds very much like Addison. He describes man as both social and charitable by nature, figuring the human race as a serene, nonviolent herd which "o'er the Mountain strays;/ Nor begs this Beast the other's Leave to graze." In this vein, Fielding will go so far as to claim that laws are unnatural and unnecessary, uttering a "Curse on all laws which Liberty subdue" (p. 37). He will assail Hobbes and Mandeville and claim that they "borrow all their information from their own savage Dispositions" (p. 119). Yet Fielding mixes his benevolism with a Scriblerian distaste for eighteenth-century England and its innovations. In one verse satire he laments, "When our old British Plainness left us, / Of ev'ry Virtue it bereft us," and once describes the world as a "vast Masquerade" in which people cultivate the "Art of *Thriving*" (pp. 116, 155, 154).

The political ramifications of this uncertainty about human nature manifest themselves in Fielding's discussion of patriotism in "An Essay on the Knowledge of the Characters of Men." Here he cannot decide whether love of country is a product of nature or of nurture, whether patriotism is a byproduct of universal benevolence—"a passion which really exists in some Natures" (p. 178)—or a learned attitude. In the *Miscellanies* Fielding will not answer this question, will not formulate a final or successful definition of patriotism or of political man. He fluctuates between Drury Lane sentiment and Scriblerian pessimism. Their opposing pulls leave his politics enigmatic and shapeless (witness the different political groups satirized in *Jonathan Wild*), and marr the structure and sense of his literary works (witness the disparate characters and plots of *Jonathan Wild*).

By threatening all that Fielding held dear, Prince Charles Edward provided him with the opportunity to define his political values.[34] *The True Patriot*, in effect, answers the question that Fielding had left unresolved when he wrote "An Essay on the Knowledge of the Characters of Men." In it, he defines patriotism as a wise, prudential concern for property, liberty, and religion, rather than as a perfect altruism. The benevolism of writers like Addison, or even Parson Adams, does not dominate Fielding's final political position; nor does the cynical, reductive quest for self-gratification that Hobbes spoke of and that Stephen Grubb embodies. Instead, Fielding proposes enlightened (not debased) self-interest as the source of virtuous political action. He modernizes Locke's conception of property as the necessary medium for enlightening self-interest and supposes that commonwealths arise because individuals wish to protect both their property and their liberty.

In line with his emphasis on enlightened self-interest, Fielding comes to believe that sound leadership, like true patriotism, depends on "Sagacity" (VIII, i, iii), on a quick perception of where the interests of both the individual and the nation lie. For all their doubts about human motivation—perhaps because of them—Bolingbroke and Swift were idealists when they considered political leadership. The Patriot King is "a sort of standing miracle" (II, p. 396), a "patriarch" who wins universal love and esteem.

He is not a politican who sagaciously links self-love and social; rather, he provides a great example of "how repugnant the interests of private ambition and those of real patriotism are" (II, p. 411). With its emphasis upon "Sagacity," Fielding's ideal for leadership integrates "private ambition" and "real patriotism," rather than separating them. Given Fielding's unflinching admission of the role of "private ambition" in politics, his definitions for true patriotism and true political greatness inevitably lack the idealism displayed by Addison, Parson Adams, Philander, or even Bolingbroke. But this reflects the general character of *The True Patriot* (and of his later political writing), which is pragmatic and prudential in the best sense—the sense defined in *Tom Jones*.

In *The True Patriot* Fielding's earlier fluctuation between political extremes resolves itself in a call for enlightened self-interest. That call depends upon his making Britons' concern for their property congruent with their concern for the survival of the Pelham ministry. Fielding undoubtedly pays a price for his consistent loyalty to Pelham. Adams moves from center stage, as his creator shifts his concern to earthly (as opposed to spiritual) estates. The Parson's exuberant, simple benevolism will never again dominate Fielding's work. But whatever the cost, in his greatest political journal Fielding arrives at a complex, mature, and strong set of principles that involve ideology as well as interest. His definition of patriotism allows him to locate impressive virtues in the Pelham ministry. His support for that ministry will not waver during the final years of his life, as a firmness of vision and purpose, which *The Jacobite's Journal* elaborates, replaces the political uncertainty of the 1730s.

VI
𝔓olitical Certaintp

True Greatness in The Jacobite's Journal *and Related Writings*

In his writings of the late 1730s and early 1740s, Fielding often used the word "great" ironically—to describe a self-ish, mercenary, and violent disposition with which we usually do not associate the word. In *Jonathan Wild* he used the word "good," if not ironically, then uniquely—to describe an obtuse and passive disposition that is power-less before the Great Man's guile. But in his poem "Of True Greatness" (January 1741) and in the preface to his *Miscellanies* (April 1743), Fielding offered more conven-tional, straightforward definitions. At one point in the latter he remarks that, although characters like Heartfree may win our love, they "often partake too little of Parts or courage to have any Pretensions to Greatness" (p. 12). He appends this judgment of Heartfree to a list of three basic types of human character: the good (as embodied by Heartfree), the great (as embodied by Wild), and the great and good (which finds no embodiment in *Jonathan Wild*). Fielding reserves his highest praise for this last character, which combines the "Benevolence, Honour, Honesty, and Charity" of "a good Man" with the "Parts, Courage

. . . the efficient Qualities of a Great Man" (p. 11). He labels such a character "truly great" and uses it as a standard for judging goodness and greatness taken by themselves. Given the absolute separation between goodness and greatness in *Jonathan Wild*, one of Fielding's comments upon them in the preface is particularly important. He claims that, "tho' the one bear no necessary Dependence on the other, neither is there any absolute repugnancy among them which may totally prevent their Union so that they may, tho' not of Necessity, assemble in the same Mind, as they actually did . . . in those of *Socrates* and *Brutus*; and perhaps in some among us" (p. 11). The preface, then, shows that the word "great" was not inevitably ironic for Fielding. Men who exemplified true greatness had lived in the past, and, as the pantheon of contemporary great men in "Of True Greatness" asserted, lived in Fielding's day.

The study of Fielding's politics becomes particularly significant if we ask why his political and literary writings of the late 1730s and early 1740s deviate so sharply from the theory advanced in the preface to the *Miscellanies*. This deviation had, at least in part, a political motive. To protect London's financiers and merchants from complicity in Walpole's sins, Fielding used several devices to suggest that Walpole's success resulted from illusion and trickery, rather than from faults in Englishmen and their institutions. Fielding's desire to isolate the London merchant from the Great Man meant that he also had to isolate the former from the latter's "efficient Qualities"—to contrast (rather than combine) active, courageous greatness and passive, benevolent goodness. The separation of greatness and goodness, apparent in both *The Champion* and *Jonathan Wild*, prevented Fielding from developing strong political allegiances and views. He could only contrast Wild and Heartfree, the sorcerer and his bewitched audience, to their mutual disadvantage; he could only speak *against* Walpole, or whomever he considered to be the most striking example of political venality, and not *for* anyone. With the exception of his praise for Dodington,[1] Lyttelton, and Carteret[2] in "Of True Greatness" and a few brief panegyrics upon the "boy Patriots" in *The Champion*, Fielding's use of the words "great" and "good" remained "odd" and uncertain prior to 1745.

When the Pelham ministry proved its mettle both during the '45 and during the crisis of the "48 hour ministry," the gap between Fielding's theory of true greatness and his politics narrowed. Pelham had recognized early the Jacobite threat, had called for the return of British troops from Holland to stop the rebels, and had spurred into action the initially lethargic George II. The failure of Granville and Bath to form a ministry clearly consolidated his power and opened the way for the political stability that would characterize the remainder of his tenure. Fielding had no direct involvement in the high-level political struggle of February 1746, although he commented upon it in *The True Patriot* No. 16 and later repeated a popular joke about the "48 hour ministry"—a joke in which people are described as hesitating to walk the streets for fear of being asked to accept a place under Granville and Bath.[3] But Pelham had one more political hurdle to jump before he could dominate the political life of Great Britain. Having won the grudging respect of George II, he faced a new challenge from an opposition that centered around Prince Frederick and that repeated many charges of the patriot opposition of 1737–41. Saddled with an unpopular and costly foreign war, Pelham tried to save his position by negotiating a peace and calling for elections before the opposition could organize itself. His need for a propagandist to justify his peace policy and his early dissolution of Parliament coincided with Fielding's need for financial aid in 1746. The result was an elaboration by Fielding, in two pamphlets and *The Jacobite's Journal*, of his faith in Pelham as first expressed in *The True Patriot*.

If we are to understand the place of *The Jacobite's Journal* in Fielding's political development, the important fact about Pelham is that he was a protégé of Walpole. While the Great Man was alive, Pelham sought and followed his counsel; after Walpole's death, Pelham governed very much as his mentor had.[4] Without careful study of Fielding's uncertainty in *The Champion* and *Jonathan Wild*, it is easy to describe his support for Walpole's protégé as a major reversal in his politics. Such a description fails to recognize that, for Fielding, the change from opposition writer to ministerial writer was not a profound one. His conflict with Walpole was more a matter of taste than of principle; his distinction between Walpole and Great Britain's economic and political elite was more convenient than true. Pelham, at once less colorful and more efficient than Walpole,[5] served the House of Brunswick and the new financial order without lapsing into the uncompromising Walpolian venality that drove Fielding into the opposition camp. Thus, while Fielding's allegiance to Walpole in the 1730s and early 1740s was hesitant, his allegiance to Pelham during and after the '45 was (with one possible exception[6]) consistent and strong. Fielding found in Pelham a practical model for true greatness—a model he had lacked during the tempestuous years of his early political career.

Fielding's diction in *The Jacobite's Journal* provides the clearest sign of his new political certainty. Most significantly, he uses the word "great" in a straightforward rather than an ironic fashion. In one passage he describes the virtues of the Pelham ministry's "broad-bottom": "We have an Administration not consisting of one absolute Prime Minister, supported only by his Tools and Dependents, and obnoxious to the *Great Men* in the Nation; but an Administration composed really of all the *Great Men*, whose Abilities of any Kind make them worthy of a Place in it" (pp. 113–14, italics mine). Other examples from *The Jacobite's Journal* illustrate Fielding's forthright use of the phrase "Great Man" or the word "greatness."[7] Suffice it to say that in the *Journal* he refers to Pelham and his supporters as "the Greatest of Men" almost as often as he uses that epithet for Wild and his gang, although the impact of the phrase is reversed. In line with this changed use of "great," Fielding also begins to combine the word with its previous antonym "good." He describes the Pelham ministry as "those Great and Good Men" and as the "greatest and best of Men" (p. 215, 311), thus indicating that he had passed beyond the convenient distinction used in his works of the 1730s. When he locates true greatness in Pelham and his men, he avoids any hint of irony in his diction.

Fielding's newfound political certainty also appears in the models to which he refers in the *Journal*. By 1747 the battles between the Scriblerians and the Cibberians, which had provided an index to Fielding's early literary and political uncertainty, were a thing of the past. Except for one essay (No. 31, 2 July 1748) in which he compares Pope's attacks on Cibber to unjust opposition attacks on Pelham, Fielding does not refer to the old dispute. The *Journal* does reopen Hercules Vinegar's "Court of Censorial Enquiry" in a section entitled the "Court of Criticism," but it ponders the critical response to *Clarissa* (pp. 119–20), describes performances by Garrick at Drury Lane (p. 153), and evaluates *The Castle of Indolence* (pp. 300–302). As Pelham had ushered the nation into a new political age, so, apparently, Fielding felt it had entered a new literary era. He relegates Pope, Swift, and Cibber to the status of past giants, and he no longer is torn between divergent loyalties to satire and sentiment.

Walpole had died in 1745, and Bolingbroke had retired to France in 1744. Fielding, however, had good reason to remember their past differences. In No. 7 (16 January 1748) he attacks Bolingbroke's *Dissertation Upon Parties* and claims that Tories are "concealed Jacobites." In No. 15 (12 March 1748) he describes one of the arts of Jacobitism as the "Art of Lying and Misrepresenting" and bitterly asserts " 'Twas by such Arts as these that the brave *Marlborough*, and the just *Godolphin* fell a Victim to the Intrigues of Harley and ***" (p. 190). In Nos. 11 (13 February 1748) and 14 (5 March 1748) he introduces Humphrey Gubbins as the embodiment of "that honest hearty *English* Spirit, which distinguishes the Country Gentlemen of this Island from all other People in the World." Fielding's persona, John Trott-plaid, echoes Swift and Bolingbroke when he observes of his cousin, Gubbins, "I have often thought what a glorious Nation we should be, if we could once see a Majority in our Senate of this kind of Man" (p. 155). The echo turns to jeering mockery, however, when Gubbins appears as a semi-literate, xenophobic, and bibulous character—a Squire Western at his worst.

While *The Jacobite's Journal* treats Bolingbroke roughly, it also makes Fielding's amends to the reputation of Robert Walpole. After his attack on Bolingbroke in No. 7, Fielding quotes at length a passage from Samuel Squires's *Historical Essay upon the Ballance of Civil Power in England.* In it Squires first claims "a true and consistent Whig is a Ballancer, a Mediator; always against Violence, and against Encroachment from whatever Quarter it is derived." He then sets up a galaxy of Whig heroes, placing Walpole, the Earl of Orford, in the best of company: "Such were the great *Clarendon* and *Southhampton*; such the Lords *Somers* and *Godolphin*; such was the late Earl of *Orford*; and such are those illustrious Persons, who are, at present, generally supposed to enjoy the greatest Share of his Majesty's Favour and Counsels" (p. 133). In No. 31 (2 July 1748) Fielding quotes from *The Fool* a slander on the ministry ("W--l--pe began, and P--m plays his part, / To fix corruption's Standard in their [the Commons'] Heart"), labeling it "Libel not only against the Dead, but against one of the greatest Men now alive" (p. 325). Early numbers of the *Journal* include prominently placed advertisements for Fielding's pamphlet, *A Proper Answer to a Late Scurrilous Libel* (24 December 1747). In it Fielding defended Walpole from a series of vituperative and senseless charges, not the least of which was that he secretly plotted to restore the Stuart pretender.[8]

The Fool's attack on Pelham and Walpole, and Fielding's

response to it, do share one revealing assumption: both agree that Walpole and Pelham were cut from the same political cloth. Fielding, the old Walpole-abuser, does not deny their close association. Instead he rehabilitates Walpole's reputation, satirizing an attack on the Great Man similar to his and Ralph's in *The Champion*. Fielding's revision of his attitude toward Walpole was more than a sign of proper respect for the recently deceased; it was a necessary first step if he was to develop a firm allegiance to the cause of Henry Pelham, Walpole's true successor. Because Bolingbroke's *Dissertation Upon Parties* and *Patriot King* (written specifically for Prince Frederick's political education) had become commonplace books for opposition attacks on Pelham, Fielding could not forgive Bolingbroke as he forgave the other Scriblerians. But even without the stimulus of Bolingbroke's political writings, criticism of him followed inevitably from Fielding's commitment to the Walpole-Pelham wing of the Whigs. To attack the political heresies of the great Tory served almost as a rite of passage into the Whig establishment.

In *The Jacobite's Journal* Fielding's reconciliation to Walpole, as well as his straightforward diction, point to the political stability he has acquired. Other brief journal references to literary models also reflect his confident Whiggism. In his one comment on the Pope-Cibber quarrel, he sided with Cibber (pp. 322–23); he also placed himself firmly in the Whig tradition in No. 36 (6 August 1748) when he lauded and reprinted in its entirety an essay from Addison's *Freeholder*.[9] Fielding's models and diction indicate, then, that by 1747–48 his flirtation with the role of Scriblerus Secundus had become a distant although potentially embarrassing memory. By then he had settled

into the political allegiance for which his family background and social status had destined him.

Fielding's political uncertainty forced him, in *The
Champion* and *Jonathan Wild*, to construct a complex rhetoric. In *The Jacobite's Journal* one more sign of his confidence
in the Pelham ministry is a relative dearth of argumenta-
tive sleight of hand. While it would be precious to label
The Champion "exciting," it does develop a variety of
suspense. Fielding's repetition of foreign analogues for the
office of prime minister, as well as his references to Harlequin, may cause us to wonder if he can "bring off" the
spurious distinction between Walpole and the eighteenth-
century British society that he dominated. The rhetoric of
The Jacobite's Journal offers no similar intrigue. With one
small exception, it is as straightforward as Fielding's diction.

The one possible source of complexity in the *Journal*'s
rhetoric is Fielding's persona, the Jacobite John Trott-
plaid. But Fielding does not establish the distance between speaker and mask that is basic to irony (and that
twentieth-century students of Swift cannot investigate too
often); rather, Trott-plaid provides little more than a straw
man, whom Fielding sets up and knocks down so easily
that ultimately the effort is not worthwhile. Before Fielding drops his "Masque," Trott-plaid's main function is to
declare his own irrationality. His standard role is to boast
of "our contempt of all Arguments drawn from Common
Sense" (p. 201), and then to introduce a carefully reasoned, pro-Pelham argument that he claims not to fear.
Typical of this habit is a statement that prefaces the ex-
tract from Squires's pamphlet, *Upon the Ballance of Civil
Power in England*. Trott-plaid glibly claims not to fear the

pamphlet's arguments because "Jacobitism is a very high unintelligible Mystery, and as it is the Glory of our Party to maintain their Doctrines in Opposition to Reason and Argument, all Attempts to shew the Inconsistency of these Doctrines with Reason contribute to raise and spread our Triumph" (p. 130). Here and in many other instances[10] he offers so little resistance to Fielding's opinions that he becomes an unnecessary and cumbersome absurdity. The passage is ironic only insofar as Trott-plaid is blind to certain implications of what he says; otherwise, he clearly says what Fielding means.

Fielding eventually would find unrewarding even the slight opportunity for irony that Trott-plaid provided. In No. 17 (26 March 1748) he claims, "it is high time to speak in a plainer Language than that of Irony, and to endeavour to raise something more than Mirth in the Mind of the Reader" (p. 212), and he drops his Jacobite "Masque." The conclusion of the sentence reveals an important reason why Fielding had to dispense with this persona: Trott-plaid's only real flaw was that he offered too easy, too laughable a foil. Because he became inimical to the more serious tone of advocacy that Fielding wished to establish, Fielding began to speak his own voice.

One change in the latter issues of the *Journal* illuminates Fielding's motive for dropping Trott-plaid. Following No. 17 Fielding engages in direct and extended vindication of the members of the Pelham ministry, which he could not have done if he had wanted to maintain the prejudices of his mouthpiece.[11] In No. 18 (2 April 1748) he defends Lyttleton from attacks in Horace Walpole's anonymously published *Second and Third Letter to the Whigs*. Subsequent issues[12] also include direct vindications of

Pelham, Walpole, and Lyttleton, along with proposals for
reform in the nation's education system and in its manner
of providing relief for the families of deceased clergymen.[13] Once Fielding freed himself from the Trott-plaid
"Masque," he could be more assertive in his political
comment. Confusion due to the small irony of the Jacobite
pose was not the reason for the change Fielding announced
in No. 17; no one could be confused about the implications
of Trott-plaid's utterances, or, after No. 5 (2 January
1748),[14] wonder who wrote the *Journal*. Trott-plaid had to
go because, after years of political uncertainty, Fielding
had found a group of men that he supported without the
slightest reservation.

Despite the shift toward more positive political comment, the rhetoric of the *Journal* changes little after No.
17. Fielding continues to link Jacobitism with irrationality
and absurdity and merely dispenses with Trott-plaid's
eager embracing of the absurdity. Fielding's principal aim
in the rest of the *Journal* is to link all opposition to the
ministry with Jacobitism—a favorite device of Walpole's
propagandists.[15] Thus in No. 24 (14 May 1748), the first
issue after the ministry announced the preliminaries of the
Treaty of Aix-la-Chapelle, Fielding argues that the treaty
will be opposed only by soldiers eager for more battle, and
Jacobites eager for the nation's ruin. Two years after
Culloden, Jacobitism was hardly a threat to the Protestant
Succession and the peace of England. To link the survival
of a free Protestant England with the survival of the
Pelham ministry, as Fielding did, was inaccurate but convenient—particularly because it enabled him to recall the
glory days of the Pelhams during the '45.

Other features of the *Journal*'s rhetoric are as standard as the opposition-equals-Jacobitism ploy. Fielding repeatedly associates Pelham with moderation and light, and the opposition with extremism and darkness.[16] Pelham wins biblical sanction for his actions—"Blessed are the peace-makers" (p. 274)—while Jacobitism is compared with Judaism, and writers for the opposition press with the lowest, most poisonous vermin.[17] For the most part, however, Fielding does not extend or elaborate these devices. Confident in a field where he once was uncertain, he apparently enjoyed saying, simply and directly, that "a Jacobite Country Squire, in his Plaid Waistcoat, is, in reality, a Disgrace to his very Species" (p. 374), and that Henry Pelham is "the best of Men."

Fielding's confidence results in a *Jacobite's Journal* that is not only less complex rhetorically, but also, at least superficially, less moralistic than much of his earlier political writing. In *The True Patriot*, Abraham Adams moved from a central to a peripheral position as Fielding elaborated the virtues of the Pelhamites. Adams makes only a brief appearance in *The Jacobite's Journal* (pp. 331–36), and Fielding, secure in his allegiance to Pelham, apparently brushes aside or overlooks variances between his old and new political positions—variances that a modern student may find disturbing.[18] I shortly will suggest connections between Fielding's politics in the *Journal* and his politics in *The Champion*, and will argue that the change in his position is not as fundamental as it may seem. But first I must point to those instances where Fielding deviates from his earlier views. While he could have avoided (and, in two important instances, did avoid) self-contradiction, his new confidence manifested itself in his failure to explain all possible discrepancies. The important point is not that

Fielding may have reversed an earlier position, but that his confidence as he wrote the *Journal* may have committed him to a position that did scant justice to his old doubts and dilemmas.

In his defense of Lyttelton in No. 18, Fielding quite clearly opens himself to charges of equivocation: "I assert, that neither he [Lyttelton] nor his particular Friends did ever *speak* or *vote*, while in *Opposition*, against *Septennial Parliaments*, as the Writer of this Libel asserts" (p. 219). The assertion may be technically true; Lyttelton and his "particular friends" perhaps avoided opposition to septennial Parliaments on the floor of the Commons. But we need only turn to *The Champion* No. 56 (22 March 1739/40) to find Ralph complaining that "The *very desirable* Attempt which was expected to be made this Session to restore *Triennial* Parliaments, seems to be no longer thought of" (II, 31). Of course, this comment is not as forceful as Ralph's comments upon Place Bills, and we have seen that Ralph's views were not always Fielding's. Nonetheless, this comment provides one case in which a journal supervised by a "Friend" of Lyttelton's, and written with Lyttelton's encouragement, did speak against septennial Parliaments.

In the same vein, Fielding, who had protested ministerial threats to curb freedom of the press during his days with *The Champion*, in the *Journal* frequently warns his adversaries they have gone too far in their slanders, and that only the great tolerance of the ministry prevents the imposition of censorship.[19] When in No. 22 (30 April 1748) the "Court of Criticism" considers the case of Samuel Foote and his *"Scandal-Shop in the Haymarket"* (p. 262), this impulse seemingly leads Fielding to legitimize

the Licensing Act that ended his career at the Haymarket
Theatre. Trott-plaid, in his role as judge, says to the
famous mimic, "I know not for what Reason, unless
. . . because the Government is concerned in more weigh-
ty Matters, that you have been suffered to go on for so long
with Impunity; for surely the Act of Parliament, which
was made to prevent Theatrical Abuse was made on much
less Occasion than you have afforded" (p. 264). The final
self-serving distinction saves Fielding from outright support for the 1737 version of stage licensing. But when we
recall that the Haymarket Theatre, during the time when
Fielding managed it, was known as "Mr. Fielding's
Scandal-Shop,"[20] his change in sympathies suggested by
his attack on Foote becomes striking. A distinction between Quidam's dance in *The Historical Register* and Foote's
mimicries would be hard to draw, and, in chastizing
Foote, Fielding risked discrediting at least some of his
earlier work.

   Even sharper changes of position appear most clearly in
Fielding's pamphlet *A Dialogue Between a Gentleman of
London . . . and An Honest Alderman of the Country Party* (23
June 1747). An 85-page apology for the Pelhamites, this
piece was published almost six months before he began
work on *The Jacobite's Journal* and anticipates its major
issues and themes. The "Gentleman of London," who
espouses urban, Whig views, tries to persuade the "honest
Alderman" to support the Pelham candidates in the
"early" election. In the opening section of the pamphlet,
the Gentleman repeats arguments that Fielding used in
The True Patriot. One opposition candidate is a Jacobite,
and thus the Gentleman emphasizes how Jacobitism en-
dangers English liberty and property; he rejects the Alder-

man's claim that Jacobitism is no longer a serious threat. But to win the Alderman's vote, the Gentleman must defend the ministry's position on specific issues not raised in *The True Patriot*, and it is in this defense that he appears to contradict positions Fielding took in *The Champion*. Indeed, the Gentleman's comments upon a Place Bill, the ministry's use of pensions, and septennial Parliaments have led one student to argue that the pamphlet signals a "reversal in political perspective" on Fielding's part which makes his "voice" almost unrecognizable.[21] The Gentleman claims, in response to three traditional opposition complaints, that the Place Bill the Alderman champions would result in "either a very sorry Parliament, or a very sorry Administration" (p. 5); that pensions are not necessarily evil, "but a necessary Part of the Royal Bounty" (p. 18); and that triennial elections would be no better than septennial because, "A Man who sells his Vote once in seven Years, will be equally ready to sell it in three" (p. 27). In all of these statements the Gentleman diverges from positions with which Fielding associated himself in *The Champion*, but whether the statements signify a "reversal in political perspective" is debatable.

Several explanations for the Gentleman's remarks are plausible. One is that Fielding, in the hire of the Pelham ministry, simply made the best possible case for them, without worrying about contradictions of his old work. Another is that the Gentleman's speeches reflect a growing political disillusionment on Fielding's part, and a growing willingness to accept Mandeville's premise that corruption and prosperity are reciprocal.[22] The problems with these explanations are quite clear. One attributes to Fielding a mercenary lack of principle which seems alien not only to his generous and moral nature, but also (Namier aside) to the political norms of his day. Fielding was too principled to support a ministry for purely financial reasons, and too experienced in the ways of eighteenth-century newspaper controversy to presume that his adversaries[23] would permit him to reverse his principles or his allegiances. The second explanation, although somewhat more likely, also has flaws. It attributes a pessimism about man and society to Fielding that his praise for the Pelhamites and bright good humor in *Tom Jones* do not reflect; it describes Fielding as disillusioned and broken long before his experiences as a magistrate and his failing health took their toll on his previously irrepressible good nature.

Another explanation for Fielding's changes in position on key issues takes into account his entire political development, and therefore perhaps is more likely: his confidence in Pelham made it possible for him to accept political customs that he had previously found unacceptable. To hold together a majority in the Commons, Pelham used pensions and places as Walpole had done, albeit more discreetly.[24] Fielding could accept and support this moderation. With a sense of how Pelham both conformed to and deviated from Walpole's model, we can begin to see as less extreme the changes Fielding announced in the *Dialogue*.

If we return to the issue of the Place Bill, for example, we find that the Gentleman argues against a "universal Place Bill," rather than against all such bills. He opposes a universal bill because he feels that some intermingling of the executive and legislative branches is necessary if the Commons is to keep its central role in the British government. He urges the Alderman to "ask any Member who hath sat there [in Commons] a single Session, and he must be candid enough to satisfy you, that the Business of the Nation cannot be (as it is) conducted in Parliament, unless those who are principally engaged in conducting it, are Members of that Body" (p. 5). The phrase "principally engaged" makes an important qualification, for, as the Gentleman points out, the ministry had supported "one Place-Bill enacted this very Parliament, by which great Numbers of inferior Place-Men are excluded from being hereafter Members of the House of Commons" (p. 21). Fielding's position in the *Dialogue* on the use of places and pensions thus elaborates, rather than reverses, his position in *The Champion*. Place-seeking must be kept in check, but the check must not be so extreme that it separates the legislative from the executive branch and clears the way for tyranny by the executive, the great evil against which *The Champion* (like all Whig journals) repeatedly warned.

Similarly, the Gentleman's arguments against triennial Parliaments hardly indicate a reversal in Fielding's position, or his surrender before a growing sense of inevitable and universal corruption. Frequent parliaments were common from 1694, the year of the Triennial Act, to 1715, when their vogue ended with the passage of the Septennial Act. Their main advocate in Fielding's day was Bolingbroke, particularly in his *Dissertation*. We might expect that Fielding would be wary of any idea of Bolingbroke's; as early as *Don Quixote in England* (XI: III, iv, p. 53) he had displayed his suspicion that frequent elections would only increase the opportunities for bribery and corruption. His later support for triennial Parliaments was perfunctory (in *The Champion* he left Ralph to talk about their virtues) and took second place to the general goal of ending abuse of the electoral process in toto. Because the gentleman argues cogently for septennial Parliaments as a curb on corruption, his speech thus refines, rather than reverses, Fielding's earlier position on the issue (pp. 24–27).

Brought up on the Tory interpretation of literature, many of us would like to say that Fielding's changes in the *Dialogue* and *The Jacobite's Journal* involve him in bald self-contradiction—that they deviate from his earlier, purer Scriblerian vein. While I deny that such is the case, I do not assume that Fielding's changes are unimportant or unrevealing. The nature of the changes is understood better if we emphasize elaboration rather than reversal of past principles, and if we recall the falsity of Fielding's position in *The Champion*. The greatest change in the *Dialogue*, the *Proper Answer*, and the *Journal* is Fielding's consistent praise for Walpole. This return to the Great Man's camp required one very important sacrifice that will loom ever more important in the final years of Fielding's life: he had to give up the convenient image of Walpole as a foreign sorcerer who bewitched the British people and derived his power from illusion rather than from reality. Fielding abandoned this fiction only at considerable cost to himself, for it had allowed him to isolate all contemporary vices in one figure, and to dissociate them from human nature and British institutions.

As Fielding, in *The Jacobite's Journal* and his other political writings of 1746–48, gives up the fiction of Walpole as harlequin, his political comment becomes less moralistic. He finds himself in a very difficult position: either he can attack the political institutions and customs of Great Britain for the vices that they encouraged, or he can apologize for practices that he once labeled corrupt. Not surprisingly, Fielding tries to take a middle course, in effect admitting that the Pelham ministry unwillingly practices some of the vices he once attacked. In the *Dialogue*, for example, the Gentleman claims that "some Degree of Corruption always hath attended, and always will attend a rich and flourishing Nation" (p. 31), and then protests that "Nothing . . . can appear more unjust than the Charge of Corruption on the present Government; which neither introduced nor can possibly cure it" (p. 32). Fielding here is very far from the righteous indignation of Abraham Adams. He justifies the electioneering of the Pelhamites by arguing that "everybody does it," and does not ask if the pervasiveness of vote-buying and bribery means that the entire system has gone wrong.

In *The Champion* Fielding remained loyal to Whig principles. His loyalty was artificial and easy because he created a satisfying (albeit false) explanation for venal politics: the Great Man was at fault. In his political comment of the late 1740s, Fielding confronted both the virtues and vices of the new political order—the order shaped and dominated by the Whig majority. His admission of widespread political corruption, however, was not a prelude to an adoption of Mandeville's doctrines. For Fielding, the confrontation with corruption did not necessarily mean a change in political ideology or allegiance. Rather, if he then could go on to describe the Pelhamites successfully linking self-love with social good, such a confrontation actually became the first step in delineating their virtues—a step toward confidence and hope.

The confidence that dominates *The Jacobite's Journal* and related writings, that seemingly leads Fielding to contradict his earlier positions, depends upon his belief in the true greatness of Henry Pelham and his associates. We have seen how at least two of Fielding's changes in the 1740s actually refined positions that he took as a member of the opposition to Walpole, but the clearest sign of how little Fielding reversed himself appears in the virtues that he attributes to the Pelham ministry. Those virtues reflect values and interests Fielding had long espoused.

According to Fielding, the first virtue of the Pelhamites was the quickness with which they recognized the Jacobite threat. Quickness of mind, of course, was not a virtue that Whigs alone admired; Swift and Bolingbroke could have admired a sharp, agile mind as easily as Fielding. But the role that Fielding gives to this quickness of mind in relating a leader's self-love to the national good does separate his ideal for leadership from Bolingbroke's. Similarly, Fielding's definition and the model for this quickness give it a particularly Whiggish cast. For example, in *The True Patriot* No. 8 (24 December 1745), he discusses the "Talents" necessary for "high Office," "adapts" Locke's term "Sagacity" as a synonym for "Quickness of Mind," and then uses the example of the Duke of Marlborough to illustrate the meaning of the term. Thus, when Fielding praises Pelham's quick response to the '45, or to crises in public finance, his praise is not as neutral and non-partisan as it might seem. He is locating a Whig virtue in this truly great man.[25]

Other virtues that Fielding ascribes to Pelham and his men reflect traditional Whig values even more directly than "Sagacity." In both the *Dialogue* and the *Journal*[26] he praises Pelham's mastery of public finance. In one instance in the *Dialogue* he lauds Pelham's acumen in a field that Swift and Bolingbroke considered ruinous to the national interest:

In the borrowing of Money, I am sure, that the Minister at the Head of the Treasury hath more to boast of than perhaps any of his Predecessors. That after the Shock of so great a Blow as Public Credit received the year before [1745], and while the Nation was still so deeply engaged in the Midst of such Perils and Dangers he should be able to raise so vast a Sum upon such easy and moderate Terms, is what none would have believed to be possible till convinced by the Fact. [p. 47]

Here again Pelham is seen as the defender of the system of public credit that was established to finance the wars of William and Marlborough. In *The True Patriot* Pelham was shown rescuing the system; here he is portrayed making it work. In both cases Fielding's loyalty is to a recognizably modern economic order based upon deficit spending, public credit, and joint stock companies.

Another great virtue of the Pelham ministry is its "broad-bottom," its inclusion of Whig leaders who had been in the opposition. Since some of these men were Fielding's friends and patrons, Lyttelton and Pitt in particular, the student of Namier might assume that Fielding's praise for the Pelham ministry's inclusiveness simply reveals his self-interest. While this motive undoubtedly played a role, we must not overlook the ideological motive that accompanied it. Walpole always excluded from his cabinets men whose talents and ambitions made them potential threats to his sway.[27] This policy brought him great personal power and made him the autocratic prime minister from whom Fielding prayed for the nation's deliverance in *The Champion*, No. 76 (8 May 1740) (II, 192). It also led to the formation of a coalition of able and powerful opponents who eventually forced his removal. Pelham, learning from Walpole's mistake, found places for a wide variety of prominent Whigs, including Fielding's friends, in his ministry. Fielding's admiration for "an Administration composed really of all the Great Men" (p. 114) thus had an ideological as well as a personal basis. Such inclusiveness showed respect not only for Fielding's friends, but also for the fundamental beliefs and values that bound all Whigs. By founding his ministry upon a "broad-bottom," Pelham showed Fielding that he would not become the kind of corrupt, venal, mercenary prime minister against which *The Champion* warned.

Another virtue of Pelham and his men was their great wealth. In the *Journal*[28] Fielding rings changes upon this comment in the *Dialogue*: "Is not the present Administration composed of a number of Men of the greatest Property in the Kingdom? Who would be so great Losers by an Injury done to the Public; by enslaving or impoverishing the Nation, as those who have the largest Possessions in it?" (p. 28).[29] Locke's basic principle of domesticating self-love through concern for property—the principle Fielding lost sight of in the midst of Walpole's excesses, but upon which he based his appeal in *The True Patriot*—finds its perfect embodiment in the Pelham ministry. Fielding's praise for Pelham's financial wizardry and personal wealth, then, is praise not only for a specifically Lockean but also for a specifically Whiggish virtue. Although George II long felt[30]—and many historians have agreed—that Pelham was only a pale imitation of Walpole, Fielding saw Pelham as a man who possessed many of Walpole's virtues while avoiding many of his vices. He would solidify the position of the Funds, the Bank, and the Hanoverian dynasty in English society without enriching himself or his family. Indeed, probably the strongest testimony to Fielding's claims for the Pelhams is the oft-noted fact that the Duke of Newcastle, Thomas Pelham-Holles, spent the family fortune even as he nurtured Whig hegemony.[31]

Fielding's political certainty in 1746–48 is revealing for the student of British political history because it developed not only after Pelham had rewarded Fielding's friends, but also after Pelham had displayed the great traditional Whig virtues. It depended upon a *combination* of ideology and interest. This new certainty did not reverse the Whig principles that Fielding held to, even when he was in opposition to Walpole; rather, it refined them. Fielding's confidence in Pelham's greatness meant that he could dispense with his old scapegoat. That *The Jacobite's Journal* sounds very different from *The Champion* should not surprise us, for we all change our tune and our tone when we move from doubt to certainty. What should impress us about the differences between *The Champion* and *The Jacobite's Journal* is that true greatness, when Fielding finally realized it, depended upon qualities that modernized standard Lockean virtues. With his family background and latitudinarian religious sympathies, Fielding's eventual alignment with the Whigs was likely, even during the uncertain 1730s. In his political writings of 1746–48 Fielding completed the transition begun in *The Opposition: A Vision* and aligned himself unequivocally with the Whig establishment. His uncertainty ended, and with it his need to work out his political creed. For the rest of his life literary accomplishment, social reform, and service to the Pelhamites would be his goals. In attaining these, however, his newfound political confidence would not always be an asset. It complicated his attitude toward Britain's property-owning upper class and made their vices (once easily attributed to the pernicious influence of one man) problematic for him. In the works of his last years he tried—not always with success—to work out this problem.

VII

The Perils of
Political Certainty

Politics and Morality in Fielding's Last Writings

That Pelham would ride out the political storm created by the surprise election of 1747 and the Treaty of Aix-la-Chapelle became apparent by mid-1748. For the rest of Fielding's life Britain would maintain an uneasy peace with her rivals, and Pelham, who had forged the peace and rescued public credit, would face no serious challenge.[1] By 5 November 1748, when the final number of *The Jacobite's Journal* was published, it had become little more than an ongoing apology for the Treaty. Meanwhile, on 11 June 1748, Fielding had received £600 from Andrew Millar for "the sole Copy Right of a Book called the History of a Foundling" (advance copies of the first two volumes of *Tom Jones* were circulating by October), and on 25 October he had been commissioned as justice of the peace for the City of Westminster—a reward for his services to the ministry.[2] Thus it seems likely that Fielding spent the months before and after he ended *The Jacobite's Journal* preparing his masterpiece for the press and learning the ins and outs of his new job. The final volumes of *Tom Jones* clearly reflect the confidence that led him to feel that the *Journal* was no longer a necessary or important

work. References to the '45 almost disappear after Book
XII, which comes to a climax with the narrator's correction
of Jones's mistaken enthusiasm for the benevolent despotism of the gypsies (XII, xii-xiii).[3] This combination probably was not coincidental; rather, it strongly implies that
Fielding was beginning to lose interest in Jacobitism. The
last issue of the *Journal* declared it to be irrelevant foolish-
ness and gave up the convenient but false notion that it
remained a threat to the British political system. The
narrator's comments in XII, xii, have the effect of a last
word on the subject of absolutism, be it Egyptian or
Stuart. Wiser in the virtues of limited monarchy than his
hero, he points to the great risk of absolute power—that an
evil ruler will exercise it—and reminds us that Satan's rule
in Hell is the prototype for the tyranny to which it often
leads. Having mastered Jones's political lesson for him and
having prevented "our History from being applied to the
Use of the most pernicious Doctrine, which Priestcraft
had ever the Wickedness or Impudence to preach" (XII,
xiii, p. 673), he sets Jones on his way to London with no
further mention of the rebellion that once loomed so
important.

The assurance with which Fielding has the narrator
correct Jones, and the pains he takes to set up this otherwise unnecessary encounter with the Egyptians, indicate
that he could handle political themes with great confidence by the time he wrote the conclusion to *Tom Jones*. An
important change followed from the end of Fielding's
political doubt: once he located true greatness in Pelham
and his men, he could no longer protect Britain's social
and economic elite from responsibility for its vices. The
action of *Tom Jones* anticipates this change. After the nar-

rator corrects Jones, the scene almost immediately shifts to London, and the tone of the novel begins to darken. The fashionable vices cultivated by Lady Bellaston, Lord Fellamar, and others momentarily become the focus of the story.

Insofar as they vindicate his arguments about the dangers of absolutism, these vices do not threaten Fielding: "Nor can the Example of the Gypsies, tho' possibly, they may have long been happy under this Form of Government, be here urged; since we must remember the very material Respect in which they differ from all other People, and to which perhaps this their Happiness is entirely owing, namely, that they have no false Honours among them, and that they look on Shame as the most grievous Punishment in the World" (xii, xii, p. 673).[4] But insofar as these vices flourish under the administration of the "best of Men," they do call into question the fundamental principle of Fielding's political ideology: his correlative beliefs that possession of property will prepare men to participate in a commonwealth, and that the wealthiest of men will best serve the public interest. Although *Tom Jones* testifies to Fielding's faith that "all other People" are not incapable of the Gypsies' simplicity and honesty, the city Tom enters holds few exceptions to the narrator's rule. Jones is fortunate enough to leave it and return to a rural paradise; however, Fielding, whose commitment to success in London was longstanding and who, in his more optimistic moments, saw the city as the truest proof of man's innate sociability,[5] could not. Instead he attempted to reform it.

The hallmark of *Tom Jones* is its superb balance between satire and sentiment. Whether he is counterpointing characters (Jones and Blifil, Sophia and Mrs. Fitzpatrick), analyzing motives (most notably those of Mrs. Honour as she decides whether to accompany Sophia or to inform Squire Western of Sophia's flight: vii, viii, pp. 353–54), or shifting his mode and his diction (the highflown, chaste language of exemplary comedy with which Jones addresses Sophia, versus the earthier vocabulary which satirizes Western's crudity), Fielding recognizes man's frailties as well as his virtues. He gives us a sense of human nature that, in its fullness and tolerance, we think of as Fieldingesque.

Political certainty, as the transition in *Tom Jones* from life on the road to life in the city suggests, threatened that balance. Recall Fielding's use of the commonplace that Britain had the best Constitution, "if well administer'd, that has been made known to the World" (*True Patriot*, xviii, i, ii). When vice flourished in Britain under the greatest of administrators, Fielding had little choice but to close his eyes to it—a luxury hardly possible even in fiction—or to revise his estimate of the British "Constitution"—a word that he used in its physical, ethical, and political senses.[6] Fielding's hesitation before the latter option appears in his social pamphlets, in his portraits of upper-class life in *Amelia* and *The Covent-Garden Journal*, and in his *Journal of a Voyage to Lisbon*. By analyzing the ways in which political concerns affect these works, as well as the political metaphors Fielding chooses to describe events that seem to lack immediate political significance, we can see how his confidence in Pelham contributed, paradoxically enough, to the darkening tone of his last writings.

The social pamphlets illustrate the extent to which Fielding's duties as a magistrate precluded his return to a rural Eden. As he justified his actions in famous criminal cases, investigated the causes of rising crime, and suggested reforms in the British poor laws, he grappled with specifically urban and contemporary problems. One of his favorite refrains, particularly when discussing the crime rate, is that old solutions will not work, that the civil power must rouse itself from its "present lethargic state" (*An Enquiry into the Causes of the Late Increase of Robbers*, p. 17) if it is to curb the power that modern innovations give to the "commonalty." Fielding's zeal for reform, however, should not cause us to mistake him for a mid-century forebear of the Clapham sect. It derived from his desire to protect the status quo. In these pamphlets Fielding described the social order as hierarchical and static; he cited English legal tradition, Christian doctrine, and mercantile economic theory to argue that the lower classes must be "coerced" and "managed" for the good of society.[7] Fielding's social conservatism reflects two persistent themes in his political thought: loyalty to Locke's theory about the role of property in politics, and loyalty to London's social and economic elite—the people who, according to Locke's theory, were most fit to rule. Political certainty made these loyalties more difficult to sustain, as Fielding struggled to avoid admitting that vicious behavior by the upper classes was responsible for urban ills. Sometimes, particularly in the case of Bosavern Penlez, Fielding's rationalizations for the existing order were ethically and intellectually equivocal.

Over two hundred years after his death, Penlez's fate will strike most who read of it as harsh and unfair. On the evenings of 1, 2, and 3 July 1749, large numbers of sailors began to attack and destroy bawdy houses along London's

Strand. On the second evening of rioting, Penlez, who
was working as gentleman's servant and living across from
one of the houses the sailors attacked, joined the mob. He
later claimed he was so drunk that he (perhaps conve-
niently) could not exactly recall his actions. On the
morning of 3 July, however, he was arrested with some
expensive linen goods concealed on his person. Brought
before Justice Fielding, Penlez could not explain how he
had acquired the linen; subsequently the Duke of Bedford
directed that Penlez be prosecuted under the Riot Act.
The information Fielding collected, including the testimony of an unsavory character named Peter Wood, led to
Penlez's conviction. Because of his central role in the case,
Fielding came in for sharp criticism: "Deep parochial
opposition to the hanging of Penlez arose," according to
one historian, "not only because his role in the riot was
incidental, but also because sympathy existed for the
object of the sailors' attack."[8] Citizens offered pleas that
Penlez and others imprisoned with him be pardoned, but,
in Penlez's case, they fell upon deaf ears. He was hanged
on 18 October 1749—a dear price to pay for a night's
drunkenness.

Fielding's treatment of Penlez was only one of his many
actions during the riots. He had returned from a brief
holiday on 3 July to encounter a very dangerous situation.
For no matter how pure their motives, the three thousand
disgruntled sailors and the many others who joined in the
riot posed a threat to life, property, and legal order; the
houses under attack had been designated brothels by ill
fame, not by process of law. He took strong action against
the rioters, calling in military units to reestablish order.
From his own day down to ours,[9] critics have accused him

of overreacting to the situation and of being overzealous in his protection of houses that not only were bawdy but also cheated their customers. In November and December 1749 his handling of the Penlez case and the July riots became an issue in a special Westminster election. The opposition tried to use the "martyrdom" of Penlez against the Pelhamite candidate, Lord Trentham, claiming that Trentham and his brother-in-law, the Duke of Bedford, Fielding's patron and secretary of state for the Southern Department, had prevented Penlez from receiving a pardon. They even went so far as to accuse Fielding of complicity with the bawds.[10]

Necessitated by Trentham's appointment as commissioner of the admiralty (one bit of evidence that the Place Bill Fielding defended did have impact and effect), the special Westminister election of 1749 was one of the most expensive and hard-fought in eighteenth-century British politics. Throughout the long and bitter campaign, Fielding remained loyal to (some might say repaid) the Pelhamites by voting for Trentham, using his authority as a magistrate to shield Trentham's "dirty tricks men" from arrest, and writing a vindication of his and the ministry's conduct during the July riots.[11] Two features of this vindication, *A True State of the Case of Bosavern Penlez*, are particularly salient. First, in defending himself, Fielding also defended the political establishment with which he had become associated and which had rewarded him financially. He had a direct personal interest in the case. Second, Fielding bases his vindication upon the need to protect property (pp. 271, 284). The course of action that Peter Linebaugh labels overzealous, if not cruel, had its source in the political ideology to which Fielding had

committed himself throughout his life—the Lockean
theory that gave private property a central role in the
formation of a political commonwealth.

Fielding builds his argument upon two points: first,
Penlez had been found with stolen property in his possession; second, the rioting sailors, whatever their intentions,
were a potential threat to property of all kinds. In support
of this second point, Fielding asserts that among the
rioters were "thieves under the pretence of reformation"
(p. 286); he refuses to countenance claims that the rioters
were selective in their targets. Fielding's concern for property appears most clearly when he explains the pardon of
John Wilson, a man arrested at the same time as Penlez
and convicted of the same charge. Wilson's pardon, he
argues, was appropriate, for Wilson was not apprehended
with stolen goods in his possession (pp. 287–88). Penlez's
contemporaries complained that, of all those arrested
during the riots, only he was put to death, but Fielding
found Penlez's punishment appropriate precisely because
he alone had stolen property. This concern for property
also leads Fielding to see his actions against the rioters as
proper, rather than overzealous.[12]

Of course, as critics from the eighteenth century until
today[13] have been quick to point out, at least one implicit
self-contradiction, one moral equivocation arises in Fielding's discussion of the riots. Only two days before they
began, Fielding had delivered a charge to the Westminster
grand jury. He spoke at length on the crime of prostitution
and reminded the jury that, "To eradicate this vice out of
society, however it may be the wish of sober and good
men, is, perhaps, an impossible attempt; but to check its
progress, and to suppress the open and more profligate

practice of it, is within the power of the magistrate, and it is his duty" (p. 213). If he could not support the rioters, Fielding should at least have been sympathetic with their aims and tolerant of their excesses. That such was not the case brings us to a basic question: How can the same man who attacked profligacy defend bawdy houses? And that question encapsulates a more general question that all of the social pamphlets raise: How can the novelist whose good nature and tolerance shine through his works (witness his treatment of criminals like Black George Seagrim and debtors like Captain Booth; witness his refusal to damn the slips of minor characters like Betty the Chambermaid and major characters like young Jones) commit himself to strenuous interpretation and enforcement of a criminal code that today seems harsh and unfair?

The answers to these questions lie not so much in Fielding's religious views, although he quoted Holy Scripture and Archbishop Tillotson in support of his opinions on the proper treatment of the poor, and not so much in his economic views, which were commonplace,[14] as in his political ideology and allegiance. We saw as early as *The True Patriot* No. 4 that Fielding could not find a role in British politics for the poor and unpropertied. He saw the lower classes as inherently dangerous because they had no access to property, the medium that he, following Locke, defined as the great curb on violent self-interest. Fielding's political theory conditioned him to fear the mob—to take a dim view of lower-class rioters, whatever claims they might make for their motives.

Fielding's concern for property and the rule of law can help us to understand his actions during the Strand riots, but it in no way resolves the ambiguity inherent in his taking the role of protector of bawdy houses. The ethical difficulties created by his allegiance to Locke and London's property owners become even more apparent when we note who owned the property in question. A bawdy house named the Bunch of Grapes, which the rioters sacked on the night of 2 July, was the property of Lord Stanhope, namesake of an old and great Whig family and distant kin of the Earl of Chesterfield.[15] The greatest property owner in Covent Garden, the man who stood to lose most should the riots spread beyond the Strand, was Fielding's patron, the Duke of Bedford.[16] In quelling the riots and punishing Penlez, Fielding not only was protecting property in the abstract, but also was serving the interest of the great Whig families who dominated London's economic and political life. If this upper class was corrupt, if it (or its distant relations) profited from vices that Fielding had set himself against, how could he continue loyal to it? Again, we return to the basic problem that political certainty created for Fielding and that the Penlez case both illustrated and intensified. In committing himself to faith in Pelham's greatness, Fielding rendered burgeoning vices like gambling, drinking, and "amusements" problematic. He found himself between the twin perils of admitting that the property owners, the London elite, were corrupt (and thus putting his political faith in doubt), or stifling his moral sense. He opened himself to the complaint that "It appeared the magistrate's duty lay less in bringing down bawdy houses than in keeping them standing."[17] All rationalizations about property aside, his loyalty to London's economic and political establishment had led him to seek the execution of a man whose crime was joining a popular outcry against prostitution and economic exploitation.[18]

Fielding dedicated to Henry Pelham his final social pamphlet, *A Proposal for Making Effectual Provision for the Poor* (January 1753). His praise for Pelham, while not extravagant, reveals no disavowal of the opinions he expressed in the mid-1740s;[19] consequently, as in the Penlez case, Fielding encounters difficulty in attempting to justify his actions. Since he cannot attribute widespread crime and vice to a bad minister, he must confront the possibility that the source of these evils may lie in the moral "Constitution" of Britons. He blanches at this confrontation, because ultimately it would require a profound reformation of his views. His loyalty to the property-owning elite of London, after all, followed from his belief that their property should enable them to control and enlighten their self-interest. Attacking this group, Fielding inevitably would attack the political ideology that he inherited and that he espoused in *The True Patriot* and *The Jacobite's Journal*. As he avoided important ethical questions in his discussion of the Penlez case (Should property used for illegal, immoral purposes receive the full protection of the law?), so in the *Proposal* he avoids basic questions about upper-class vice. In this pamphlet, as in *The Champion*, he attacks "Luxury" as the source of drinking, gaming, poverty, and eventually crime. The important change from *The Champion* is that his faith in Pelham prevents him from blaming luxury upon one foreign sorcerer.

Malvin R. Zirker has pointed out that Fielding invariably considers the "hows" of social problems, rather than the "whys." In the *Proposal* his opening question is: How can administrators stop the poor from drinking, gaming, or stealing?, rather than Why do the poor drink, game, or steal? The reason for Fielding's approach manifests itself if we first note that he traces all these miscellaneous vices of London life to one seminal vice, "Luxury." As in *The Champion*, he describes luxury as an unnecessary excrescence that has insinuated itself into an otherwise sound system. If we ask where luxury comes from and why it flourishes, we return to the political dilemma that troubled Fielding's last years.

The desire of the poor to imitate the diversions of their social betters is, Fielding reluctantly admits, the cause of ruinous luxury. He is not eager to criticize the diversions of the elite; instead, he hits upon a formula that Zirker has analyzed astutely in his study of Fielding's other great social tract, *An Enquiry Into the Causes of the Late Increase of Robbers* (1751). Fielding's impulse generally is to describe luxury as "licentious activity unbefitting *one's social rank*" (italics mine) and to insist "that the extravagances of the rich, while morally reprehensible and certainly stupid, do not have the disastrous effects on the well-being of the country that are implicit in the social and moral vagaries of the poor." In several crucial instances (pp. 27–28, 37–38) the disappointing moral of the *Enquiry*—a moral echoed in the *Proposal*—is that gaming, masquerades, and other fashionable vices are punishable only insofar as the individual cannot afford them. As a magistrate Fielding adhered to this double standard, releasing socially prominent masqueraders and jailing poor ones.[20] His policy as a magistrate, as well as his equivocal definition of luxury, reveal him once more trying to isolate London's elite from complicity in contemporary ills.

We can understand (although hardly vindicate) Fielding's double standard if we recall his earlier political writings, particularly *The Champion*. Protection of successful Londoners in his social theory and judicial practice reflected Fielding's loyalty to those "sturdy Scrubs," the traders and financiers, to whom he appealed in *The Champion*. He viewed them as the chosen people at least politically, those whose possession of property qualified them to rise above narrow, violent self-interest. But although both writings protect the propertied elite, Fielding's position in *The Champion* is neither as false nor as lacking in moral rectitude as his position in the social pamphlets. In the earlier work Fielding, however spuriously, denies the direct involvement of Britons in the sins of the Great Vizier, alias Harlequin. In the social pamphlets he accepts these sins as part of British life, turning to an obvious and unfair double standard to avoid criticizing their practice by the upper classes. Beyond the compromise of his ethical integrity, Fielding also limited his previously democratic good nature. In the *Enquiry* he repeatedly warns "the good-natured and tender-hearted Man" (p. 110, 118–20) not to treat criminals too generously. It seems that Fielding the magistrate might well have transported a poor postillion for "robbing a Hen Roost."[21]

Other explanations for the double standard that Fielding proposes in his social pamphlets are possible and perhaps valid. Zirker sees it following from Fielding's (uncomfortable) acceptance of "the public values of that time"[22] and assiduously traces sources and analogues for Fielding's views. (But because innovation characterizes Fielding's literary work, might we not wonder why so little of this quality appears in his social pamphlets?) His basic fear of the unpropertied may well have intensified as his magisterial duties brought him into constant contact with them, and perhaps pushed him toward the double standard. Certainly, as a pragmatic reformer, he did not wish to insult those who would decide whether to implement his reforms. Nevertheless, the role of political considerations in shaping his social writings cannot be underestimated. Fielding's habit of protecting London's upper classes first appeared in his opposition pamphlets; so did his willingness to claim that the "Machine" of government and the "Constitution" of British society are sound. By focusing so narrowly upon the poor and offering a definition for luxury that established a double standard, he was again able to call for social change without questioning the social order. He could scold wealthy Londoners without questioning the economic, social, and political principles on which the city was built.

When the rich fail to set a proper example for the poor yet incur no punishment for their failings, Fielding must find another check on lower-class licentiousness. In the social pamphlets that check becomes the law, properly administered. Fielding tries to extend the model of Pelham by emphasizing that, in their dealings with the poor, administrators of the law, ranging from watchmen to the king,[23] must be intelligent, strong, and dedicated. In his proposal for a workhouse he "emphasizes time and again the need for honest management"[24] and makes good administration the key to solving the problem presented by the indigent poor (*Enquiry*, pp. 55–56; *Proposal*, p. 139). Given the administration-constitution framework in which Fielding worked, and given his reluctance to attack the "Constitution" of one class, the call for strong administration was a logical step for him. So long as Pelham dominated the London scene, Fielding's confidence in the efficacy of good administration was such that he could

view upper-class vice with sometimes surprising tolerance. However, this confidence was not without its
dangers. For while Fielding's calls for strong administration are somewhat limited by appeals to legal precedent,
the social pamphlets (particularly the *Proposal*) eventually
call for administrative control so complete that it verges on
tyranny.[25] In the social pamphlets, then, Fielding's unwillingness to attack the wealthy, in combination with the
threat posed by the unruly poor, forced him to call for ever
more powerful administrators. His proposals begin verge,
however hesitantly, on the absolutism against which he
had fought.

Fielding's toleration of upper-class vice was neither
complacent nor absolute. Indeed, as George Sherburn has
pointed out, readers who generalize about Fielding on the
basis of his novels alone may mistakenly "conclude that his
sympathies lay with the humbler classes and that he disliked the upper circles into which he was born and from
which perhaps poverty chiefly separated him."[26] Zirker,
whose work destroyed the notion of Fielding as a liberal
social reformer, also has noted "the disparity between the
pamphlets and the fiction"; he attributes it to a split between Fielding's "private values" and "the public values of
that time,"[27] implying that Fielding was not truly free to
speak his mind in the social pamphlets. What has not been
observed about Fielding's free expression of a negative
attitude toward the upper circles is that he was capable of
it only when addressing issues outside of a political context. *The Covent-Garden Journal*, on which he worked from
4 January to 25 November 1752, provided such freedom
for Fielding. In it he expresses his moral sense with in-
tensity and wit.

Fielding begins *The Covent-Garden Journal* by claiming,

"First, then I disclaim any Dealing in Politics" (I, 135). In it he takes positions very different from those announced in the *Enquiry* and the *Proposal*. He lashes the rich for their indifference to the suffering of the poor (I, 203–4), for their loss of Christian faith and virtue (I, 296), and for their bad taste. He even goes so far as to praise the lower classes for their "Decency" (I, 297), claiming that "it is, perhaps, the Awe of the Mob alone which prevents People of Condition, as they call themselves, from becoming more egregious Apes than they are already, of all the extravagant Modes and Follies of Europe" (I, 297–98). In this positive reference to the mob we may discern a good bit of equivocation and irony,[28] but this does not change the fact that in the *Journal* Fielding censures a decadent, corrupt elite. When he urges the wealthy to learn "a noble Lesson of Christian Patience and Contentment" (I, 294) from those who endure poverty with good cheer, he is not ironic, and he clearly reveals a radical departure from the tone of his social pamphlets.

While *The Covent-Garden Journal*, with one important exception, lives up to its promise not to deal in politics, the political situation in 1752 affected it in important ways. As personal rivalries split the alliance of the nation's great men, the "broad-bottom" of Pelham's ministry began to shrink. With the death of Prince Frederick in March 1751 (an elegy for whom Fielding "mislaid" and published late: I, 298), the Leicester House opposition, which had challenged Pelham in 1747 and 1749, lost its leader and ceased to threaten the ministry. This gave the Duke of Newcastle an opportunity to work for the removal of his rival and Fielding's patron, the Duke of Bedford[29]—an end which was accomplished with Bedford's resignation as secretary of state in June 1751. Bedford's efforts to form an opposition, which led him to hire the pen of James Ralph and fund a journal entitled *The Protester*,[30] were unsuccessful; however, they did make brave talk about a "perfect Unanimity among all Parties" (I, 235) more wishful than realistic. In No. 16, Fielding gives such comments to a simple, idealistic persona. As Pelham's ministry began to split, as the wealthy began to lose their political halo, Fielding became less tolerant of their moral lapses. In the *Journal* he considered those lapses outside of a political context, returning to the Scriblerian pose of savage indignation that he had dropped in *The True Patriot* and *The Jacobite's Journal*.

This return to Scriblerian models is central to the differences of *The Covent-Garden Journal* from Fielding's political and social writings. Barely a number passes without mention of the satires of Swift, Pope, and Gay: Swift's *Modest Proposal* provides the model for Fielding's comment about mistreatment of the poor in Britain (I, 201–4); Pope's *Peri Bathus* for Fielding's satire, "A Treatise on the Confident and the Pert" (I, 360–61); and Gay's *Beggar's Opera* for Fielding's attack on his enemy, Dr. John Hill (I, 163). Throughout the *Journal* Fielding not only quotes the Scriblerians, he also takes up their battle against dullness and bad taste. Engaging in his own "war" with Grub Street, he returns to his earlier role as Scriblerus Secundus.

The preponderance of Scriblerian allusions is not the only sign of a decline in Fielding's political confidence. His use of the words "greatness" and "goodness" once again becomes ironic and odd,[31] and his definitions for patriotism and politics (I, 157) emphasize venality and place-seeking. As in *The Champion*, his comments upon the times

in which he lives are confusing and equivocal. His assertion that he lives in "one of the most Virtuous Ages, that
hath ever yet appeared in the World" (I, 142) is obviously
ironic.

However, in one instance the *Journal* praises Pelham's
greatness and the blessings it has brought to Britain. This
praise comes in a letter from Axylus, a good-natured man
who blinds himself to evil and unhappiness and seeks to
foster good. Because the virtue of Axylus is so resolutely
fugitive and cloistered, Gerard Edward Jensen dismisses
the persona's comments as not expressing Fielding's true
views. In doing so, he oversimplifies the problem that
Fielding creates. The words of Axylus only paraphrase
and repeat comments in *The True Patriot* and *The Jacobite's
Journal*. He takes pleasure in the political quiet that followed Frederick's death: "I never enjoyed so happy a
Winter as this last, in which there hath been such perfect
Unanimity among all Parties, and the sole Attention of all
our great Men seems to have been the Good of the Public."
He attends "a certain Levee in Arlington Street [Pelham's
home], with more Devotion than any of the Candidates for
Preferment" to give thanks to the principal author of this
"political Happiness" (I, 235). Since Fielding expressed
similar views in previous works, and would offer more
praise for Pelham in his dedication to the *Proposal*, I do not
think he is being ironic here. Rather, the letter from
Axylus reveals the incongruity between Fielding's political views, most particularly his faith in Pelham, and the
sharp social satire that dominates the *Journal*. Given the
descriptions of British life that we encounter throughout
the *Journal*, we find it difficult to take Axylus seriously;
yet, particularly in his panegyric upon Pelham, I think we

must. His words are ironic only insofar as they point to the equivocal thread that runs through Fielding's last writings —his inability to combine political confidence and social criticism.

The praise of Axylus for Pelham is crucial if we are to understand the relation of the *Journal* to Fielding's other writings of the 1750s. The numerous references to the Scriblerians might lead scholars raised on the Tory interpretation to think that Fielding here returned to his true, proper literary role. But the praise for Pelham points to the political allegiance that always set Fielding apart from Swift, Bolingbroke, and Pope. In a journal that did not deal in politics, Fielding could strike a Scriblerian note. He could attack the taste and behavior of the London elite and hold up the patient poor as a model for the rich. When political issues came to the fore, however, as in the letter from Axylus, Fielding's family background, personal interest,[32] and political ideology all led him to espouse the virtues of Pelham and the Whig establishment. Thus we perhaps best view the *Journal* as Fielding's working vacation from politics, an enterprise to which he turned after his frustrating experience with *Amelia*, and in which he briefly escaped his equivocal attitude toward fashionable vice. It committed him to no new political or social theory, however. He gives voice to the standard Scriblerian complaints but does not take up their ideology—a point that appears most clearly when we note one of his more subtle insults to Bolingbroke. In No. 29 (1, 306) he quotes with approval the opening lines of Pope's *Essay on Man*, but he cuts the reference to St. John. Fielding will not compliment, or even mention, the great Tory ideologue, and while he may flirt with Scriblerian pessimism and cynicism, he cannot drop his commitment to the city and its values.

The Covent-Garden Journal, then, is an important but in several ways anomalous production of Fielding's later years. The echo of the Fielding of the 1730s and early 1740s is important, because it reminds us that his moral sense remained acute, that his embracing of the political and economic establishment was not blind. The *Journal*, however, is not anomalous in its treatment of Pelham. Even as he grew dubious about the taste and virtue of London's elite, Fielding remained convinced of Pelham's greatness. While this faith in Pelham stopped Fielding from becoming totally cynical about London life, it also meant that his roles as social censor and political advocate would conflict in often frustrating ways.

We have already traced the effect of this conflict upon the treatment of upper-class vice in the social pamphlets; *Amelia* provides another example of the difficulty Fielding faced, after attaining political certainty, in defining his attitude toward the ruling class. The perils of political certainty for Fielding are clear in *Amelia*, XI, ii, a chapter he entitles "Matters Political." In it Dr. Harrison attempts to win a noble lord's patronage for Booth, but the lord is uninterested in Booth's virtues, and will help him only if Harrison supports his candidate in the upcoming election. (*Amelia* is set in 1733.) Harrison refuses and thus fails in his mission. Before parting, the two men discuss corruption in the British body politic; Harrison's comments are particularly important, because he calls for enlightened and strong administration as the remedy for social ills. He holds up Oliver Cromwell, a leader whose absolutism Fielding earlier had criticized,[33] as a model administrator and argues that ministers can reform society if they reward "men of merit" like Booth. He castigates ministers who use patronage to "baffle an opposition" and thus seems, at least implicitly, to attack Pelham.

In the course of his argument, Harrison also claims that a good administrator "requires no very extraordinary parts, nor any extraordinary degree of virtue." He begs "one simple question" (II, 231) from the lord—a question Fielding avoided in his social pamphlets. The lord asks why, if political virtue is such a simple matter, his contemporaries act so roguishly. Harrison's reply links the politics of *Amelia* with the politics of 1746–48, turning an attack on political corruption into an apology for Pelham:

Perhaps the opinion of the world may sometimes mislead men to think those measures necessary which in reality are not so. Or the truth may be, that a man of good inclinations finds his office filled with such corruption by the iniquity of his predecessors that he may despair of being capable of purging it; and so sits down contented, as Augeus did with the filth of his stables, not because he thought them better, or that such filth was really necessary to a stable, but that he despaired of sufficient force to cleanse them. [II, 231]

The summary image of Fielding's apologetic politics in *Amelia*, as well as in the social pamphlets, is that of a despairing Augeus in a stable whose filth defies cleansing.[34] The image elaborates the justification Fielding made in the *Dialogue* (1747), when he claimed that Pelham should not be held accountable for corrupt practices that he did not initiate and could not stop. Although his care in dating *Amelia* saves Pelham from direct criticism, it certainly calls Walpole's honor into question—a lapse from the praise for the Great Man that Fielding, after the mid-

1740s, consistently offered. The troublesome question raised by the lord leads Fielding once again to seek a convenient scapegoat.

Fielding does not allow Harrison to continue long in this apologetic vein, for to do so would lead to questions about who fouled the stable and an attack not only on Walpole, but also on the interests he served. So, having come to the verge of criticizing widespread corruption in British politics and British society, Harrison retreats. He does not challenge the lord's complacent venality, and he accepts the comparison of the British "Constitution" to a decaying natural body. He is "sorry" when the lord claims that politics and religion bear no relation to each other, but he tailors his argument to fit the lord's distinction. In line with the social pamphlets, Harrison, who will not attack the lord, can only propose the remedy of a powerful and finally (as his praise for Cromwell indicates) absolute minister. The image of a despairing Augeus only hints at Fielding's suspicion that not even strong, Cromwellian medicine can cure the ills of the body politic.

The problems that political certainty created for Fielding appear explicitly in Harrison's surprising toleration of the corrupt lord. They are also implicit in other, more general features of *Amelia*: in its return to unsuccessful use of a double plot, and in its passive, guileless heroine. The two actions of the novel—Booth's spiritual journey to a religious faith that rescues him from his own worst impulses,[35] and his efforts in the city to receive a military command commensurate with his merits—ultimately bear no relation to each other. Booth's spiritual rebirth and subsequent reward have no effect on the London scene; rather, they permit him to imitate Jones's escape to a rural world ruled by a benevolent despot. They speak not at all to the problem of corruption in London and involve no reward for his *military* virtues. Similarly, Amelia's oft-criticized lack of spirit[36] derives from her own inability to question the vices of London life. She has great moral recititude but little moral force; her virtue is lame because Fielding will not permit it to combat the vice it encounters. Fielding's hesitancy to criticize London life is at the heart of both these features of *Amelia*, and again reveals how political considerations account for some of the more puzzling, unsuccessful features of his later work. (Harrison's behavior before the lord, particularly after Booth's case is lost, is preposterous, totally improbable for a man of his character; we cannot explain it without placing it in a political context.) Fielding's hesitancy to criticize venal property-owners also underlies his calls for better administration in *Amelia*—a theme he typically illustrates by multiplying examples of bad administrators: Justice Thrasher, the bailiffs who guard Booth, the venal lord, Booth himself in his first attempt at being a country gentleman.

Fielding's ideas about strong administration as a political and social remedy achieve their final, starkest expression in *The Journal of a Voyage to Lisbon*, a work which must trouble any admirer of his. Not only must we share the physical and mental torment of the dying author, but we also must wonder how much the dark tone of the narrative—the recounting of seemingly endless instances of malicious, cruel behavior—requires modification of generalizations about Fielding's faith in the power of human reason and good nature. Perhaps for this reason critics have been loath to say much about the *Voyage to Lisbon*.

This is unfortunate, for besides being a compelling and brave last literary testament, the *Voyage* is an important work because it provides another example of the close, almost inevitable tie between Fielding's political and literary activities. Against the background of his earlier political writings, we can see that, as he describes his physical condition in essentially political terms, he is doing more than spinning metaphors. Rather, he is grappling one last time with the themes of corruption and administration that dominated his final political, social, and literary writings. Without attempting a conclusive interpretation of the *Voyage*, I shall point out how it summarizes the changeable and the constant elements in Fielding's politics, and how its genre and its form reflect political considerations.

The *Voyage* begins with Fielding describing his service as a magistrate. His tone almost immediately darkens as he recalls an instance when the Duke of Newcastle (Pelham's brother and political partner) summoned him to discuss plans for reducing crime but then did not meet with him; Fielding then recounts his efforts to devise such a plan, asserting that Newcastle's rudeness did not weaken his dedication to the task, and speaks proudly of his success. The tone of his account darkens permanently with the conjunction of two events, the significance of one of which is revealed only by a full understanding of his politics. Describing a bout of illness in early 1754, he notes: "I was at my worst on that memorable day [6 March] when the public lost Mr. Pelham. From that day I began slowly, as it were, to draw my feet out of the grave; till in two months' time I had acquired some little degree of strength, but was again full of water" (196). In this passage, as

Fielding reports an incurable breakdown in his health, so he also reports an irremediable political loss. In the remainder of the *Voyage* he will parallel the effects of these two blows by offering political analogies for his physical and mental state. Never content to be a historian who merely recites details, he will use the political metaphors to give his own suffering greater significance.

Fielding's worsening physical state has a political counterpart, as the reference to Pelham's death implies. In his description of a passenger's lot—a lot he now must share—Fielding points out the relation between physical and political illness that becomes one of the central themes of the *Voyage*. A passenger must make

a perfect resignation both of body and soul to the disposal of another; after which resignation, during a certain time, his subject retains no more power over his own will than an Asiatic slave, or an English wife . . . If I should mention the instance of a stage-coachman, many of my readers would recognize the truth of what I have here observed; all, indeed, that ever have been under the dominion of that tyrant, who in this free country is as absolute as a Turkish bashaw. [p. 207]

With passengerhood established as a metaphor for political slavery (an institution that he still tries to distance from the norms of "this free country"),[37] Fielding connects his physical decay, and most specifically the conditions it imposes upon him, with the fate of his long-held anti-absolutism.

In the *Voyage* changes in Fielding's physical condition occur in a vicious cycle, such that "if my strength had increased a little my water daily increased much more" (p. 198). The only relief from this condition is for Fielding to have his body tapped by a "trochar" and drained of fluid, which reduces him once more to a weakened state. Similarly, to protect himself from the malevolent reactions that his weakness provokes, Fielding must choose the harsh remedy of placing himself in the hands of people whom he describes as tyrants. The pilot who guides Fielding's ship to the Downs is the "worst tempered" of all "the petty bashaws or turbulent tyrants that I ever beheld" (p. 210). While waiting for a good wind off Gravesend, Fielding observes, "Every commander of a vessel here seems to think himself entirely free from all those rules of decency and civility which direct and restrain the conduct of the members of a society on shore; and each claiming absolute dominion in his little wooden world, rules by his own laws and his own discretion" (p. 222). Again Fielding tries to separate this world of "absolute dominion" from the norms of "society on shore"—the British society in which the "rules" of a social contract supposedly "restrain" the self-interest of individuals. Fielding's weakness, however, forces him into "this little wooden world." The captain of the ship in which he sails differs from these "petty tyrants" only in being one of "the best natured fellows alive" (p. 271)—a debased version of the Allworthy-Harrison type of benevolent despot. And Fielding briefly escapes the captain's shipboard tyranny only to encounter Mrs. Francis, the innkeeper who also is "a tyrant," and who has made her husband "an absolute slave" (p. 235). The *Voyage*, then, forms a panorama of the despotism that Fielding rebels against but, with his weakened "Constitution," cannot escape. The fullest meaning of this panorama reveals itself only when we observe the fundamental paradox of Fielding, a Protestant and a Whig, voyaging to Catholic and totalitarian Portugal to save his life. That

Portugal held no elixir for his ills could only provide the grimmest of consolations for him.

Once we understand how Fielding gives his failing "Constitution" a political significance, we also can begin to see the *Voyage* as a political as well as personal testament. The absolutism of "captain bashaw," anticipated in the social pamphlets' call for powerful administration, became necessary because Newcastle disappointed him and Pelham died, leaving Fielding without a practical model for the enlightened self-interest that made limited sovereignty possible and effective. His reference to Pelham's death reveals that he lacked political (and physical) resources, just when he faced human nature at its most anarchic. Physically helpless before the cruel "insults and jests" of the watermen, Fielding turns to a "petty tyrant" for protection. In another central passage, he supports the captain's refusal to let his men go ashore by reasoning, "They acknowledged him to be their master while they remained on shipboard, but did not allow his power to extend to the shores, where they had no sooner set their feet than every man became *sui juris*, and thought himself at full liberty to return when he pleased" (p. 255).

In the relation between the captain and his men, the twin perils of absolutism and anarchy clearly are present. Lacking is the possibility for mediation between them, for the kind of commonwealth that Fielding referred to in *The True Patriot* and *The Jacobite's Journal*. Confronted with "a pure state of anarchy," such as results from the sailors' "vague and uncertain use of a word called liberty" (p. 238), Fielding supports stern, absolute measures he otherwise might view with disdain.[38] One crucial difference between the *Voyage* and his earlier work is largely responsible for its dark tone: here he has no model for the essential political virtue of enlightened self-interest. While the loss of Pelham frees him from his equivocal loyalty to London's elite (he notes bitterly that the "regulation of the mob is below the notice of our great men" [p. 238]), it leads to a political alternation that parallels the changes in his physical condition. It sets him to moving between absolutism and anarchy, two equally extreme deviations from the politics of enlightened self-interest and limited sovereignty. Forced to choose, he opts for absolutism—but his return to bitter and ironic use of the word "great," and his persistence in describing the tyrants he encounters as "petty," reveal the unwillingness with which he does so. His description of boarding the ship becomes one of the most poignant episodes in all his works, not only because the taunts of the watermen humiliate him personally, but also because they mock the brave definitions of patriotism and political greatness that he gave in earlier writings. The "cruelty and inhumanity" of the watermen, which "is an excrescence of an uncontrolled licentiousness mistaken for liberty" (p. 202), reduces the lifelong Whig to seeking protection from a "petty bashaw."

Fielding enters Lisbon only to describe it as "the nastiest city in the world" (p. 285). "New," "strange," and arbitrary laws impede his landing. He is greeted by customs officers who strut imperiously, and by innkeepers who charge exorbitant prices. His dim view of Lisbon has many sources; fear of impending death and a yearning for absent loved ones undoubtedly contributed to his gloom. Nevertheless, the vocabulary with which he describes Lisbon indicates that he responds to it in basically political terms. He does not mention his imminent death or his absent children, and he is moderate in his criticism of Catholicism. Lisbon becomes an earthly analogue for Hell, not because of its priestcraft, but because its laws and officialdom prove it to be governed by pure, capricious political absolutism.

Even at the end of his life Fielding tries˙ to set political abuses apart from British norms, and thus derives some solace from the fact that Lisbon is not London. The irony of his final description of a supper in Lisbon, at which "we were as well charged as if the bill had been made on the Bath Road between Newbury and London" (p. 286), is bitter but potentially instructive. Fielding disdains the mercenary self-interest of the Portuguese and asks his British readers to do the same. He thrusts the analogy to British life upon his audience as a rebuke and offers them the chance to declare venality and greed, absolutism and anarchy, alien to British custom.

The *Voyage to Lisbon* is an important final statement of Fielding's political views, then, because in it his fundamental problems of political certainty find a stark resolution. In his immediately preceding work, Fielding's admiration for Pelham's virtues made him suspicious of the British "Constitution"—physical, political, moral. This suspicion became particularly problematic when Fielding confronted upper-class vice. Lower-class riotousness appalled and frightened him, but he knew how to respond to it; upper-class riotousness ultimately was more difficult, because it challenged a basic tenet of his political faith. Thus, when luxury flourished during the administration of the "best of Men," and Fielding struggled, in face of his awareness of their moral failings, to remain loyal to the urban bourgeoisie, his ethics became uncharacteristically

shoddy. Avoiding outright criticism of those who pros-
pered under the Whig economic system, he turned to
strong administration as the remedy for social ills. He
spent his time and energy in an Augean effort to administer better a system he could not admit to be flawed.[39]

This dependence upon strong administration contributed to the second peril that political certainty created for
Fielding. The licentiousness of the lower classes increasingly led him to promote tyrannical and cruel-seeming
means for controlling them. As failing health left him at
the mercy of all that is anarchic and cruel in human nature,
and as Pelham's death left him without a model for political true greatness, Fielding became an unwilling passenger in a microcosm for the Hobbesian state against
which he had fought during his entire political career. The
Voyage also reveals, however, that the repression inherent
to the maritime code and Portuguese politics remained
foreign to Fielding's Whig heritage and political ideology.
His disdain for the customs of Lisbon testifies to his
continuing, almost congenital dislike for absolutism. This
dislike also reveals itself in his descriptions of the ship in
which he traveled, with its unruly crew and petty tyrant,
as little more than a grim version of Charon's vessel bound
for Hell.

The conjunction of his illness and Pelham's death shook
the confidence that Fielding had developed during the
1740s, bringing him once more to a position that involved
equivocations and self-contradictions. In the *Voyage* he
repeats the standard Addisonian praise for trade as the
strength of the nation (pp. 211, 219) but then encounters a
series of mercenary merchants. His faith in the rule of law,
so important in *The True Patriot*, also suffers. Lisbon's

statutes and regulations, instead of protecting citizens and travelers from the caprice of their governors, embody it. But Fielding's faith, although shaken, is not lost. The genre of the *Voyage to Lisbon* suggests that British society remains capable of returning to political greatness. The *Voyage*, Fielding insists, is a travel book, meant to inform Britons of customs and manners different from their own (pp. 183–84). Thus, while the signs of loss of political confidence are obvious—the return to uncertain use of the word "great," the panorama of tyranny—they do not reveal Fielding returning to his political uncertainty of the 1730s. As he voyaged to Lisbon, he once more was preparing to attack Bolingbroke's "pernicious doctrines"—to equate, in one instance, the Viscount's misguided philosophy with his misguided politics.[40] This final attack on Bolingbroke, his description of Lisbon as the anti-type of all that is just and good, and his disdain for the petty tyrants upon whom he must depend, express political ideals that were his touchstones throughout his political career.

Given time and health, Fielding might have resurrected his political faith and found a new leader to embody it—perhaps his old schoolmate William Pitt. Such speculation merely joins the student of Fielding's political writings with the student of his novels in the wish that their subject's life might not have been cut short. As the student of the novels must solace himself with the fact that Fielding did live to envision and produce one masterwork, so the student of the political writings must assert that, whatever doubts assailed Fielding during his last voyage, he did, in the mid-1740s, give clear expression to his political faith. While in the *Voyage to Lisbon* he lacked time, strength, and opportunity to realize again his political ideal, only in light of his definition of a politics of enlightened self-interest in the 1740s did Lisbon become for him such a dark and shadowy port. His treatment of Lisbon, and his final praise for Walpole as "one of the best of men and of ministers" (p. 247), reflect his enduring loyalty to the Whig tradition of Marlborough and Godolphin, Addison and Steele, and his father. His loyalty to the Whig principles rarely wavered, even in his late writings. Only his estimation of the ability of frail men to live by those principles was subject to substantial, yet grudging, revaluation.

Conclusion

If we are to discuss the art of an author or the form which he
impresses on his material, it seems a necessary preliminary in
the case of an intellectual novelist to see how far his opinions
shape his work, both as a whole and as seen in individual
episodes. It would be a mistake to take Fielding very seriously as
a systematic thinker; but only the casual reader can fail to see
that his thinking does shape his stories.   —George Sherburn

This study has attempted to do two things at once. On one
hand I have used the particular case of Henry Fielding to
test generalizations about the nature and structure of mid-
eighteenth-century British politics. On the other, I have
used my study of the political norms that held during
Fielding's lifetime to explain important and problematic
features of his art. My hope is that, by combining these
two issues, I have been able to discover new truths that
would go unremarked if each were considered separately.

Fielding's particular case does shed considerable light
on "the historiographical quarrel between the Namierians
and anti-Namierians." These two groups have been ham-
mering each other for years, and I suspect their quarrel has
gone on for so long because the period offers both of them
such abundant evidence. Certainly personal interest had
an important role in Fielding's political career. The likeli-

hood that he accepted payments from Walpole to acquiesce in the Licensing Act and to withhold publication of
Jonathan Wild, his eager support of the Pelham ministry
after it gave places to his friends and to himself, and his
work for Bedford during the Westminster election of 1749
all reveal how his political interest ran parallel to his
financial. But if we can show that Fielding profited by
supporting Bedford and Pelham, we should also note that,
when Bedford left the ministry in 1751, Fielding's loyalty
to Pelham did not waver. Even though he had a continuous and growing debt to Bedford, a debt he could not
pay,[1] Fielding still sided with the man in whom he had
found true greatness. James Ralph, not he, edited Bedford's opposition newspaper.

Fielding's relations with Pelham and Bedford during
the 1750s provide additional evidence that ideology was an
important factor in his politics. His persistent focusing on
the relation between property and interest reveals his
assimilation of the ideas of John Locke; his persistent
loyalty to Marlborough, and to the financial order that
grew out of Marlborough's war, reveals his loyalty to the
political principles that had separated Whigs from Tories
at the opening of the century. If a Namierian were to point
to Fielding's extensive discussions of property as a sign
that personal interest was the dominant force in the politics of mid-eighteenth-century England, the anti-Namierian could rejoin that Fielding's definition of property
clearly aligned him with a movement based on principles
greater than mere family ties. If the anti-Namierian were
to point to Fielding's debt to Locke as a clear sign that
ideology was the dominant force in the politics of mid-
eighteenth-century England, the Namierian could retort

that Locke's ideas exerted well-nigh universal sway (even Tories like Swift were influenced by them), and that allusions to them do not necessarily distinguish one individual's politics from another's.

Both Namierians and anti-Namierians seem to miss an important point: Locke's theory became so powerful and attractive because it combined the two opposites they so resolutely have separated. Responding to Hobbes, Locke admitted that self-love inevitably plays a role in any society. But, as he attempted to offer an alternative to Hobbes's repressive, absolute sovereign, Locke tried to establish the conditions under which self-interest might be enlightened rather than violent, under which men could choose to form commonwealths rather than be forced to submit to one absolute ruler. Locke hit upon property as the medium for enlightening self-interest. His canny observation that men, in order to protect their own property, will recognize and respect the property of others is at the heart of his theory of commonwealth. While this theory of property ultimately and obviously involved personal interest, it also led to important ideas about the nature of the state: that the sovereign should be limited in his power; that he should serve only with the consent of those whom he governed; that the law should be more powerful than he, and should protect the citizen. Of course, today it is easy to say that, instead of taming the rude beast described by Hobbes, Locke merely camouflaged it—that his ideas emphasize self-interest as much as those of Hobbes, that his differences derive more from style than from substance. While these charges may be true in the abstract, in the real world of mid-eighteenth-century politics the predominance of Locke's ideas led to a much different political structure than that visualized by Hobbes. The notions of limited sovereignty, popular will, and rule by law took on a life of their own as the century progressed. Though they served the interests of a group that wanted to protect its property, they became principles that even poor men (like Fielding) could claim to hold apart from their personal interests. By basing his political theory on property, then, Locke originated the thorny interaction between ideology and interest that we have seen in Fielding's politics. Indeed, we can guess that Locke's work went unrivaled because it freed men from the dark spectre of absolutism but still allowed them to pursue their interests. With his ambiguous use of the word "property," Locke tied ideology and interest into a Gordian knot that eighteenth-century Englishmen found appealing, but that twentieth-century philosophers and historians have severed.

Fielding's politics, with their focus on property and interest, also say much about recent and important work by E. P. Thompson and his students. Following Namier, Thompson sees English life during this period as dominated by a clash of interests, although he describes them as class (rather than family) interests. Dismissing the politics of the period as dominated by and serving one homogeneous ruling class, Thompson and his circle have concentrated upon social (as opposed to political) history and have detailed the ways in which the law became a means of social oppression. In tracing the lower-class response to this oppression—widespread, sometimes violent disobedience—Thompson portrays English society as volatile rather than stable, as not unlike the society of prerevolutionary France. He does not explain why, given the conditions he describes, England was spared a reign of terror.

Fielding's particular case points to both strengths and weaknesses in Thompson's analysis. A lawyer who was suspicious of lawyers, a man who enforced the law rigorously even as he repeatedly portrayed unjust laws and unfair punishments, Fielding combines the two attitudes that Thompson describes: oppression and rebellion. His suspicions about the law and its administration are most important, for they reveal a member of the ruling class willing to question an institution that, according to Thompson, was sacrosanct for Englishmen of this era. At this point the question raised in the previous chapter becomes crucial: If Fielding was suspicious of the law, if he was aware that it sometimes protected unfair, corrupt practices, why did he use it to coerce the poor? The answer, of course, is that Fielding used the law to protect property. At the root of his social conservatism was not a powerful, almost irrational commitment to the law, as Thompson would have it, but a powerful, almost irrational commitment to property. Of course, Thompson's analysis remains astute and accurate insofar as loyalty to property and to the law were congruent for men like Fielding. But we must recognize that the concern for property came first, for only then can we explain how and why Fielding remained a social conservative even as he remained suspicious of lawyers and magistrates.

By observing the central role of property in Fielding's political and social writings, we also may begin to answer the question that looms so unsatisfyingly over recent work by Thompson and his circle: Why, given the massive resistance to certain laws, did England avoid a revolution? Obviously a complete answer to this question is not pos-

sible, but the example of Fielding suggests some possi-
bilities. France and England both had legal codes that
served as means of social oppression, and both had large
groups of people who rebelled against those codes. But
England, unlike France, had a popular theory of the role of
property in politics that both curbed absolutism and vindicated harsh treatment of the unpropertied. The French
monarchy was both absolute and weak—weak precisely
because it could not offer (and did not care to offer) a
plausible rationalization for the absolute power it claimed
for itself. The English monarchy, to the contrary, was
limited but strong; the very theory that limited its power
also justified its role in a legal and social system that
Thompson and others have shown to be oppressive and
cruel. As Thompson and his followers document, much of
the systematic lawbreaking in eighteenth-century England was done by people who were asserting rights and
privileges. English monarchs, who by Locke's theory
were at the center of a commonwealth devoted to protecting property, could mobilize support from lower-,
middle-, and upper-class property-holders; Louis XVI
could not. Englishmen who were suspicious of the law
could remain loyal to the sovereign because their commitment to a theory of property was more fundamental
than their commitment to a theory of law. This theory of
property was particularly central to the survival of the
English status quo because, once the Whig definition of
property triumphed, all manner of new men came directly
into the political process. French financiers and merchants
watched Louis fall; in contrast, their English counterparts
had taken a central role in English politics even by Fielding's day, and they actively supported George III in the

crises of the 1790s. The fact that some of these men sprang from humble origins gave the English system powerful claims to fairness and democracy that the French lacked.

Fielding's political career thus points to a social *telos* rather different from that which Thompson has studied in such detail. Despite his suspicions about the English legal system, Fielding was unequivocal and unsparing in his defense of property. If that defense led him to actions that today seem oppressive, it also led him to support a version of the state that is, by the standards of Hobbes, liberal, and to enfranchise large groups of people who at one time would have been excluded from politics. Thus Fielding's political career not only manifests the interaction between ideology and interest in eighteenth-century British politics; it also manifests a change in the role of Locke's political theory. When first introduced, that theory was liberal—a challenge to traditional ideas about royal power and royal prerogative. By Fielding's day it had become an instrument of social conservatism, not to say oppression. In charting changing attitudes toward the law, Thompson gives great insight into social discontent in eighteenth-century England. But by charting the changing function of Locke's theory of property and interest, Fielding's political writings help to explain, as Thompson's work cannot, why that strife-ridden society avoided revolution.

If Fielding's writings can tell us much about the politics of mid-eighteenth-century England, the study of his politics can tell us much about his art. By scrutinizing his political career in its entirety, students of Fielding derive one great benefit: they see that he was by nature and heritage a Whig, and that his satires on Robert Walpole were essentially a deviation from his otherwise consistent loyalty to the Whig establishment. This finding can free Fielding studies from the confusion created by attempts to make him a good Tory. Fielding's politics inevitably separated him from Bolingbroke and his circle; despite his espousal of aristocratic values in matters of taste and style, he never joined the Scriblerians in their contempt for the city and its ways. Seeking literary success in 1730–31, he took the pseudonym Scriblerus Secundus. But his flirtation with the role of a second-generation Tory wit was brief; the Scriblerians apparently did not respond to his overtures, and he soon returned to Drury Lane and equivocal but nonetheless Whig political allegiances.

Recognition of Fielding's fundamental and persistent Whig loyalties can spare scholars the need to explain away his pro-Walpole pieces—to assert that poems like his *Epistles to Walpole* and pamphlets like *The Opposition: A Vision* do not say what they seem to say. Scholars have misread these pieces because they have not wished to see Fielding moving from the Tory camp to the Whig—a misreading that recognition of Fielding's Whiggism makes unnecessary. By labelling Fielding a Whig, we do not spare him from charges of opportunism, but we may spare him from charges of tergiversation. With Namier's demystification of party labels clearly in mind, we can see that Fielding's shifts between Whig factions did not compromise his most important principles; with the nature of Fielding's earliest political allegiance clearly in mind, we can see that his support for Henry Pelham did not compromise his political heritage. Necessarily a quester after the political main chance, Fielding sometimes let money buy his pen—but never the money of men whose ideology differed from his.

Besides permitting a clearer look at some of Fielding's minor poems and pamphlets, recognition of his Whiggism also encourages fuller understanding of his literary accomplishment. In the third chapter we saw how the Tory interpretation has sharply narrowed our focus on Fielding's plays; we study only the imitations of Gay, the farces and ballad operas, and neglect the imitations of Steele and Cibber, the conventional Drury Lane comedies. This narrow focus also characterizes studies of Fielding's masterpieces. His borrowings from Swift, Pope, and Gay are noted with great sensitivity and care, but his allusions to Addison and Steele, if noted, are dismissed as surprising; his debts to Cibber go completely unremarked. If we are to perceive the true nature of Fielding's literary accomplishment, we must begin to appreciate that his borrowings from Addison and Steele are as extensive as his borrowings from Swift and Pope,[2] that he could see virtues in the work of Cibber to which we presently are blind.[3] Fielding's genius in *Joseph Andrews* and *Tom Jones* lies in his ability to combine satire and sentiment—to give us a sense of good nature that is knowing rather than naive, sage rather than simple. This combination, which he struggled so fitfully to attain in his plays and in *Jonathan Wild*, reflects his integration of the two great literary traditions of the preceding generation: the Scriblerian tradition of Swift and Pope, and the sentimental tradition of Addison and Steele. Because the Tory interpretation has reduced the role of Addison and Steele in eighteenth-century literature, it also has reduced our ability to appreciate the marvelous balancing act that Fielding performs in his fiction. Yet our understanding of *Joseph Andrews* and *Tom Jones* can be full and rich only when we recognize them for what they are: carefully nurtured literary hybrids. While we have several admirable studies of these works as generic hybrids—as comic romances, or modernizations of classical forms[4]—the Tory interpretation has left our study of Fielding's models largely incomplete. Insofar as the study of Fielding's political writings points to his great debts to Addison and Steele, to his fundamental Whiggism, it can open our eyes to the literary counterpart of this political debt. It can refocus our attention upon Fielding's borrowings from the sentimental tradition and correct our presently unbalanced perspective on his relations with his most immediate literary forebears. We never must forget that Fielding opened his theatrical career by professing his regard for both Gay and Cibber. In one sense his career takes its unique shape from his efforts, at first unsuccessful but later triumphant, to join the very different literary modes those two playwrights represented.

The extent to which the Tory interpretation has narrowed our focus on Fielding perhaps appears most clearly when we compare the range of opinions held by students of his politics with the range held by students of his art. Those who have commented upon Fielding's political writings have offered a dizzying but ultimately suggestive array of opinions. One student, overlooking Fielding's disdain for Bolingbroke and commitment to the City and its ways, has argued that he joined Bolingbroke and his circle in their nostalgic, conservative politics. Caroline Robbins, on the other hand, places Fielding within the tradition of English liberal thought, characterizing him as a reformer.[5] Careful study of Fielding's political writings reveals how both of these views point to important truths, even as they err. Fielding's Whiggism, his loyalty to the principles of Locke, to urban financial interests, and to Henry Pelham clearly set him apart from Bolingbroke. His concern for property and loyalty to London's upper circle made him a reformer, but one whose conservative goals included harsh, oppressive treatment of the poor. His political career is understood most exactly, most truthfully, as one instance of the transformation of Whiggism from a revolutionary political philosophy that challenged royal authority to a conservative political philosophy that protected the values and interests of a property-owning elite.

Despite the reputation of literary critics for contentiousness, commentators upon Fielding's literary writings actually have offered more homogeneous opinions than their stimulating, if misguided political counterparts. In general they have picked up Fielding's allusion to himself as Scriblerus Secundus and carried it much further than he himself ever did. Whatever his other limitations, Austin Dobson[6] was capable of perceiving Fielding's admiration for Addison and Steele; most recent commentators are not, reading only a select group of Fielding's plays and certain parts of his fiction. They dismiss the love scenes between Tom and Sophia in *Tom Jones* as reflecting Fielding's inability to express true or deep emotion, failing to note how those scenes look back to the traditions of sentimental drama. They explain at great length Fielding's relations to the Scriblerian mock heroic, but find less congenial (and describe in less positive terms) the exemplary figure of Allworthy. They understand a part of Fielding very well, but are blind to the whole. Brought up on the Tory interpretation, they misread him.

Is this misreading to be criticized? That is a question I only can raise, not answer. If, as Harold Bloom argues, all poems are misreadings of earlier poems, then does not literary criticism become an art form as it too misreads or deconstructs texts, as it breaks free of the meanings to which the text would constrain it? Should we not rejoice in the misprision to which the Tory interpretation has led? I think not. Because I fear the study of literature becomes little more than an act of immense and ultimately harmful vanity if it does not offer students the opportunity to seek truth. While Fielding's political writings have no intrinsic worth for us, to establish their context and meaning requires that we temporarily drop our own assumptions and values and try instead to re-create those of a different age. Inevitably, our re-creation will be imperfect, but to give up on the process for this reason is to deprive ourselves of the past as a resource, of history as a means of instruction. Even if we reject the ideas that Fielding brought to his political, social, and literary writings, we must try to understand them and to scrutinize our ideas in light of that understanding. Otherwise we learn nothing about Fielding, and nothing about ourselves.

I can offer no better defense for my return to an old-fashioned type of literary history than Herbert Butter-field's brilliant essay on the Whig interpretation of history and the misreading to which it led. Butterfield could point out both the colossal vanity and, ultimately, the wasteful-ness of contemporary literary criticism's frenetic quest after misprision. For, as we misread literary works, we refuse to understand them in their own terms. Instead, we understand them in our own terms: they become mere reflections of our own prejudices, neuroses, and values. If a work does not fit our needs, we throw it away. (We do not read Fielding's conventional plays; we skirt the sentimental portions of *Tom Jones*.) In doing this, we engage in a kind of poetic misprision, but we lose the past as a source of knowledge. Butterfield fought the misunderstanding that the Whig interpretation caused, not because he wanted to defend men long dead, or to take a side in controversies long past. He exploded the Whig interpretation because he saw it reflecting a vanity, a prejudice, that distorted the understanding of historians and blinded them to certain truths. The truths were not as important as the act of understanding, the escape from deleterious vanity.

Similarly, by trying to reconstruct rather than deconstruct Fielding's political writings, I have tried to combat the Tory interpretation of literature. I have fought this battle not because I think Colley Cibber was a literary great, or because I care deeply about long-forgotten sentimental comedies, but because I fear the vanity that underlies the Tory interpretation. Our unwillingness to reconstruct Fielding's politics, and our subsequent inability to see all facets of his literary work, mean that Fielding's work is a wasted resource for us. We learn from it nothing we do not already know, because we are too proud to approach it on its own terms.

This is not to say that "old" literary history is the only way to talk about texts. Like Johnson's lexicographer, the critic who commits himself to historical reconstruction risks all sorts of futile drudgery. His reproduction never can be perfect; his subject matter often will seem petty and arcane. Misprision obviously is more fun, and, in the hands of a great critic like Harold Bloom, often provides insights whose strength and power I certainly cannot equal. But I think that the dangers of misprision finally outweigh its advantages. The misreader verges always upon solipsism, whereas the drudge attempts to suspend his own values and assumptions in order to learn about those of others. The misreader's only resource is his own mind, which must be infinitely inventive. The drudge's great resource is the past, and the minds of the men and women who made it. This book reflects my sense that an imperfect dialogue with Henry Fielding is preferable to a perfect echo of ourselves—an echo that the Tory interpretation constructs.

Notes

Preface

1. Bertrand A. Goldgar, *Walpole and the Wits* (Lincoln: University of Nebraska Press, 1976), p. 5.

Chapter I
The Political Background

1. Wilbur L. Cross, *The History of Henry Fielding* (1918; rpt. New York: Russell and Russell, 1963), I, 55–57, and B. M. Jones, *Henry Fielding: Novelist and Magistrate* (London: George Allen and Unwin, 1933), pp. 25–26, discuss the circumstances of Fielding's coming to London in 1727.

2. J. H. Plumb, *Sir Robert Walpole: The King's Minister* (Boston: Houghton Mifflin Company, 1961), pp. 176–85.

3. H. T. Dickinson, *Bolingbroke* (London: Constable, 1970), p. 177.

4. For a history of the Whig interpretation, see Herbert Butterfield, *George III and the Historians*, 2d rev. ed. (1957; rpt. New York: Macmillan, 1959), pp. 151–82.

5. Herbert Butterfield, *The Whig Interpretation of History* (1931; rpt. New York: W. W. Norton, 1965), pp. 11, 16.

6. In his *George III and the Historians*, however, Butterfield sharply criticizes the Namierians for giving too little attention to

"those higher political considerations" that motivated Englishman during the eighteenth century (p. 203). He argues that their
focus upon personal interest is too narrow, just as the Whig
historians' focus upon ideology was too narrow, and calls for a
history of the period that recognizes both interest and ideology
as important political forces.

7. Lewis Namier, *Crossroads of Power* (London: H. Hamilton, 1962), p. 230.

8. Robert Walcott, Jr., *English Politics in the Early Eighteenth
Century* (Cambridge, Mass.: Harvard University Press, 1956).

9. See Robert J. Allen, *The Clubs of Augustan London* (1933;
rpt. Hamden, Conn.: Archon, 1967), pp. 35–43, 232, 246,
Geoffrey Holmes, *British Politics in the Age of Anne* (New York:
St. Martin's Press, 1967), pp. 22–23, Bertrand A. Goldgar, *The
Curse of Party: Swift's Relations with Addison and Steele* (Lincoln:
University of Nebraska Press, 1961), pp. 77–135, and Dickinson, *Bolingbroke*, pp. 18–20. Holmes, *British Politics*, pp. 1–9,
summarizes the roles of both Namier and Walcott in studies of
eighteenth-century politics.

10. Dickinson, *Bolingbroke*, pp. 191, 197, 182, 269–70. See
also John B. Owen, *The Rise of the Pelhams* (London: Methuen,
1957), pp. 3–4.

11. As Plumb does in his chapter entitled "Victory, 1724–6,"
in his *Walpole*, pp. 110–12.

12. See particularly E. P. Thompson's chapter entitled
"Offenders and Antagonists" in his *Whigs and Hunters: The
Origins of the Black Act* (New York: Pantheon, 1975), pp. 81–115.
Thompson shows that the Waltham Blacks tended to be
members of "a declining gentry and yeoman class confronted by
incomers with greater command of money and of influence" (p.
108). For the work of Thompson's associates, see Douglas Hay
et al., *Albion's Fatal Tree: Crime and Society in Eighteenth-Century
England* (New York: Pantheon, 1975).

13. Dickinson, *Bolingbroke*, pp. 187–89, 274, describes "the
plight of the lesser gentry and even of the middling gentry"
during the 1730s and 40s, and how Bolingbroke spoke to the
fears of this class. He points out that this plight was not universal—many of the gentry families survived to prosper later in

the century. This point is important, for it reveals why Boling-broke's political program finally failed. As the century pro-gressed, his division of English society into a landed interest and a moneyed interest became irrelevant. The two tended to merge, whereas Bolingbroke could profit only if they remained distinct.

14. Isaac Kramnick, *Bolingbroke and His Circle: The Politics of Nostalgia in the Age of Walpole* (Cambridge, Mass.: Harvard University Press, 1968), pp. 4–5.

15. See Archibald S. Foord, *His Majesty's Opposition 1714–1830* (Oxford: Clarendon Press, 1964), pp. 20–21, for an example of the common practice of citing a work by Namier—in this case, *England in the Age of the American Revolution*—and then applying it, without comment or qualification, to a period fifty years earlier.

16. See Holmes, *British Politics*, pp. 52–54, for discussion of the motive behind Bolingbroke's claim, and analysis of its falsity.

17. Dumas Malone, *Jefferson and the Rights of Man* (Boston: Little, Brown, 1951), pp. 291–92, 436.

18. Bolingbroke's sense of the relation between a state of war and economic divisions within English society perhaps appears most clearly in a letter he wrote to Lord Orrery in July 1709:

We have now been twenty years engaged in the two most expensive wars that Europe ever saw. The whole burthen of this charge has lain upon the landed interest during the whole time. The men of estates have generally speaking, neither served in the fleets nor the armies, nor meddled in the public funds and management of the Treasury.

A new interest has been created out of their fortunes, and a sort of property which was not known twenty years ago, is now increased to be almost equal to the terra firma of our island. The consequence of all this is that the landed men are become poor and dispirited. They either abandon all thoughts of the public, turn arrant farmers, and improve the estates they have left: or else seek to repair their shattered fortunes by listing at court, or under the heads of partys. In the meanwhile those men are become their masters, who formerly would with joy have been their servants" (quoted in Dickinson, *Bolingbroke*, p. 69).

19. Vern D. Bailey, "Fielding's Politics" (Ph.D. dissertation, University of California, Berkeley, 1970), refers often to Kramnick and describes Fielding as a follower of Bolingbroke. He overlooks Fielding's attacks on Bolingbroke, as well as his basic loyalty to Whig principles and politicians.

20. Isobel M. Grundy, "New Verse by Henry Fielding," *PMLA* 87 (1972): 213–45. Grundy dates the composition of the unfinished burlesque epic by Fielding that she discovered in the Montagu papers at 1729 (p. 214).

21. J. W. Gough, *John Locke's Political Philosophy*, 2d ed. (Oxford: Clarendon Press, 1973), speaks for the traditional view; C. B. Macpherson, *The Political Theory of Possessive Individualism* (Oxford: Clarendon Press, 1962), treats Locke as a Hobbesian; John Dunn, *The Political Thought of John Locke* (Cambridge: Cambridge University Press, 1969), elaborates Locke's religious motives; Geraint Parry, *John Locke* (London: George Allen and Unwin, 1978), summarizes the recent work on Locke and speaks to the question of inconsistency.

22. John Locke, *Several Papers Relating to Money, Interest and Trade, etc.* (1696; rpt. New York: Augustus M. Kelley, 1968), pp. 12–14, 56–58, 85–88, 116.

23. See Parry, *Locke*, p. 49.

24. Fielding's library included the volume *Locke on Government* (1698). See Ethel Margaret Thornbury, *Henry Fielding's Theory of the Comic Prose Epic* (Madison: University of Wisconsin Press, 1931), p. 176. See also Fielding's references to Locke in *The True Patriot* Nos. 8 and 12 and in *The Covent-Garden Journal* No. 1.

25. Sections of *Patriarcha* were published as early as 1648, 1652, and 1653. See Peter Laslett's introduction to John Locke, *Locke's Two Treatises of Government* (New York: Mentor, 1963), p. 71.

26. Thomas Hobbes, *Leviathan*, ed. Michael Oakeshott (New York: Collier, 1962), p. 186.

27. Goldgar, *Walpole*, pp. 98, 115, summarizes this discussion.

28. This tendency is so pervasive that to select just one example of it is difficult. But we might note William Kupersmith's review essay, "Studies in Augustan Literature," *Philological Quarterly* 55 (1976): 533–52, in which he discusses only works dealing with Swift, Pope, and Mandeville.

29. See Leslie Stephen's *Alexander Pope* (1880; rpt. London: Macmillan, 1900), p. 25, and his *English Literature and Society in the Eighteenth Century* (New York: G. P. Putnam's, 1904), pp. 71–86, for discussions in which he emphasizes the roles of Steele and Addison, as well as those of Swift and Pope, in the literary life of Anne's reign. For a typical example of Cibber's adopting a pose in which he expresses great admiration for Pope and accepts with tolerance Pope's criticism, see his *Apology*, ed. B. R. S. Fone (Ann Arbor: University of Michigan Press, 1968), p. 16. I would not suggest that Cibber was a great playwright, but anyone who studies the history of the London stage during Fielding's lifetime immediately confronts his omnipresence. His plays were the most popular, most successful of his age; even rival theatres produced them with great frequency.

30. Owen, *Rise*, p. 42.

31. Donald J. Greene, *The Politics of Samuel Johnson* (New Haven: Yale University Press, 1960), p. 20.

32. Basil Williams, *The Whig Supremacy* (Oxford: Oxford University Press, 1939), pp. 4, 3. For a differing view of Locke's popularity see Dunn, *Political Thought*, p. 8.

33. B. Williams, *Whig Supremacy*, pp. 101–2.

34. This passage also is quoted in Martin C. Battestin, "Fielding's Changing Politics in *Joseph Andrews*," *Philological Quarterly* 39 (1960): 55, and in Goldgar, *Walpole*, p. 208.

35. Grundy, "New Verse," p. 215.

36. Owen, *Rise*, p. 34.

37. W. B. Coley, "Henry Fielding and the Two Walpoles," *Philological Quarterly* 46 (1966): 162–78. Hugh Amory, "Henry Fielding's *Epistles to Walpole*: A Reconsideration," *Philological Quarterly* 46 (1967): 236–47.

38. Plumb, *Walpole*, pp. 179–82.

Chapter II
Family Background

1. See [J. H. Leslie], "An English Army List of 1740," *Notes and Queries* 3 (14 April 1917): 267, and Cross, *History*, I, 5–7, 11.

2. Fielding's mother, Sarah, died in 1718, and her children were reared by her mother, Sarah Davidge Gould. Fielding's maternal grandfather, Sir Henry Gould, who died in 1710, was a famous and successful lawyer, rising to the title of Judge of the King's Bench. When Fielding came to London in 1727, he separated himself from his aged grandmother and committed himself to his father's world. See Cross, *History*, I, 15–16, and Jones, *Fielding*, pp. 19–26.

3. My source is an original edition of the pamphlet in the Yale University Library: *A Plan of the Universal Register Office* (London, 1753), p. 6. For the publication history of this piece, which has never been reprinted, see Cross, *History*, III, 321.

4. Bailey, "Fielding's Politics," p. 11.

5. "An English Army List of 1740," p. 267.

6. Dickinson, *Bolingbroke*, pp. 18–20.

7. Holmes, *British Politics*, pp. 148–58, describes the conflict between old landed economic interests and new moneyed economic interests to which the war led.

8. See George Edward Cokayne, *The Complete Peerage of England, Scotland, Ireland, Great Britain, and the United Kingdom*, ed. Vicary Gibbs and H. A. Doubleday (1921; rpt. London: St. Catherine's Press, 1926), IV, 181; Holmes, *British Politics*, pp. 231, 330; and Mrs. S. C. Lomas's introduction to Historical Manuscripts Commission, *Report on the Manuscripts of the Earl of Denbigh at Newnham Paddox*, Part V (London, 1911), pp. xviii–xxviii. Generally, Lady Denbigh and the Marquise discuss matters of health, but political issues intrude quite frequently; see pp. 124, 127, 129, 130, 131, 153.

9. Daniel Defoe, *A Tour Through the Whole Island of Great Britain*, ed. Pat Rogers (Baltimore, Md.: Penguin Books, 1971), p. 307.

10. Donald J. Greene, "Swift: Some Caveats," *Studies in the Eighteenth Century*, ed. R. F. Brissenden (Toronto: University of Toronto Press, 1973), II, 342–58, esp. 342–43, 345.

11. Jonathan Swift, *Correspondence*, ed. Harold Williams (Oxford: Clarendon Press, 1963–65), IV, 100, 230.

12. Irvin Ehrenpreis, "Swift on Liberty," *Journal of the History of Ideas* 13 (1952): 146, 140.

13. Ibid., p. 132.

14. Swift attacks Steele's Low Church views in *The Publick Spirit of the Whigs* and *The Importance of the Guardian Considered*, but only after Steele, with typical insouciance, presumed to speak for all Anglican clergymen without being one himself.

15. Ehrenpreis, "Swift," p. 146.

16. Compare this to Fielding's praise for Godolphin in *The True Patriot* No. 25 as "one of the wisest, ablest, and best ministers that was ever at the Head of our Affairs" (XXV, iii, iii).

17. Joseph Addison, *The Spectator* No. 69 (19 May 1711), in Addison and Richard Steele, *The Spectator*, ed. Donald F. Bond (Oxford: Clarendon Press, 1965), I, 276.

18. John Loftis, *The Politics of Drama in Augustan England* (Oxford: Clarendon Press, 1963), pp. 125–27.

19. Fielding praises Marlborough in ch. IV of *A Journey from This World to the Next* and in the poem *Of True Greatness* for winning his victories at the least possible cost. He lauds Marlborough's "Sagacity" in *The True Patriot* No. 8 and his bravery in *The Jacobite's Journal* No. 15. In *A Proper Answer to a Late Scurrilous Libel* (1747), he refers to "the great Duke of Marlborough" and "the unparallel'd Successes of our Arms, under the Conduct of the Great, the Protestant, the Whig Duke of *Marlborough*" (*The Jacobite's Journal and Related Writings*, ed. W. B. Coley, pp. 64, 65). In his introduction to the *Voyage to Lisbon* he describes Parliament's rewards to Marlborough—the rewards Swift attacked—as "deservedly liberal." Add to this Fielding's *Full Vindication of the Dutchess Dowager of Marlborough* (April 1742), written in behalf of Marlborough's widow, and Fielding's admiration for the Duke becomes very clear.

20. Christopher Hill, "Clarissa Harlow and Her Times," *Essays in Criticism* 5 (1955): 315–40.

21. Raymond Williams, *The Country and the City* (New York: Oxford University Press, 1973), pp. 11–32.

22. Herbert Davis's introduction to Jonathan Swift, *The Prose Works* (Oxford: Basil Blackwell, 1939–68), VI, xii.

23. See Dickinson, *Bolingbroke*, pp. 210–11, Gay to Swift, 27 April 1731, *The Letters of John Gay*, ed. C. F. Burgess (Oxford: Clarendon Press 1966), p. 108, and Defoe, *Tour*, pp. 109, 177.

24. See Cross, *History*, I, 34–37, and Jones, *Fielding*, pp. 20–28, esp. p. 21.

25. Arthur Murphy claims that Fielding went to Leyden in 1728 with his father's help (perhaps, with his promotion in 1727, Edmund Fielding's finances were temporarily healthy) and returned when that help stopped abruptly.

26. Fielding's first publication was a pair of poems written on the occasion of George II's coronation and his birthday. No copy of this publication has survived, but it is listed in the *Monthly Catalogue* for 1727; for details see David Fairweather Foxon, *English Verse 1701–1750: A Catalogue of Separately Printed Poems With Notes on Contemporary Collected Editions* (London: Cambridge University Press, 1975), I, 273.

Chapter III
Fielding's "Undistinguished Career as a Dramatist"

1. Attempting to give a historical model for his own battles against censorship, Shaw wrote, in his preface to *Plays Pleasant and Unpleasant* (New York: Herbert S. Stone, 1898), I, xvii–xviii: "In 1737 the greatest dramatist, with the single exception of Shakespeare, produced by England between the Middle Ages and the nineteenth century—Henry Fielding—devoted his genius to the task of exposing and destroying parliamentary corruption, then at its height. Walpole, unable to govern without corruption, promptly gagged the stage by a censorship which is in full force at the present." Quoted in the introduction to Henry Fielding, *The Author's Farce*, ed. Charles B. Woods (Lincoln: University of Nebraska Press, 1966), p. xii.

2. Most prominent among them are J. Paul Hunter, "Fielding's Reflexive Plays and the Rhetoric of Discovery," *Studies in the Literary Imagination* 5 (1972): 65–100; Jean B. Kern, "Fielding's Dramatic Satire," *Philological Quarterly* 54 (1975): 239–57; Sheridan Baker, "Political Allusion in Fielding's *Author's Farce, Mock Doctor*, and *Tumble-Down Dick*," *PMLA* 77 (1962): 221–31. Marsha Kinder, "Fielding's Dramatic Experimentation" (Ph.D. dissertation, University of California, Los Angeles, 1967), provides an extensive study of the formal features of Fielding's plays, particularly as they point toward his techniques as a novelist. Ronald K. Paulson, *Satire and the Novel in Eighteenth Century England* (New Haven: Yale University Press, 1967), pp. 72–95, comments briefly and suggestively upon the satiric elements in Fielding's conventional plays.

3. Fielding did produce *Don Quixote in England* at the Haymarket Theatre in April 1734, but only after he spent months trying to get it performed at Drury Lane. See *The London Stage 1660–1800*, Part 3: 1729–1747, ed. Arthur H. Scouten (Carbondale: Southern Illinois University Press, 1961), p. cxlv. In those instances where I cite specific productions of plays, readers need merely locate the date in Scouten to find my source. But when I have derived important generalizations from Scouten—i.e., that Cibber dominated the stage during Fielding's years as a playwright, or that Fielding's plays were widely produced at rival theatres both before and after the Licensing Act—I cannot refer to one clearly delimited section. I must ask my reader to take me at my word, or to repeat my own long journey through the day-by-day history of the London stage that Scouten provides—a task made easier by his superb index.

4. Hunter, *Occasional Form*, p. 51, observes that London audiences brought different expectations to different theatres: the Haymarket Theatre "specialized in topical satire, and its audiences supported an anti-Establishment theatre of ideas rather than the revivals and conventional five-act plays presented at other houses."

5. I define the word "sentimental" here, and throughout the rest of the chapter, as John Harrington Smith defines it in *The Gay Couple in Restoration Comedy* (Cambridge, Mass.: Harvard

University Press, 1948), pp. 231–33. According to Smith, the comedy of Steele and Cibber is sentimental only if we define sentimental as "sententious, moralizing." He claims that "exemplary comedy" is a better descriptive term for the comedy of Steele—a claim I accept and follow. When I refer to Fielding's exemplary or sentimental plot, then, I refer to those parts of his comedies and satires characterized by "the use of examples for conveying edification."

     6. See *The London Stage*, ed. Scouten, 20, 28 September, 22 October, 27 November 1733, 16 February, 19 March 1734.

     7. Holmes, *British Politics*, p. 24.

     8. See Loftis, *Politics of Drama*, pp. 57–60, and his *Steele at Drury Lane* (1952; rpt. Westport, Conn.: Greenwood Press, 1973), pp. 155–56.

     9. With the exception of one production of *Pasquin* at Lincoln's Inn Fields on 25 January 1737.

     10. Historical Manuscripts Commission, *The Diary of the Earl of Egmont*, ed. R. A. Roberts (London, 1920–23), II, 390.

     11. In discussing Fielding's Haymarket plays of 1730–31, which critics have supposed to satirize Walpole, Bertrand A. Goldgar pointedly observes: "there is not the slightest scrap of evidence which suggests that the first three of these four plays [*The Author's Farce, Tom Thumb*, and *Rape upon Rape*] were read or viewed at that time as satirizing Walpole" (*Walpole and the Wits*, p. 102). Yet, as Goldgar notes, many scholars, himself included, have traced political allusions in these plays. His response to this phenomenon is to discredit the work of the scholars, including his own (p. 110n). Perhaps, however, the relative decline in the importance of party labels may explain the failure of Fielding's contemporaries to give his early political allusions great significance. His slaps at Walpole in these early plays are obvious but unsystematic. They serve no party program, no dogma. Thus a politically sensitive man like the Earl of Egmont easily could have attended *The Author's Farce* or *Tom Thumb*, noted their bits of political satire, yet not classified them as party or even political works. See *Walpole and the Wits*, p. 105.

     12. During Fielding's lifetime, seven of his five-act comedies were performed. Five of them—*Love in Several Masques, The*

Modern Husband, The Miser, The Universal Gallant, The Wedding Day—were staged at Drury Lane; a sixth, *The Temple Beau*, was apparently written for Drury Lane but rejected by Cibber and Wilkes. The numbers indicate that Fielding associated Drury Lane with literary orthodoxy—with conventional, five-act drama. During Fielding's lifetime, eighteen of his ballad operas, farces, and three-act comedies were performed, ten at the Haymarket, eight at Drury Lane. The Drury Lane irregular plays generally served as afterpieces, however, while the Haymarket plays generally were performed as main pieces. Fielding clearly felt that farce and burlesque were appropriate at the Haymarket, but at Drury Lane he gave them only a limited, secondary role.

13. Robert Halsband, *The Life of Lady Mary Wortley Montagu* (New York: Oxford University Press, 1960), pp. 17–18, 32, 76.

14. Grundy, "New Verse," p. 213.

15. *The Spectator* No. 40 (16 April 1711), in Addison and Steele, *The Spectator* (1965), I, 171.

16. This line captures Fielding's political ambivalence. Initially it seems an indictment of Walpole's use of bribery, though a second look reveals an equally strong criticism of Bolingbroke's calls for frequent, even yearly, elections.

17. Most scholars assume that Fielding's dedication of *The Modern Husband* to Walpole must be ironic; e.g., see Hunter, *Occasional Form*, p. 57. Goldgar challenges this assumption rightly, I think, in *Walpole and the Wits*, p. 102. If we note that Fielding let his *Grub-Street Opera* die without complaint or protest, that he did not authorize its publication and try to profit from its banishment *à la* Gay, we can guess that he was ready to return to Drury Lane by mid-1731. If he was eager to curry both the literary and political favor of the Whig establishment, he may well have wanted *The Grub-Street Opera* to die. He could have anticipated that its presence would evoke the response to *The Modern Husband*, and to its dedication, that so many modern scholars have shared. See Edgar V. Roberts's introduction to Henry Fielding, *The Grub-Street Opera* (Lincoln: University of Nebraska Press, 1968), pp. xi-xii, xvii.

18. James T. Hillhouse, *The Grub-Street Journal* (1928; rpt.

New York: Benjamin Blom, 1967), p. 45, claims the *Journal* "was unmistakably undertaken as an organ for Pope." Bertrand A. Goldgar, "Pope and the *Grub-Street Journal*," *Modern Philology* 74 (1977): 360–80, argues convincingly that Pope's role in the *Journal* was very modest.

19. Ronald K. Paulson and Thomas Lockwood, eds., *Henry Fielding: The Critical Heritage* (New York: Barnes and Noble, 1969), p. 2.

20. William W. Appleton's introduction to Henry Fielding, *The Historical Register for the Year 1736 and Eurydice Hissed* (Lincoln: University of Nebraska Press, 1967), p. xi.

21. Paulson and Lockwood, eds., *Critical Heritage*, p. 2. All citations of the paper war between Fielding and Dramaticus are taken from the reprints in the *Critical Heritage* text. Page numbers are included in parentheses.

22. Hillhouse, *Grub-Street Journal*, p. 45.

23. John Harrington Smith discusses the role of the female audience in stage reform and links it with Steele's. See his chapter entitled "Forces in Opposition: The Reforming Dramatists, 'The Ladies,' " in *The Gay Couple*.

24. Hunter, "Fielding's Reflexive Plays," pp. 84–5.

25. Paulson and Lockwood, eds., *Critical Heritage*, p. 83.

26. Baker, "Political Allusion," traces the standard opposition ploy of linking Walpole with Harlequin; see pp. 228–30.

27. P. J. Crean, "The Stage Licensing Act of 1737," *Modern Philology* 35 (1938): 250, argues against the traditional view that Fielding's plays were directly responsible for the Licensing Act and shows how this view, shared by Shaw and others, overlooks the long history of the stage reform movement in England. Loftis, *Politics of Drama*, in his chapter on "Fielding and the Stage Licensing Act of 1737," also traces the history of the stage reform movement and claims that the Act of 1737 was "in a restricted sense the culmination of the stage controversy initiated by Collier's *Short View* in 1698" (p. 128).

28. Fielding still was shifting between playhouses as late as 1737—a fact that should make us wary of viewing his final dramatic satires as partisan documents. On 19 February he had

a benefit night at Drury Lane, with his ill-fated afterpiece *Eurydice* and *Cato* forming the program. Barely a month later (21 March) *The Historical Register* debuted at the Haymarket, to be joined on 13 April by *Eurydice Hissed*.

Chapter IV
The Uncertain Opposition

1. Austin Dobson, *Henry Fielding* (New York and London: Harper, 1901), pp. 50–51; Cross, *History*, 1, 233–37; Frederic T. Blanchard, *Fielding the Novelist* (1926; rpt. New York: Russell and Russell, 1966) p. 4; William T. Laprade, *Public Opinion and Politics in Eighteenth-Century England to the Fall of Walpole* (New York: Macmillan, 1936), p. 383.

2. Fielding had rushed an edition of *The Historical Register* and *Eurydice Hissed* into print on 12 May 1737 (Cross, *History*, 1, 222). While *The Vision of the Golden Rump*, the play that Walpole used to justify the Licensing Act, perhaps was not Fielding's (ibid., pp. 226–28) and was hardly suitable for publication, Fielding certainly could have used any play he had at hand to test the Act and, assuming it was banned, publish. His acquiescence in this case seemingly parallels his acquiescence in the demise of *The Grub-Street Opera*, which was also a prelude to support for Walpole.

3. As he did with his afterpiece *Miss Lucy in Town* on 6 May 1742, and his five-act comedy *The Wedding Day* in 1743.

4. Bailey, "Fielding's Politics," p. 130.

5. Goldgar, *Walpole*, p. 197.

6. Ibid., pp. 10, 14, 34, and E. P. Thompson, *Whigs and Hunters*, pp. 278–94.

7. Goldgar, *Walpole*, p. 102.

8. See Battestin, "Fielding's Changing Politics," pp. 40–41, and Coley, "Fielding and Two Walpoles," pp. 157–78.

9. John Edwin Wells, "Fielding's Signatures in *The Champion* and the Date of *His Of Good Nature*," *Modern Language Review* 7 (1912): 97–98.

10. Ten of Ralph's leaders in the 1741 reprint bear no motto: 24, 29 November, 1 December 1739, 19 January 1739/40, 3, 17, 24 April, 1, 29 May, 14 June 1740. Five bear Latin mottoes: 20 December 1739, 23 February, 18 March 1739/40, 10 April, 22 May 1740. One bears a motto from Pope's *Essay on Criticism*: 8 March 1739/40. One bears a motto from Milton: 26 April 1740.

11. Fielding did sign the Index of the 13 December 1739 issue, which merely transcribes a long satiric poem attacking Walpole's manipulation of George II. And he surely wrote the eulogy for George Lillo in the issue of 26 February 1739/40.

12. See I, 216, 265, II, 61, 242 for other comments on the Place Bill. See I, 145, II, 322 for additional bitter comments on the standing army. See II, 178, 233, 241 for complaints about royal visits to Hanover, and the power they left in Walpole's hands.

13. The name "Hercules Vinegar" may be another sign of Fielding's political uncertainty, for it had been used first in a pamphlet, "An Answer to one Part of the Infamous Libel reflecting on Captain *Vinegar*, and the late worthy *Jonathan Wild*, etc. By *Hercules Vinegar*, of Hockley-in-the-Hole, Esq.," advertised in *The Grub-Street Journal* of 24 July 1731. John Edwin Wells in *The Nation* (16 January 1913) suggested that this pamphlet parodied William Pulteney's "Answer to one Part of a Late Infamous Libel intitled Remarks on the *Craftsman*'s Vindication of his Two Honourable Patrons, in which the Character and conduct of Mr. P. is fully vindicated," and satirized Pulteney. If Wells is right, Vinegar first appeared in the paper war between Walpole and the opposition on the side of the ministry.

14. Bailey, "Fielding's Politics," pp. 111–21, also claims that Fielding began *The Champion* with great uncertainty and cites the bookseller's letter as a turning point, but he draws no distinction between the work of Fielding and the work of Ralph after the 4 December 1739 issue.

15. Certainly such a distinction was clear to Fielding's rivals, although they attacked him for it. *The Gazetteer* for 12 November 1740 included this description of the respective roles of

Fielding and Ralph: ". . . when the Hero has harangu'd the better sort of his Customers in the initial Letter, then comes his *Myrmidion* with two or three staring Paragraphs, full of the old Ornaments,—Lying and Detraction, to satisfy the Mob." An earlier number of *The Gazetteer* made the charge in sharper language: "To have been obliged to write thrice a Week a Medley of Scrurrility and Politicks, and at the same Time to have burlesqued the Daily Occurences, would have been a Task too hard for *Hercules* himself; on this occasion, therefore, he judiciously introduced a Second to take the Augean Stable and other nasty Adventures off His hands" (cited in William B. Coley, "The 'Remarkable Queries' in the *Champion*," *Philological Quarterly* 41 [1962]: 435). Coley also points out one instance in which Ralph, in the 1741 reprint, substituted a more politically inflammatory essay for one of Fielding's; Coley notes, "the *Champion* was most didactic politically sometime *after* the terminal date of the collected edition"—i.e., after Fielding's participation in it ended (p. 427). Certainly Ralph's later career as a political journalist placed him in opposition to Fielding as he supervised *The Remembrancer* and *The Protester*, journals that attacked Henry Pelham. See Foord, *Opposition*, pp. 267, 280.

16. See I, 354, II, 55, 198 for particularly dark comments upon the times.

17. The Index of No. 68 (19 April 1740) includes the following comment: "According to the *Gazetteer*, Lord *Marchmont*, Sir *William Wyndham*, and *William Chetwind*, Esq.; are gone to pay a visit to the late *Lord Bolingbroke* in France.—If this Paragraph is meant as a Reflection, the Author should have first consider'd, that a Man, to the full as obnoxious, is much more visited at Home" (II, 126).

18. See Cross, *History*, I, 255, for a brief summary of how Fielding's initials, and his use of a motto to open his paper and an initial to close it, hark back to Addison and *The Spectator*. Fielding's C and L are the first two letters of Addison's Clio.

19. Loftis, *Steele*, pp. 7–10. It is important to note here that Lyttelton, as a member of the Patriot opposition, often heaped scorn upon these groups. See particularly his attacks upon

226 Notes to Pages 91–103

stock-jobbers and his dark portraits of the Exchange in his *Persian Letters* Nos. 7, 25, and 43. Lyttelton here shows far greater influence by Bolingbroke's ideas than Fielding ever did—a point we do well to bear in mind before we mistakenly place Fielding in Bolingbroke's camp. Fielding obviously admired and supported Lyttelton, but did not share his aristocratic bias. His different economic and social loyalties meant that his allegiance to the Boy Patriots was far from absolute; he returned to the Whig establishment long before Lyttelton did.

20. No. 10 (6 December 1739) includes Fielding's most sustained treatment of Walpole as the child of "fortune."

21. This device is used by Lyttelton in his Persian Letter No. 12. *George Lyttelton's Political Tracts 1735–1748*, ed. Stephen Parks (New York and London: Garland, 1974), p. 55.

22. See John Edwin Wells, "Fielding's Political Purpose in *Jonathan Wild*," *PMLA* 28 (1914): 12; Goldgar, *Walpole*, pp. 197–98, and William Robert Irwin, *The Making of Jonathan Wild* (1941; rpt. Hamden, Conn.: Archon, 1965), pp. 29–30.

23. J. H. Plumb, *Men and Places* (London: Cresset Press, 1963), p. 286.

24. "Notes" to the Shakespeare Head edition of *Jonathan Wild*, p. 255.

25. Richard J. Dircks, "The Perils of Heartfree: A Sociological Review of Fielding's Adaptation of a Dramatic Convention," *Texas Studies in Language and Literature* 8 (1966): 8, catalogues the techniques of the drama of sensibility that Fielding uses in *Jonathan Wild*.

26. C. J. Rawson, *Henry Fielding and the Augustan Ideal Under Stress* (London: Routledge and Kegan Paul, 1972), pp. 112–14.

27. Irwin, *Making of Wild*, p. 65.

28. Battestin, "Fielding's Changing Politics," p. 46.

29. Cross, *History*, I, 298.

30. Coley, "Fielding and Two Walpoles," pp. 157–78.

31. Cited in Battestin, "Fielding's Changing Politics," p. 55, and in Goldgar, *Walpole*, p. 208.

32. Henry Knight Miller, *Essays on Fielding's Miscellanies* (Princeton, N.J.: Princeton University Press, 1961), p. 20.

Chapter V
True Patriotism and Political Certainty

1. See Cross, *History*, i, 375–76, ii, 1–10, Battestin, "Fielding's Changing Politics," pp. 44–46, and Miller, *Essays*, pp. 3–10, for fuller accounts of Fielding's activities during this difficult period.

2. See Battestin, "Fielding's Changing Politics" and "Fielding's Revisions of *Joseph Andrews*," *Studies in Bibliography* 16 (1963): 89, 91. The crucial additions to the second edition include the revelation of Bellarmine's political tergiversation (ii, iv, p. 112), and Fanny's fear, after her rescue by Adams, that he might use her "as some very honest Men have used their Country; and rescued her out of the Hands of one Rifler, in order to rifle her himself" (ii, x, p. 140). Both these additions clearly impugn the motives of the Pulteney-Carteret opposition.

3. Martin C. Battestin, *The Moral Basis of Fielding's Art* (Middletown, Conn.: Wesleyan University Press, 1959), pp. 121–29; Sheldon Sacks, *Fiction and the Shape of Belief* (Berkeley and Los Angeles: University of California Press, 1967), pp. 206–16; I. B. Cauthen Jr., "Fielding's Digressions in *Joseph Andrews*," *College English* 17 (1956): 379–82.

4. Battestin, *Moral Basis*, pp. 94–104.

5. Dick Taylor, Jr., "Joseph as Hero in *Joseph Andrews*," *Tulane Studies in English* 7 (1957): 91–109.

6. See Owen, *Rise*, pp. 278–80, 282–83, 293–94, and B. Williams, *Whig Supremacy*, pp. 257–58. Granville pleased George by suggesting an aggressive English role in the War of the Austrian Succession. Pelham was committed to seeking peace.

7. Gerard E. Jensen, "A Fielding Discovery," *Yale University Library Gazette* 10 (1935): 27–28.

8. Owen, *Rise*, pp. 295–300.

9. It is important to note that, except for a perfunctory compliment to him upon his birthday in No. 1, Fielding in *The True Patriot* makes few references to George II until the political

crisis revolved itself in Pelham's favor. Fielding frequently praises George's sons: William for his military greatness (see esp. Nos. 18, 25, 26, 27) and Frederick for his generosity (Nos. 11 and 12). But not until No. 17 (25 February 1745), the issue immediately following that which details the rise and fall of the 48 hour ministry, does Fielding praise George as the "best of Princes," thus anticipating his praise for all the members of the royal family in No. 27 (6 May 1746).

10. The only way Bath and Granville could have set up a ministry was by employing Tories; this George II recognized not to be in his best interest. See Owen, *Rise*, p. 296.

11. Arthur Murphy felt *The True Patriot* was "a project of the same kind" as *The Freeholder*; Paulson and Lockwood, *Fielding*, p. 423. See No. 2 (12 November 1745) for a direct reference to *The Freeholder*, and No. 15 (11 February 1746) for satire on the luxury and affectation of hoopskirts modelled on Addison's satires on petticoats in *The Tatler* No. 116 (5 January 1710) and *The Spectator* No. 127 (26 July 1711). Noted by M. A. Locke in Fielding, *True Patriot*, p. 51. For references to Locke see VIII, i, iii, and XII, i, ii.

12. B. Williams, *Whig Supremacy*, p. 20. For a good example of the antipathy that the excursions to Hanover aroused, see *The Champion* No. 80 (17 May 1740), II, 233, and No. 81 (20 May 1740), II, 241.

13. Rupert C. Jarvis, *Collected Papers on the Jacobite Risings* (New York: Barnes and Noble, 1972), II, 172–73, 170. *The Hanover Rat* pamphlet also appeared during the period of Fielding's so-called silence. The three pamphlets are: *A Serious Address to the People of Great Britain; The History of the Present Rebellion in Scotland;* and *A Dialogue Between the Devil, the Pope, and the Pretender.* Announcements in *The Daily Advertiser* place their publication dates respectively on 3, 8, and 15 October 1745.

14. "General Introduction" to Henry Fielding, *The History of Tom Jones A Foundling*, pp. xxv–xxix.

15. M. A. Locke, in Fielding, *True Patriot*, p. 163, describes No. 18 (4 March 1746) as "the turning point in the course of *The True Patriot*." She points out that "Although there is still some variety in subject matter, most of the remaining essays are

primarily in support of and in praise of the ministry. The Lenten Assizes on the Western Circuit opening on March 4, followed by the sittings of the King's Bench in London and Westminster, doubtless filled most of Fielding's time during the spring. Preoccupation with legal matters appears to have prevented the close personal attention to *The True Patriot* that earlier numbers had received. A falling off in style was inevitable."

16. Paulson and Lockwood, *Fielding*, p. 423.

17. M. A. Locke, introduction to Fielding, *True Patriot*, p. 7.

18. No. 28 (13 May 1746) includes only "Bankrupts." No. 33 (17 June 1746) currently is lost, and only a reprint of the lead essay survives.

19. See the letter from an old gentlewoman (II, ii, i), the story of a ruined prisoner of the Jacobites (II, i, iii), and the letter from A. X. (VII, iv, ii), all of which warn against the disavowal of the national debt and the economic ruin it would bring.

20. Kramnick, *Bolingbroke*, p. 262.

21. No. 16 (13 February 1715/16), Joseph Addison, *The Freeholder* (London: J. and R. Tonson, 1751), p. 91. All other citations of *The Freeholder* are taken from the 1751 edition; page numbers are included in parentheses.

22. Swift to the Reverend Thomas Sheridan, 11 September 1725, in *Correspondence*, III, 94.

23. Addison refers to the historical analogue of the Roman Commonwealth (pp. 93–94) and to previous suspensions of the Habeas Corpus Act in the reigns of William and Mary, William, and Anne (p. 95). For a brief sample of his other uses of analogy, see No. 24 (12 March 1715/16), in which he compares his task to that of a doctor dosing a patient; No. 5 (6 January 1715/16), in which he compares his audience's "Love of Country" to that of the ancient Hebrews; and No. 17 (17 February 1715/16), in which he compares how slander is treated in Britain with how it is treated in Turkey.

24. Examples of this tendency are particularly abundant in *The Conduct of the Allies*. See Swift, *Prose Works*, VI, pp. 5, 16, 19, 41, 43, 53–58.

25. See my "Romances, Newspapers, and the Style of Field-

ing's True History," *Studies in English Literature 1500–1900*
(forthcoming), in which I discuss Fielding's impulse to integrate
different types of literary truth.

26. Glenn W. Hatfield, *Henry Fielding and the Language of
Irony* (Chicago: University of Chicago Press, 1968), pp. 7–24.

27. M. A. Locke (Fielding, *True Patriot*, p. 157) guesses that
Fielding here may have in mind the famous saying attributed to
Walpole that "every man has his price." If Fielding is echoing
Walpole here, he also is improving him. For, as is typical of his
comments upon self-interest throughout *The True Patriot*, Fielding here makes it an important but not absolute motive: the
statement dismisses idealistic notions about human motivation
but does not commit Fielding, or the Great Man, to the cynical
notion that every man can be bought. We may see this passage
capturing in small the rehabilitation of Walpole's reputation
that Fielding makes in his writings from *The Opposition: A Vision*
until the end of his life. Actually, the strongest echo of the
statement attributed to Walpole comes in XI, i, i, when Stephen
Grubb imagines that "every Man, Woman, and Thing . . .
have their Price." Fielding clearly asks us to reject Grubb, and
his recasting of "the Saying of a Great Man" may reveal him
trying to spare Walpole from association with Grubb.

28. In *The Importance of the Guardian Consider'd*, Swift's argument is almost entirely ad hominem. He claims, for example,
that Steele, "after the first Bottle . . . is no disagreeable Com-
panion" (*Prose Works*, VIII, 6). In *The Publick Spirit of the Whigs*,
the vituperation is more extreme and bitter; Swift once goes so
far as to describe Steele licking up and regurgitating "the Spittle
of the Bishop of *Sarum*" (VIII, 38). This dealing in innuendo
comes only when Swift becomes frustrated by the inability of
his logic to sway those who do not share his assumptions about
property and society. He will try to reason with a Whig lord,
even though he believes the lord has acted as a traitor. He
merely abuses Steele, who does not share the landed interest of
the lord.

29. Jarvis, *Collected Papers*, II, 194–95, 29.

30. Swift's defense of the Anglican establishment differs
from that of Addison or Fielding because he sees dissent and

latitudinarianism as more immediate threats to the Church than
Roman Catholicism. Swift often uses the terms "Whig" and
"Low Church" synonymously, for example, referring in *An
Enquiry into the Behaviour of the Queen's Last Ministry* to a time
when "the Favour of the Court was almost perpetually turned
toward those who in the Party Term are called the Whigs, or the
low-Church" (*Prose Works*, VIII, p. 148). Obviously, then, Swift
disagreed with the latitudinarianism of men like Addison and
Fielding, and this disagreement had political consequences. But
I think that religious differences were not the main reason Swift
split with the Whigs, and I take *Some Reasons . . . in a Letter to a
Whig Lord* as the source for my view. Here Swift argues that
religious differences do not separate him from the lord; rather,
the war does. He, Addison, and Fielding all start from the same
rhetorical position when they consider the Church, casting
themselves in the role of its defender. Such is not the case when
they consider the economic and social character of British life.
For comments on the legal system, see Addison's careful appeal
to precedent to justify the suspension of the Habeas Corpus Act
during the Jacobite rising of 1715, in *The Freeholder* No. 16 (13
February 1715/16), and his opening statement of support for the
British system of laws in No. 1 (23 December 1715), p. 2. See
Swift's assertions that both the Queen and the Harley ministry
are pledged to preserving the English Constitution and the
Protestant Succession in *The Publick Spirit of the Whigs* (*Prose
Works*, VIII, 66), and in *Some Reasons . . . in a Letter to a Whig Lord*
(VI, pp. 126–27).

31. George Sherburn, "Fielding's Social Outlook," *Philological Quarterly* 25 (1956): 10, points out that Fielding's art
becomes darker and more pessimistic when he dwells on London life.

32. Martin C. Battestin, "Fielding's Definition of Wisdom:
Some Functions of Ambiguity and Emblem in *Tom Jones*," *ELH*
35 (1968): 188–217.

33. Like Addison's, Adams's arguments rely on analogy—in
this case, the biblical analogy of Sodom and Gomorrah. He will
not try to link syllogistically private interest to a specific definition of the nation's economic and social good.

34. The ten years of relative political calm following the '45 and the crisis of February 1746 suggest that Fielding was quite representative in this regard. Having reaffirmed the Whig principles (Bonnie Prince Charlie was a perfect enemy toward this end) and rescued public credit, Pelham never again would face a serious challenge. See Owen, *Rise*, p. 320.

Chapter VI
Political Certainty

1. Fielding's relationship with Dodington requires a brief summary, because it might seem to indicate deviation from his loyalty to Pelham. Fielding's early praise for Dodington came when they both, after serving Walpole, joined the opposition in 1739. Dodington, like Fielding, was not long in finding his way back to the Whig establishment, serving as treasurer of the navy under Pelham from 1744 to 1749. Thus the praise for Dodington in Fielding's *Miscellanies* and in *The True Patriot* (x, i, ii) was reciprocal with his loyalty to Pelham. In March 1749, however, Dodington resigned his post, split with Pelham, and joined the Leicester House opposition that centered around Prince Frederick. Dodington was probably gambling on advancement to a higher place in a new reign than Pelham's sway would allow in the old; he lost when Frederick died on 20 March 1751, and then began a long effort at rapprochement with Pelham. Thus Fielding's allusion to Dodington in *Amelia* xi, ii, as "one of the greatest men this country ever produced," while its hyperbole inevitably shocks us, is not an anti-Pelham statement. By late 1751 Dodington was on the verge of moving back to the Whig establishment, preparing to offer his electoral interest in Weymouth in exchange for Pelham's vindication of his reputation with the king. Fielding's hyperbole probably is due to the generous treatment that he received from Dodington; we know he dined frequently with Dodington in 1751 and 1752. The political impact of the allusion in *Amelia* probably is best understood if we look forward to May 1752, when Dodington was

dining with Pelham, praising his character, and serving his electoral interests. See *The Political Journal of George Bubb Dodington*, ed. John Carswell and L. A. Dralle (Oxford: Clarendon Press, 1965), pp. 3–5 (for Dodington's break with Pelham), 67, 130, 132, 134, 143, 148, 149, 163 (for Fielding's meetings with Dodington), 154–60, 163–65, 219–20, 225 (for Dodington's efforts to return to the good graces of Pelham and the King). Note particularly that the one meal Fielding had with Dodington while Dodington still was in opposition also was attended by Walter Carey, an officeholder under Pelham. Perhaps Fielding (or, as seems more likely, Carey) was a tie between Dodington and the ministry. Certainly in his later vindications of himself, Dodington claimed that during his years in opposition he tried to reconcile the differences between Frederick and his father and to stop the opposition from becoming intemperate. A clever politician, he obviously kept open his lines to the ministry; Fielding may have been one of them.

2. Fielding's faith in Carteret's "true greatness" soon failed. But, as Miller, *Essays*, p. 44, points out, the poem shows Fielding in a very optimistic vein.

3. *A Dialogue Between A Gentleman of London . . . and An Honest Alderman*, p. 31.

4. Most notably in his decision, in 1743, to split with Carteret and negotiate with the "broad-bottom" opposition. See Foord, *Opposition*, p. 247, and Owen, *Rise*, p. 40.

5. Owen points out that Pelham, "by converting to Administration the most able of his opponents," rendered patronage less necessary that it had been for Walpole, and thus ran a less "financially extravagan[t]" administration. He quotes a letter from Newcastle to Pelham in which Newcastle describes the king remarking of Walpole, "that he managed money matters very ill: he did not indeed give money abroad, but he gave it away liberally at home; that he was a great man, he understood the country; but that with regard to money matters, your brother does that, understands that, much better." See Owen, *Rise*, pp. 319–20.

6. This would be the praise for Dodington in *Amelia*, XI, ii.

7. See No. 26 (28 May 1748), p. 289; No. 29 (18 June 1748),

pp. 308, 311; No. 31 (2 July 1748), p. 325; No. 45 (8 October 1748), p. 404; No. 47 (22 October 1748), p. 415; No. 48 (29 October 1748), p. 421.

8. In his introduction to the Wesleyan edition of the *Journal*, pp. xxix-xlii, William B. Coley summarizes the circumstances and content of *A Proper Answer to a Late Scurrilous Libel*.

9. For other references to Addison, see No. 9 (30 January 1748), p. 146; No. 30 (25 June 1748), p. 317; No. 38 (20 August 1748), p. 373. Coley, in his introduction to *The Jacobite's Journal*, pp. lvi-lvii, describes Fielding's "number of indebtednesses" to Addison as "surprising." Actually, Fielding's debts to Addison typify his Whiggism and will surprise only those who over-emphasize his ties to the Scriblerus Club and the Tory politics of Bolingbroke.

10. For a short sample, see No. 1 (5 December 1747), p. 91; No. 2 (12 December 1747), p. 102; No. 3 (19 December 1747), pp. 103–4; No. 4 (26 December 1747), p. 110.

11. Bailey, "Fielding's Politics," pp. 223–24, describes several inconsistencies in early numbers of the *Journal* that "indicate the constraint Fielding felt in providing affirmation within a negative form." Trott-plaid's comments on war news become particularly confused, as Fielding occasionally forgets a Jacobite should cheer French successes.

12. See No. 40 (3 September 1748), pp. 382–83, for a defense of Pelham; No. 33 (16 July 1748), pp. 342–45, for a defense of Pelham and Walpole; No. 28 (11 June 1748), pp. 303–4, for another defense of Lyttelton.

13. For reforms in the laws regarding education, see No. 22 (30 April 1748), pp. 259–61, and No. 27 (4 June 1748), p. 297. For the scheme to maintain relicts of clergymen, see No. 21 (23 April 1748), pp. 251–54; No. 29 (18 June 1748), pp. 313–15; No. 30 (25 June 1748), pp. 320–22; No. 31 (2 July 1748), pp. 328–30; No. 32 (9 July 1748), pp. 336–39.

14. Trott-plaid publishes a letter that opens, "Welcome, old *Trot*, welcome into the World, under whatever Title thou dost please to appear; Champion, Patriot, Jacobite, anything" (p. 120).

15. Dickinson, *Bolingbroke*, pp. 194–97.

16. See No. 43 (24 September 1748), pp. 397–98; No. 45 (8 October 1748), pp. 406–7; No. 46 (15 October 1748), p. 413.

17. See No. 25 (21 May 1748), pp. 281–87; No. 26 (28 May 1748), p. 287; No. 43 (24 September 1748), p. 394; No. 47 (8 October 1748), p. 407; No. 32 (9 July 1748), pp. 331–33.

18. Bailey, "Fielding's Politics," p. 233.

19. See esp. No. 26 (28 May 1748), pp. 289–93, and the extended attack upon opposition journals in No. 43 (24 September 1748), pp. 394–98.

20. Laprade, *Public Opinion*, p. 383.

21. Bailey, "Fielding's Politics," p. 219, p. 221.

22. This explanation is Bailey's; ibid., pp. 221–24.

23. See Blanchard, *Fielding the Novelist*, pp. 20–22, for a brief summary of the political opposition that Fielding knew always lay in wait for him.

24. Owen, *Rise*, p. 231.

25. See *A Dialogue Between A Gentleman of London . . . and an Honest Alderman*, pp. 47, 48–49.

26. See No. 47 (22 October 1748), p. 416; No. 48 (29 October 1748), p. 422.

27. Owen, *Rise*, p. 54.

28. See, e.g., No. 43 (24 September 1748), p. 398, in which Fielding claims "That in the Circle of this Administration are contained Men of the most known Abilities, of the longest Experience in Business, of the largest Property, and of the most confirmed Integrity that are to be found in the whole Kingdom." Note also that when Fielding defended his patron, the Duke of Bedford, from opposition attacks, he described him as "a Noble Duke of the highest Rank, *the most extensive Property*, and the most unblemished Honour" (No. 10 [6 February 1748], p. 456; italics mine). See also No. 10, p. 148.

29. Fielding shortly continues, "Their Situation in Business makes them the best Judges of the Public Good; and their larger Share of Property makes them the most interested in its Promotion" (p. 29).

30. Owen, *Rise*, p. 267. George II's opinion changed greatly by the time of Pelham's death: ibid., p. 320.

31. See Ray A. Kelch, *Newcastle: A Duke Without Money*

(Berkeley and Los Angeles: University of California Press, 1974), pp. 198–200, for a summary of the relation between Newcastle's electioneering and the ruin of the Pelham-Holles family fortune. Kelch argues against the traditional view that Newcastle spent the family fortune building his electoral interest and focuses upon Newcastle's prodigious personal expenses, but he does see Newcastle's political activity as contributing to his financial ruin. Certainly Newcastle and Pelham did not use their offices to build a family fortune as Walpole did.

Chapter VII
The Perils of Political Certainty

1. Owen, *Rise*, pp. 318–20.

2. See Cross, *History*, II, 108, and M. C. with R. R. Battestin, "Fielding, Bedford, and the Westminster Election of 1749," *Eighteenth-Century Studies* 11 (1977–78): 143–53, esp. p. 145.

3. Thomas Cleary, "Jacobitism in *Tom Jones*: The Basis for an Hypothesis," *Philological Quarterly* 52 (1973): 241, claims there are no allusions to the '45 after Book XII. For two small exceptions to his rule, see XVIII, v, p. 933, and XVIII, viii, p. 946. Martin C. Battestin, "Tom Jones and His Egyptian Majesty: Fielding's Parable of Government," *PMLA* 82 (1967): 68–77, first explained the political significance of the Gypsy episode.

4. Fielding is fascinated by, but ultimately skeptical of, the notion of benevolent despotism. Allworthy, in his trial of Partridge (II, iv), like the Gypsy King, rules in a paternal and wise rather than in a purely legal way. His power as a magistrate is absolute, but only his great virtue prevents it from being tyrannical. In *Amelia*, Harrison exercises a similar absolute power when in the country, and Booth and Amelia, like Jones, leave the city to live under it. Fielding's wariness of this ideal of wise absolute rule by a beneficent patriarch—the ideal of Bolingbroke—appears when we note that Allworthy, despite his great virtues, errs repeatedly.

5. See the opening paragraphs of his *Plan for a Universal Register Office*.

6. Malvin R. Zirker, *Fielding's Social Pamphlets* (Berkeley and Los Angeles: University of California Press, 1966), pp. 65–70, outlines Fielding's reliance upon analogies between the human body and the body politic.

7. Ibid., p. 136. See also Sherburn, "Fielding's Social Outlook," p. 2.

8. Peter Linebaugh, "The Tyburn Riot Against the Surgeons," *Albion's Fatal Tree*, p. 94.

9. Linebaugh, "Tyburn Riot," p. 91, calls Fielding's decision to employ military units "ill-judged." The most famous contemporary attack on Fielding was *The Case of the Unfortunate Bosavern Penlez* (London, 1749).

10. For the fullest summary of Fielding's role in this election, see M. C. with R. R. Battestin, "Fielding, Bedford," pp. 154–66. The author of *Old England* (25 November 1749) claimed that Fielding had "interested his foul Hands and bad Heart in the Protection of the Bawdyhouses . . . and shared in the Wages of their Iniquity" (cited by the Battestins, p. 166). Even Linebaugh, "Tyburn Riot," p. 95, finds no evidence for these charges.

11. Nicholas Rogers, "Aristocratic Clientage, Trade, and Independency: Popular Politics in Pre-Radical Westminster," *Past and Present* 61 (1973): 70–106; M. C. with R. R. Battestin "Fielding, Bedford," pp. 159, 156, 150–52.

12. I part company with Linebaugh at this point. He guesses that the government killed Penlez in order to vindicate the strong actions it took in July, and he describes Fielding supporting the severe penalty in order to vindicate what actually was an overreaction on his part (pp. 97–98). This strikes me not only as unfair to Fielding but also as oversubtle. My own view is that, because property was threatened, Fielding probably never saw his actions as inappropriate or overzealous. I do not think he felt Penlez must hang in order to vindicate his behavior; rather, he felt Penlez must hang because Penlez had stolen. Such is the thrust of his comments in the *True Case*. See also Patrick Pringle, *Hue and Cry: The Story of Henry and John Fielding and Their Bow-Street Runners* (London: William Morrow, n.d.), pp. 85–86.

13. Linebaugh, "Tyburn Riot," p. 95.

14. Zirker, *Fielding's Social Pamphlets*, pp. 24–28, 103–9, 112–14. See also the *Enquiry*, p. 24, and the *Proposal*, pp. 183–87.

15. Linebaugh, "Tyburn Riot," p. 90.

16. M. C. with R. R. Battestin, "Fielding, Bedford," p. 147.

17. Linebaugh, "Tyburn Riot," p. 96.

18. While Fielding emphasized that Penlez stole property, the actual charge lodged against him was violating the Riot Act—a fact that both complicates and weakens Fielding's defense.

19. Fielding compares Pelham (p. 133) to "a skilful governor of a ship [who] hath brought his vessel through rocks, quicksands, and storms, to ride safely before the wind. . . ."

20. Zirker, *Fielding's Social Pamphlets*, pp. 46–47, 96–97. For a similar but less scholarly summary of Fielding's double standard, see Pringle, *Hue and Cry*, pp. 92–94.

21. See Cross, *History*, II, 224–25, for examples of the types of punishments that Fielding meted out for thefts. Cross also notes, however, cases that show Fielding was "invariably considerate in dealing with juvenile offenders . . . and with the aged and infirm who found their way into his court not so much because of wilful crime as indigence and distress" (II, 229).

22. Zirker, *Fielding's Social Pamphlets*, p. 140.

23. See Fielding's discussion of the need for the King to restrict his use of royal pardons in *Enquiry*, pp. 118–20.

24. Zirker, *Fielding's Social Pamphlets*, p. 127.

25. Ibid., p. 131, concludes that Fielding's workhouse, if ever it had been built, would have been "more like a prison than a factory."

26. Sherburn, "Fielding's Social Outlook," pp. 1–2.

27. Zirker, *Fielding's Social Pamphlets*, pp. 138, 140.

28. See Sherburn, "Fielding's Social Outlook," p. 2, for an allusion to this praise for the mob as "somewhat equivocal." In his note on this number (II, 211), Jensen claims the treatment of the mob is ironic.

29. For the standard history of the Newcastle–Bedford rivalry, see B. Williams, *Whig Supremacy*, p. 342. For a contemporary account of it, see the Denbigh papers in Historical Manuscripts Commission, *Report*, VIII, 232.

30. See Foord, *His Majesty's Opposition*, p. 280, and Dodington, *Political Journal*, pp. 218-19.

31. For a small sample of Fielding's return to ironic use of "great" and "good," see I, 156, 163, 231, 240, 251, 276, 294–98.

32. Self-interest was not absolute in Fielding's case. After Bedford split with Pelham, Fielding remained loyal to the latter, even as he continued under great financial obligations to the former. See M. C. with R. R. Battestin, "Fielding, Bedford," pp. 151–52.

33. In *A Journey from This World to the Next*, Cromwell, on his first visit, is denied admission to the Elysian Fields, and must return to earth as a cavalier. Fielding directly attacks his absolutism in *The Champion* No. 10 (6 December 1739), I, 66–67.

34. Fielding often turned to this image in his final works. In the *Enquiry* (p. 73), he compares the task of reforming the poor to the hopeless task of Augeus. In *The Covent-Garden Journal*, as he attacks rather than apologizes for contemporary vice, he reverses the image and casts himself once again in the role of Hercules, who can and will cleanse the stable. See No. 5 (I, 164).

35. See Martin C. Battestin, "The Problem of *Amelia*: Hume, Barrow, and the Conversion of Captain Booth," *ELH* 41 (1974): 632–34, for a summary of this plot and the religious and philosophical issues that it raises.

36. See Fielding's defense of his heroine in *The Covent-Garden Journal*, No. 9 (I, 178–79).

37. I am aware that Fielding's descriptions of English wives as equivalent to slaves might qualify the idea that he is trying to separate tyranny from English norms, but I think his comment reflects more on the status of women in mid-eighteenth-century England than on the politics of the era.

38. In *The Covent-Garden Journal*, No. 23 (21 March 1752), Fielding expresses his fear of "that dreadful State of Anarchy" that has come to prevail in the Kingdom of Letters. In No. 58 (8 August 1752), he warns against introducing "that Anarchy which is sure to end in some Species of Tyranny or other," thus anticipating his treatment of anarchy in the *Voyage*. His comments upon the mob in the *Journal* are not as fearful and harsh as they are in the *Voyage*, because there he concentrates on upper-class rather than lower-class vices.

39. In *Amelia*, I, ii, the description of Justice Thrasher's court, Fielding returns to the analogy of the machine of government and admits that, at the lowest levels, some parts of the British machine are flawed. Again, however, in I, ii, his main emphasis is on the soundness of the British Constitution. His call for reform is circumscribed sharply, and he still asserts that proper administration can correct the flaws in the machine, remedying social injustices and ills.

40. See *A Fragment of a Comment on Lord Bolingbroke's Essays*, in Fielding, *Complete Works*, XVI, esp. p. 314. Fielding claims of Bolingbroke, "That as the temporal happiness, the civil liberties and properties of Europe, were the game of his earliest youth, there could be no sport so adequate to the entertainment of his advanced age, as the eternal and final happiness of all mankind."

Conclusion

1. M. C. with R. R. Battestin, "Fielding, Bedford," pp. 151–52.

2. For a particularly significant example in support of this claim, see the famous passage in *Tom Jones* (IV, i, p. 150) in which Fielding defines his mode. The passage is spiced with allusions to both Addison and Pope. As Fielding here combines literary modes, so he combines literary models. See my "Romances, Newspapers."

3. For an exception to this rule, and a discussion of how Fielding, anticipating Sterne, adapts the digressive mode of Cibber's *Apology*, see Melvyn New, "The Dunce Revisited: Colley Cibber and Tristram Shandy," *South Atlantic Quarterly* 72 (1973): 547–59.

4. Sheridan Baker, "Henry Fielding's Comic Romances," *Papers of the Michigan Academy of Science, Arts, and Letters* 45 (1960): 411–19, and Hunter, *Occasional Form*, pp. 4, 9, 17.

5. Bailey, "Fielding's Politics," pp. 10–12, and Caroline Robbins, *The Eighteenth-Century Commonwealthman* (Cambridge, Mass.: Harvard University Press, 1959), pp. 375, 384.

6. Dobson, *Fielding*, p. 97.

Bibliography

Addison, Joseph. *The Freeholder*. London: J. and R. Tonson, 1751.

———, and Steele, Richard. *The Spectator*. Ed. Donald F. Bond. 5 vols. Oxford: Clarendon Press, 1965.

Allen, Robert J. *The Clubs of Augustan London*. 1933. Rpt. Hamden, Conn.: Archon, 1967.

Amory, Hugh. "Henry Fielding's *Epistles to Walpole*: A Reconsideration." *Philological Quarterly* 46 (1967): 236–47.

Avery, Emmett L. "Fielding's Last Season with the Haymarket Theatre." *Modern Philology* 36 (1939): 283–92.

Bailey, Vern D. "Fielding's Politics." Ph.D. dissertation, University of California, Berkeley, 1970.

Baker, Sheridan. "Henry Fielding's Comic Romances." *Papers of the Michigan Academy of Science, Arts, and Letters* 45 (1960): 411–19.

———. "Political Allusion in Fielding's *Author's Farce, Mock Doctor*, and *Tumble-Down Dick*." *PMLA* 77 (1962): 221–31.

Battestin, Martin C. "Fielding's Changing Politics in *Joseph Andrews*." *Philological Quarterly* 39 (1960): 39–55.

———. "Fielding's Definition of Wisdom: Some Functions of Ambiguity and Emblem in *Tom Jones*." *ELH* 35 (1968): 188–217.

———. "Fielding's Revisions of Joseph Andrews." *Studies in Bibliography* 16 (1963): 81–117.

———. "Lord Hervey's Role in *Joseph Andrews*." *Philological Quarterly* 42 (1963): 226–41.

————. *The Moral Basis of Fielding's Art: A Study of Joseph Andrews*. Middletown, Conn.: Wesleyan University Press, 1959.

————. "Pope's 'Magus' in Fielding's *Vernoniad*: The Satire of Walpole." *Philological Quarterly* 46 (1967): 137–41.

————. "The Problem of *Amelia*: Hume, Barrow, and the Conversion of Captain Booth." *ELH* 41 (1974): 613–48.

————. "Tom Jones and His Egyptian Majesty: Fielding's Parable of Government," *PMLA* 82 (1967): 68–77.

————, with Battestin, R. R. "Fielding, Bedford, and the Westminster Election of 1749." *Eighteenth-Century Studies* 11 (1977–78): 143–85.

Blanchard, Frederic T. *Fielding the Novelist: A Study in Historical Criticism*. 1926. Rpt. New York: Russell and Russell, 1966.

Blanchard, Rae, ed. *Richard Steele's Periodical Journalism 1714–1716*. Oxford: Clarendon Press, 1959.

Bolingbroke, Henry St. John, Viscount. *The Works of Lord Bolingbroke*. 2 vols. 1844. Rpt. London: Frank Cass, 1967.

Butterfield, Herbert. *George III and the Historians*. 2d rev. ed. New York: Macmillan, 1959.

————. *The Whig Interpretation of History*. 1931. Rpt. New York: W. W. Norton, 1965.

Cauthen, I. B., Jr. "Fielding's Digressions in *Joseph Andrews*." *College English* 17 (1956): 379–82.

Cibber, Colley. *An Apology for the Life of Colley Cibber*. Ed. B. R. S. Fone. Ann Arbor: University of Michigan Press, 1968.

Cleary, Thomas. "Jacobitism in *Tom Jones*: The Basis for an Hypothesis." *Philological Quarterly* 52 (1973): 239–51.

Cokayne, George Edward. *The Complete Peerage of England, Scotland, Ireland, Great Britain, and the United Kingdom*. Ed. Vicary Gibbs and H. A. Doubleday. 1921. Rpt. London: St. Catherine's Press, 1926.

Coley, William B. "Fielding's Two Appointments to the Magistracy." *Modern Philology* 63 (1965): 144–49.

————. "Henry Fielding and the Two Walpoles." *Philological Quarterly* 46 (1966): 162–78.

————. "The 'Remarkable Queries' in the *Champion*." *Philological Quarterly* 41 (1962): 426–36.

Congreve, William. *Complete Plays*. Ed. Alexander Charles Ewald. New York: Hill and Wang, 1956.

Cox, Richard H. *Locke on War and Peace*. Oxford: Clarendon Press, 1960.

Crean, P. J. "The Stage Licensing Act of 1737." *Modern Philology* 35 (1938): 239–55.

Cross, Wilbur L. *The History of Henry Fielding*. 3 vols. 1918. Rpt. New York: Russell and Russell, 1963.

Defoe, Daniel. *A Tour Through the Whole Island of Great Britain*. Ed. Pat Rogers. Baltimore, Md.: Penguin Books, 1971.

Dickinson, H. T. *Bolingbroke*. London: Constable, 1970.

Digeon, Aurelien. *The Novels of Fielding*, 1925. Rpt. New York: Russell and Russell, 1962.

Dircks, Richard J. "The Perils of Heartfree: A Sociological Review of Fielding's Adaptation of a Dramatic Convention." *Texas Studies in Language and Literature* 8 (1966): 5–13.

Dobson, Austin. *Henry Fielding*. English Men of Letters, ed. John Morley. 1883. Rpt. New York and London: Harper, 1901.

Dodington, George Bubb. *The Political Journal of George Bubb Dodington*. Ed. John Carswell and L. A. Dralle. Oxford: Clarendon Press, 1965.

Dunn, John. *The Political Thought of John Locke: An Historical Account of the Argument of the Two Treatises of Government*. Cambridge: Cambridge University Press, 1969.

Ehrenpreis, Irvin. "Swift on Liberty." *Journal of the History of Ideas* 13 (1952): 131–46.

Fielding, Henry. *Amelia*. 2 vols. London: J. M. Dent and Sons; New York: E. P. Dutton, 1962.

———. *The Author's Farce*. Regents Restoration Drama Series. Ed. Charles B. Woods. Lincoln: University of Nebraska Press, 1966.

———. *The Complete Works of Henry Fielding*. Ed. William Ernest Henley. 16 vols. New York: Croscup and Sterling, 1902.

———. *The Covent-Garden Journal*. Ed. Gerard Edward Jensen. New Haven: Yale University Press, 1915.

———. *The Grub-Street Opera*. Regents Restoration Drama Series. Ed. Edgar V. Roberts. Lincoln: University of Nebraska Press, 1968.

———. *The Historical Register for the Year 1736 and Eurydice*

Hissed. Regents Restoration Drama Series. Ed. William W. Appleton. Lincoln: University of Nebraska Press, 1967.

————. *The Jacobite's Journal and Related Writings*. Wesleyan edition. Ed. W. B. Coley. Middletown, Conn.: Wesleyan University Press, 1975.

————. *Jonathan Wild*. Shakespeare Head Edition. Oxford: Basil Blackwell, 1926.

————. *Jonathan Wild* and *The Voyage to Lisbon*. London: J. M. Dent and Sons; New York: E. P. Dutton, 1964.

————. *Joseph Andrews*. Wesleyan Edition. Ed. Martin C. Battestin. Middletown, Conn.: Wesleyan University Press, 1967.

————. *Miscellanies, Volume I*. Wesleyan edition. Ed. Henry Knight Miller. Middletown, Conn.: Wesleyan University Press, 1964.

————. *A Plan of the Universal Register Office*. London, 1753.

————. *Tom Jones*. Wesleyan edition. Ed. Martin C. Battestin and Fredson Bowers. Middletown, Conn.: Wesleyan University Press, 1975.

————. *The True Patriot and The History of Our Own Times*. Ed. Miriam Austin Locke. University: University of Alabama Press, 1964.

————, and Ralph, James. *The Champion*. 2 vols. London: J. Huggonson, 1741.

Foord, Archibald S. *His Majesty's Opposition 1714–1830*. Oxford: Clarendon Press, 1964.

Foxon, David Fairweather. *English Verse 1701–1750: A Catalogue of Separately Printed Poems with Notes on Contemporary Collected Editions*. 2 vols. London and New York: Cambridge University Press, 1975.

Gay, John. *The Letters of John Gay*. Ed. C. F. Burgess. Oxford: Clarendon Press, 1966.

Goldgar, Bertrand A. *The Curse of Party: Swift's Relations with Addison and Steele*. Lincoln: University of Nebraska Press, 1961.

————. "The Politics of Fielding's *Coffee-House Politician*." *Philological Quarterly* 49 (1970): 424–29.

————. "Pope and the *Grub-Street Journal*." *Modern Philology* 74 (1977): 360–80.

————. *Walpole and the Wits: The Relation of Politics to Literature, 1722–1742*. Lincoln: University of Nebraska Press, 1976.

Gough, J. W. *John Locke's Political Philosophy*. 2d ed. Oxford: Clarendon Press, 1973.

Greason, A. Leroy, Jr. "Fielding's *An Address to the Electors of Great Britain*." *Philological Quarterly* 33 (1954): 347–52.

————. "Fielding's *The History of the Present Rebellion in Scotland*." *Philological Quarterly* 37 (1958): 119–23.

Greene, Donald J. *The Politics of Samuel Johnson*. New Haven: Yale University Press, 1960.

————. "Swift: Some Caveats." *Studies in the Eighteenth Century*. Ed. R. F. Brissenden. 2 vols. Toronto: University of Toronto Press, 1973.

Grundy, Isobel M. "New Verse by Henry Fielding." *PMLA* 87 (1972): 213–45.

Halsband, Robert. *The Life of Lady Mary Wortley Montagu*. New York: Oxford University Press, 1960.

Hatfield, Glenn W. *Henry Fielding and the Language of Irony*. Chicago: University of Chicago Press, 1968.

————. "Puffs and Pollitricks: *Jonathan Wild* and the Political Corruption of Language." *Philological Quarterly* 46 (1957): 250–67.

Hay, Douglas; Linebaugh, Peter; Rule, John G.; Thompson, E. P.; and Winslow, Cal. *Albion's Fatal Tree: Crime and Society in Eighteenth-Century England*. New York: Pantheon, 1975.

Hill, Christopher. "Clarissa Harlow and Her Times." *Essays in Criticism* 5 (1955): 315–40.

Hillhouse, James T. *The Grub-Street Journal*. 1928. Rpt. New York: Benjamin Blom, 1967.

Historical Manuscripts Commission. *The Diary of the Earl of Egmont*. Ed. R. A. Roberts. 3 vols. London, 1920–23.

————. *Report on the Manuscripts of the Earl of Denbigh at Newnham Paddox*. Ed. Mrs. S. C. Lomas. London, 1911.

Hobbes, Thomas. *Leviathan: Or the Matter, Form and Power of a Commonwealth Ecclesiastical and Civil*. Ed. Michael Oakeshott. New York: Collier, 1962.

Holmes, Geoffrey. *British Politics in the Age of Anne*. New York: St. Martin's Press, 1967.

Hunter, J. Paul. "Fielding's Reflexive Plays and the Rhetoric of

Discovery." *Studies in the Literary Imagination* 5 (1972): 65–100.

———. *Occasional Form: Henry Fielding and the Chains of Circumstance.* Baltimore: Johns Hopkins University Press, 1975.

Irwin, William Robert. *The Making of Jonathan Wild.* 1941. Rpt. Hamden, Conn.: Archon, 1965.

Jarvis, Rupert C. *Collected Papers on the Jacobite Risings.* 2 vols. New York: Barnes and Noble, 1972.

———. "The Death of Walpole: Henry Fielding and a Forgotten Cause Célèbre." *Modern Language Review* 41 (1946): 113–30.

Jensen, Gerard E. "A Fielding Discovery." *Yale University Library Gazette* 10 (1935): 23–32.

Jones, B. M. *Henry Fielding: Novelist and Magistrate.* London: George Allen and Unwin, 1933.

Kelch, Ray A. *Newcastle: A Duke Without Money.* Berkeley and Los Angeles: University of California Press, 1974.

Kern, Jean B. "Fielding's Dramatic Satire." *Philological Quarterly* 54 (1975): 239–57.

Kinder, Marsha. "Fielding's Dramatic Experimentation." Ph.D. dissertation, University of California, Los Angeles, 1967.

Kramnick, Isaac. *Bolingbroke and His Circle: The Politics of Nostalgia in the Age of Walpole.* Cambridge, Mass.: Harvard University Press, 1968.

Kupersmith, William. "Studies in Augustan Literature." *Philological Quarterly* 55 (1976): 533–52.

Laprade, William T. *Public Opinion and Politics in Eighteenth Century England to the Fall of Walpole.* New York: Macmillan, 1936.

Lemos, Ramon M. *Hobbes and Locke: Power and Consent.* Athens: University of Georgia Press, 1978.

[Leslie, J. H.] "An English Army List of 1740." *Notes and Queries* 3 (1917): 267.

Linebaugh, Peter. "The Tyburn Riot Against the Surgeons." In *Albion's Fatal Tree.* New York: Pantheon, 1975.

Locke, John. *Locke's Two Treatises of Government.* Ed. Peter Laslett. New York: Mentor, 1963.

————. *Several Papers Relating to Money, Interest and Trade, etc.* 1696. Rpt. New York: Augustus M. Kelley, 1968.

Loftis, John. *The Politics of Drama in Augustan England.* Oxford: Clarendon Press, 1963.

————. *Steele at Drury Lane.* 1952. Rpt. Westport, Conn.: Greenwood Press, 1973.

The London Stage, 1660–1800. A Calendar of Plays, Entertainments and Afterpieces Together with Casts, Box-Receipts and Contemporary Comment, Compiled from the Playbills, Newspapers and Theatrical Diaries of the Period. Part 3: 1729–47. Ed. Arthur H. Scouten. 2 vols. Carbondale: Southern Illinois University Press, 1961.

Lyttelton, George. *George Lyttelton's Political Tracts 1735–1748.* Ed. Stephen Parks. New York and London: Garland, 1974.

Macaulay, Thomas Babington, Lord. *The History of England.* Ed. Hugh Trevor-Roper. Harmondsworth, England: Penguin Books, 1974.

McCrea, Brian. "Fielding's Role in *The Champion*: A Reminder." *South Atlantic Bulletin* 42 (1977): 19–24.

————. "Fielding's Trial of A. P. Esquire and a Problematic Episode in the Life of Pope." *Eighteenth-Century Life* 5 (1978): 30–37.

————. "Romances, Newspapers, and the Style of Fielding's True History." *Studies in English Literature 1500–1900* (forthcoming).

McKillop, Alan D. "The Personal Relations Between Fielding and Richardson." *Modern Philology* 28 (1931): 423–33.

Macpherson, C. B. *The Political Theory of Possessive Individualism.* Oxford: Clarendon Press, 1962.

Malone, Dumas. *Jefferson and the Rights of Man.* Boston: Little, Brown, 1951.

Miller, Henry Knight. *Essays on Fielding's Miscellanies: A Commentary on Volume One.* Princeton, N.J.: Princeton University Press, 1961.

Namier, Lewis. *Crossroads of Power.* London: H. Hamilton, 1962.

————. *England in the Age of the American Revolution,* 2d ed. New York: St. Martin's Press, 1961.

————. *The Structure of Politics at the Accession of George III*. 1928. Rpt. New York: St. Martin's Press, 1961.

New, Melvyn. "The Dunce Revisited: Colley Cibber and Tristram Shandy." *South Atlantic Quarterly* 72 (1973): 547–59.

Owen, John B. *The Rise of the Pelhams*. London: Methuen, 1957.

Parry, Geraint. *John Locke*. Political Thinkers, Vol. 8. London: George Allen and Unwin, 1978.

Paulson, Ronald K. *Satire and the Novel in Eighteenth-Century England*. New Haven: Yale University Press, 1967.

————, and Lockwood, Thomas, eds. *Henry Fielding: The Critical Heritage*. New York: Barnes and Noble, 1969.

Plumb, J. H. *Men and Places*. London: Cresset Press, 1963.

————. *Sir Robert Walpole: The King's Minister*. Boston: Houghton Mifflin, 1961.

Pringle, Patrick. *Hue and Cry: The Story of Henry and John Fielding and Their Bow-Street Runners*. London: William Morrow, n.d.

Quintana, Ricardo. *Two Augustans: John Locke, Jonathan Swift*. Madison: University of Wisconsin Press, 1978.

Ralph, James. *The Case of Authors By Profession or Trade* (1758) *Together with The Champion (1739–1740)*. Ed. Philip Stevick. Gainesville, Fla.: Scholar's Facsimiles and Reprints, 1966.

Rawson, C. J. *Henry Fielding and the Augustan Ideal Under Stress*. London: Routledge and Kegan Paul, 1972.

Robbins, Caroline. *The Eighteenth-Century Commonwealthman*. Cambridge, Mass.: Harvard University Press, 1959.

Rogers, Nicholas. "Aristocratic Clientage, Trade and Independency: Popular Politics in Pre-Radical Westminster." *Past and Present* 61 (1973): 70–106.

Sackett, S. J. "Fielding and Pope." *Notes and Queries* 6 (1959): 200–204.

Sacks, Sheldon. *Fiction and the Shape of Belief: A Study of Henry Fielding with Glances at Swift, Johnson, and Richardson*. Berkeley and Los Angeles: University of California Press, 1967.

Seliger, Martin. *The Liberal Politics of John Locke*. New York: Frederick A. Praeger, 1968.

Shaw, George Bernard. *Plays Pleasant and Unpleasant*. 2 vols. New York: Herbert S. Stone, 1898.

Sherburn, George. "Fielding's Social Outlook." *Philological Quarterly* 25 (1956): 1–23.

Shipley, John B. "Essays from Fielding's *Champion*." *Notes and Queries* 198 (1953): 468–69.

———. "The 'M' in Fielding's *Champion*." *Notes and Queries* 2 (1955): 240–245, 345–51.

———. "On the Date of the *Champion*." *Notes and Queries* 198 (1953): 441.

Smith, John Harrington. *The Gay Couple in Restoration Comedy*. Cambridge, Mass.: Harvard University Press, 1948.

Steele, Richard. *The Conscious Lovers*. Regents Restoration Drama Series. Ed. Shirley Strum Kenny. Lincoln: University of Nebraska Press, 1968.

Stephen, Leslie. *Alexander Pope*. English Men of Letters, ed. John Morley. 1880. Rpt. London: Macmillan, 1900.

———. *English Literature and Society in the Eighteenth Century*. New York: G. P. Putnam's, 1904.

Strauss, Leo. *Natural Right and History*. Chicago: University of Chicago Press, 1953.

Swift, Jonathan. *Correspondence*. Ed. Harold Williams. 5 vols. Oxford: Clarendon Press, 1963–65.

———. *The Prose Works of Jonathan Swift*. Ed. Herbert Davis. 14 vols. Oxford: Basil Blackwell, 1939–68.

Taylor, Dick, Jr. "Joseph as Hero of *Joseph Andrews*." *Tulane Studies in English* 7 (1957): 91–109.

Taylor, Houghton W. "Fielding upon Cibber." *Modern Philology* 29 (1931): 73–90.

Thompson, E. P. *Whigs and Hunters: The Origins of the Black Act*. New York: Pantheon, 1975.

Thornbury, Ethel Margaret. *Henry Fielding's Theory of the Comic Prose Epic*. University of Wisconsin Studies in Language and Literature, No. 30. Madison: University of Wisconsin Press, 1931.

Walcott, Robert, Jr. *English Politics in the Early Eighteenth Century*. Cambridge, Mass.: Harvard University Press, 1956.

Wells, John Edwin. "Fielding's *Champion* and Captain Hercules Vinegar." *Modern Language Review* 8 (1913): 165–72.

———. "Fielding's *Champion*—More Notes." *Modern Language Notes* 35 (1920): 18–23.

———. "Fielding's Political Purpose in *Jonathan Wild*." *PMLA* 28 (1914): 1–54.

————. "Fielding's Signatures in *The Champion* and the Date of His *Of Good Nature*." *Modern Language Review* 7 (1912): 97–98.

————. Untitled Letter. *The Nation*, 16 January 1913, pp. 53–54.

Williams, Basil. *The Whig Supremacy*. Oxford: Oxford University Press, 1939.

Williams, Raymond. *The Country and the City*. New York: Oxford University Press, 1973.

————. *The Long Revolution*. New York: Columbia University Press, 1961.

Woods, Charles B. "Cibber in Fielding's *Author's Farce*: Three Notes." *Philological Quarterly* 44 (1965): 145–51.

————. "Notes on Three of Fielding's Plays." *PMLA* 52 (1937): 359–73.

Work, James A. "Henry Fielding Christian Censor." In *The Age of Johnson*. Ed. Frederick W. Hilles, pp. 139–48. New Haven: Yale University Press, 1949.

Zirker, Malvin R. *Fielding's Social Pamphlets*. Berkeley and Los Angeles: University of California Press, 1966.

Index

DATE DUE

XXXXXXXX

MAY 1 8 1989